Madrid

Cities of the Imagination

Cities of the Imagination

Madrid

A cultural and literary companion

Elizabeth Nash

INTERLINK BOOKS
An imprint of Interlink Publishing Group, Inc.
New York • Northampton

First published 2001 by
INTERLINK BOOKS
An imprint of Interlink Publishing Group, Inc.
99 Seventh Avenue • Brooklyn, New York 11215 and
46 Crosby Street • Northampton, Massachusetts 01060

Library of Congress Cataloging-in-Publication Data

Nash, Elizabeth, 1949–
  Madrid: a cultural and literary companion / by Elizabeth Nash.
    p. cm. — (Cities of the imagination)
  Includes bibliographical references.
  ISBN 1-56656-368-2
1. Madrid (Spain)—Description and travel.   2. Madrid (Spain)—History.
3. Madrid (Spain)—Social life and customs.   4. Popular culture—Spain—Madrid.
I. Title. II. Series.
DP362 .N37 2000
946'.41—dc21   00-058055
                                                       CIP

Design: Baseline Arts
Cover images: Dirección General de Turismo,
Comunidad de Madrid; Prado Museum
Printed and bound in Canada
10 9 8 7 6 5 4 3 2 1

Contents

Foreword

Few people are likely to fall in love with Madrid for its appearance alone. Spread out over a flat, dusty and largely featureless landscape, and without the compensations either of a proper river, or of a generally distinguished architecture, Madrid is a city whose charms are not immediately obvious. From at least the nineteenth century onwards foreigners have unfailingly commented on its scarcity of major old monuments, on its uniform brash modernity, and on the way it fails to live up to stereotypical notions of romantic Spain. Today's tourists tend to compare it unfavorably with Barcelona, while most Spaniards from outside Madrid criticize not only its look, but also its climate of extremes, its proverbially arrogant people, and even its food, which, in the words of the fictional Catalan detective Pepe Carvalho, "has given no more than a stew, an omelette, and a dish of tripe to the gastronomic culture of our country."

It was largely the prospect of seeing the treasures of the Prado Museum that had kept my spirits raised when I caught my first glimpses of Madrid in the mid-1960s. I was arriving by train from the north, and remember vividly the descent from the exhilarating granite heights of the Sierra Guadarrama into what eventually became an expanse of sun-scorched high-rise dwellings that rose abruptly above an ochre wasteland. Many years later, when I had fallen completely under the city's spell, I would look more sympathetically at such daunting urban vistas after seeing how much they had inspired the outstanding contemporary realist painter Antonio López. Significantly, López's minutely detailed panoramas— perhaps the most memorable depictions of Madrid since those of Goya— were not intended as commentaries on the bleakness of the modern urban world but rather as affectionate records of the artist's beloved adopted city.

Madrid, a place whose true or *castizo* inhabitants have traditionally feared and hated the countryside, is a city that will probably be appreciated principally by the dedicated urbanite. Though my first and rather timorous first visit to Madrid was largely spent endlessly escaping into the Prado and its elegant, verdant surroundings, I was struck even then by the city's extraordinary vitality, and by the sense of scale that, in combination with all the neo-baroque and other eclectic detailing on the buildings, gave to the place the air of some metropolis dreamed up in the 1920s.

I did not go back to Madrid until the late 1970s, after which I began spending ever longer periods in a radically changing city that was experiencing all the excitement and new-found freedom following Franco's death and the return of democracy. These were heady and potentially ridiculous days when Madrid suddenly took over from Barcelona as Spain's thriving center of fashion and modernity, and when the city's already celebrated nightlife was inflated to such a degree that the artery of the Paseo de la Castellana was almost clogged up by the proliferating outdoor bars or *terrazas*. Very much in the spirit of these times were such establishments as the notorious swimming pool known as El Lago (where transsexual prostitutes displayed on astroturf the results of their recent operations), and the aptly named Bar Universal, where a strikingly broad cross-section of Madrilenian society gathered under the shadow of the mad, drunken poet Leopoldo Panero. Essential to the success of these places was their being favored by prominent members of the *movida*, a group of young and mainly pampered writers, fashion designers, artists and filmmakers who celebrated the ephemeral and often insalubrious elements that I came now to perceive as being central to Madrid's elusive appeal. Thus the film director Pedro Almodóvar, by far the most successful associate of the *movida*, expressed his enormous love for Madrid in rough-edged films that glorified the kitsch, the surreal, and the downright tacky.

The more I got to know Madrid, the more I discovered it to be a place full of surprises and quirky small details. Influenced by the passionate and eccentric *Madrilenista* of the early twentieth century, Ramón Gómez de la Serna, to whom even the most apparently trivial aspect of Madrid was worth recording, I started obsessively trailing the city's back streets, marveling, for instance, at how the plainest of buildings were brought to life by brilliant ceramic decorations promoting perhaps cures for tooth pain or diarrhea. I kept on coming across window displays that appeared virtually unaltered since the early years of the twentieth century, as well as unexpected and little known survivals from much earlier periods in the city's history, such as the magnificent but perpetually closed Capilla del Obispo, a jewel of the early Spanish Renaissance.

Madrid's past came ever sharper into focus as I realized the extent to which it lay barely concealed beneath the city's sprawling and chaotic facade. Despite extensive rebuilding, certain districts had retained much of the character of the period when they were first built, and sometimes appeared like enclaves of small town Castille. Soon I was tracing the whole development of Madrid by walking from one part of the city to the next, beginning with the once remarkably shabby and neglected Plaza de la Paja, which had been the palace-lined main square of the medieval town. The story of Madrid after its emergence as capital of Spain in 1561 was told in the imposingly somber streets that extended between the Plazas de la Villa and Mayor, while the extraordinary literary and theatrical boom that accompanied the city's rapid extension eastwards at the beginning of the seventeenth century was evoked in the nearby Barrio de los Literatos, with its plethora of plaques and ghost-like air. Moving on to the Paseo del Prado, I was suddenly immersed in the enlightened world of Bourbon king Charles III before heading northwards to explore Madrid's nineteenth-century past, which was conveyed both in the narrow blackened streets of run-down Chueca and Malasaña, and in the smart grid of residential and shopping avenues built under the impetus of the dynamic banker and entrepreneur the Marquis of Salamanca. Finally, to savor to the full the twentieth-century city I once walked the whole length of the exuberant Paseo de la Castellana, which leads past magnificent, soaring examples of recent Spanish architecture before culminating in Philip Johnson's twin tower-blocks that slope inwards as if to form some futuristic triumphal arch.

Sustaining me during these endless wanderings were the many bars, cafés, and restaurants that were often far more eloquent of Madrid's history and character than any museum or architectural monument. Spectacular new establishments, such as Philippe Starck's gloriously theatrical if inherently vacuous Teatriz, were opening up all the time, and were essential to visit so as to gauge the zeitgeist of a Spain preparing itself for its coming-of-age celebrations of 1992. But my attention was drawn above all to the survival in Madrid of more old-fashioned eating and drinking establishments than in almost any other city I had ever known. The tourist-loved Casa Botín, which claims to be the oldest restaurant in the world, turned out to be one of numerous places where Madrid's traditionally simple cuisine could be eaten in ceramic-covered surroundings so unchanged that—in the case of the Casa Ciriaco—you could identify the very spot where the important early twentieth-century painter Ignacio Zuloaga ate the last meal of his life. Then there were such vastly contrasting places as the Art Deco cocktail bar known as the Museo Chicote, the staggeringly cheap and grimily atmospheric restaurant popularly referred to as "El Comunista," and the celebrated Lhardy's, with its silver samovar from which consommé is daily served in an intimate gilded setting straight out of the late nineteenth century.

Many of these long-established institutions had the additional fascination for me of having been frequented by those writers who had helped turn Madrid into what had been one of the most intense café societies of Europe. Literature, as I came increasingly to realize, had played a critical role in the history of Madrid; and it was to literature that I repeatedly turned for a deeper understanding of this complex city. The actual tombs of Golden Age writers such as Cervantes, Lope de Vega and the marvelously cynical poet Quevedo might have gone; but the memories of these figures were very much alive, as was indicated by the existence at the very heart of Hapsburg Madrid of a district named after "*los literatos.*" And there were other, later writers whose presence was no less inescapable, most notably the romantic essayist Larra (the true inheritor of Quevedo), and the brilliant late nineteenth-century novelist Pérez Galdós, whose epic work *Fortunata and Jacinta* is one of the greatest panoramic portrayals of urban society in western literature.

The qualities that make Madrid such an exciting city are difficult to capture in a straightforward guidebook. For all the remarkable wealth of art treasures that is now concentrated in the museums around the Paseo del Prado, Madrid is a place whose major sightseeing attractions form only a very limited part of its overall appeal. What is clearly needed is someone to guide visitors beyond the standard tourist image of Madrid, to make them look more closely at the city's less obviously enticing aspects, and to encourage a greater familiarity with its essentially literary culture. Elizabeth Nash has performed this role with an engaging enthusiasm that is likely to disarm even those severe and myopic critics who fail to see in Madrid little more than traffic, pollution, and a dish of tripe.

—Michael Jacobs

Preface

Madrid may not grab you at first. It has few splendid buildings or views, and its culture may initially confirm clichés rather than beckon you to deeper understanding. Isolated behind the Pyrenees, Spain and its landlocked capital produced a distinctive cultural style. Of all Europe's capitals Madrid is perhaps the one that most preserves, indeed celebrates, a unique identity whose quirky customs have come to define the city. Fiestas, siestas, tapas, paseos, late lunches, midnight dinners, shouted conversations, partying 'til sunrise are social habits associated with Madrid even by those who may know little else of the city.

Madrid isn't easy to know, though its people have an open friendliness rare in comparable European capitals. Few here speak English. Fewer still understand the Anglo-Saxon mindset, or are aware that there is one different from their own. Yet any visitor may recognize and admire their directness and honesty. *Madrileños*, the city's inhabitants, can be brusque, and enchanting, frenetic and lazy, pompous and ironical. Countless visitors who end up staying for years say that what keeps them there is this fizzing, vibrant human exchange, a lust for enjoyment elevated to an art form.

This book is an attempt to identify the city's personality and to explain how it might have come about. Starting from a number of particular spots identifiable from any guidebook, I have tried to explore something of what *Madrileños* are like, and why. Obviously such an approach is fraught with pitfalls. The most obvious is that of falling into stereotypes, or assuming that it is even possible to classify the personality of a city; another is to take people's own self-assessment at face value. Still another is to seize upon a particular trait forged by a moment in history that may today be no more than romantic nostalgia. In reality, the spirit of Madrid is certainly more flexible and subtle than I have managed to convey.

I believe that the city's often cruel history holds the key to explaining why Madrid is as it is. And because the people of Madrid and their customs are mostly far more interesting than the monuments they have made, I have concentrated on the personalities, heroes, heroines and villains, and their adventures real or fictional, that often receive only a tantalizing few lines in the many excellent guidebooks produced for English-speaking visitors.

Spain has known democracy only since 1975. Before then, apart from a few short interludes, Madrid's history is that of a string of absolute rulers, stupid or enlightened, and of a subject people. *Madrileños'* characteristic mixture of deference and insolence, of pride and insecurity, are rooted in the city's historic role as the royal court. Madrid emerged as the heart of the world's most powerful empire. Its rulers were rarely effectively challenged even as empire fell about their ears. On the couple of occasions when the people of Madrid rose up against tyranny, they were bloodily defeated. But Madrid pioneered a unique literature of satire, mocking a society where appearance and display were everything. It created Europe's first modern theater and some of its finest artists, who portrayed real people in real settings for the first time. Despite, or perhaps because of, successive absolute dynasties, Madrid produced a fiercely idiosyncratic popular culture that simultaneously mocked and deferred to its rulers, and revealed a capacity for both partying and suffering that most Europeans would consider extreme.

Madrid rarely looked out to the wider world, as did Barcelona or Bilbao or Seville. Marooned in its vast rocky tableland, it remained largely immune to outside influences, apart from throwbacks to Arabic times and those European fashions imported via the dynastic alliances of the monarchs. At the same time, since most *Madrileños* came originally from elsewhere in Spain, the city developed an openness and tolerance that visitors still find irresistible. Perhaps the greatest achievement of this city adept in the art of improvisation is the extent to which, impoverished, demoralized and frozen in time by forty years of Franco's dictatorship, Madrid became within a generation an eager and effective participant in modern Europe, while losing almost none of its sharply defined identity.

Experts in art and literature have written specialist books on Madrid's painters and writers down the centuries, and described their haunts in the city. Others have captured the youthful zest of the modern capital to guide visitors to the nightspots and hottest fashions. I have drawn extensively upon these indispensable works. But I wanted to write a book for those who have visited the Prado, sampled the nightlife, half-adjusted to the crazy hours, and are curious about what makes the place tick, socially and psychologically. Why, for instance, are *Madrileños* so insufferably rude? Why are they so extraordinarily generous, so superficial, so profound, so extravagantly affectionate, so coolly indifferent? I have no particular qualifications for undertaking such a subjective investigation, beyond curiosity and growing affection for a city I initially found formless and exasperating—if, always, loads of fun. What results is a personal, even arbitrary, view, but I have tried to be as accurate in my facts and observations as I could. The opinions and the mistakes are mostly mine.

Special thanks to Ann Bateson and Harvey Holtom; and to Peter Besas, Miguel Angel Bastenier, David Boardman, Anunciación Bremón, Tom Burns, Borja Casani, David Castillejo, Miguel Angel Coso, John Dew, Stephen Drake-Jones, Joanne Episcopo, Ian and Carole Gibson, Mercedes Herranz, Carlos Mendo, Antonio de Miguel, Simon Moore, Catherine Olive, Andrés Ortega, Terry Otero, Edward Owen, Michael Palin, Carmen Rodriguez, Damaso Santos at the Prado Museum, Juan Sanz, Daniel Schweimler, Jo Tuckman and Jane Walker. Thanks too to my editor James Ferguson, to *El País* newspaper and the foreign desk of *The Independent*, especially Leonard Doyle and Andrew Marshall, who encouraged me and allowed me time to write.

This book is dedicated to my parents, Gladys and Frederick Nash.

Elizabeth Nash
Madrid, November 2000

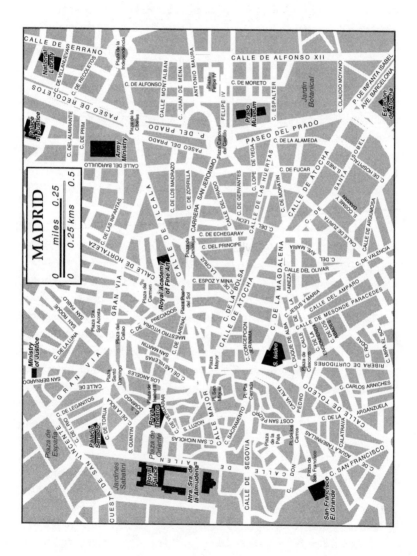

MADRID

miles 0.25 0.5
0 0.25 kms

CHAPTER ONE

Paseo del Prado:
From Siesta to Fiesta

Madrid in high summer—when July burns into August—is a terrible place, a searing empty frying pan, in the words of the city's best-known chronicler, Benito Pérez Galdós. The heat buffets your face as if you had stepped inside an oven. The sun spikes your eyeballs like a spear to the brain. Every step, every breath, requires superhuman effort. Your eyelids droop, your body sags; thought processes all but close down. If you make the mistake of entering the city in the afternoon of such a day, when the sky is as fiercely white as the heart of a blast furnace, you will find the streets silent and deserted. Europe's most vivacious city is smothered in a pall of indolence, engulfed in soporific languor. Madrid, wrote the Spanish socialist Arturo Barea in 1920, "smells of sun." Traditionally the only way to protect yourself from its intolerable heat, what the French poet and traveler Théophile Gautier called "this torrent of fire," was to cower in a basement in virtual darkness, keeping cool by filling earthenware jugs with water. The nineteenth-century author describes this homemade cooling system in heartfelt detail:

> Put seven or eight jugs on marble window sills, mantelpieces or corner shelves, fill them with water and go and lie on a couch to wait for them to take effect and savour in quiet seclusion the pleasure they provide. The clay becomes darker, the water penetrates its pores, and

> *the jugs begin to "sweat", producing a perfume that recalls the scent*
> *of wet plaster or a damp cellar long shut up. This evaporation is so*
> *intense that within an hour half the water is gone; and what remains*
> *is as cold as ice and has the dank taste of a well or a tank. It's like a*
> *cold steam bath.*

Only someone who has truly suffered the torments of summer in Madrid could write with such passion about the art of cooling off.

Since a summer afternoon in Madrid is considered to last until eight or nine in the evening, you begin to understand what has been called Spain's greatest contribution to western civilization: the siesta. The siesta is more than a nap. That slight and hasty Anglo-Saxon concept does no justice to the solemn rhythm of the Spanish day that builds up to the siesta after hours of hectic social activity, serious meals and copious quantities of wine. In Madrid you don't "take" (*tomar*) a siesta as we English-speakers would take a nap. You "throw yourself" (*echarse*) into a siesta or "sleep" (*dormir*) the siesta; someone even told me they "practice" (*practicar*) the siesta, as if it were a rite of deep philosophical or spiritual significance. These are strong prolonged actions that testify to the seriousness of the whole business. The siesta amounts to a little night in the middle of the day; it enables you to resume the cycle of activity and meals with renewed strength until the early hours. As a character says in Pedro Almodóvar's melodramatic film *El Flor de mi Secreto* (The Flower of My Secret): "It's never late in Madrid."

Legend has it that the siesta was invented by the Holy Roman Emperor Carlos V, who after lunch would take one of the iron keys of his palace chambers and retire, not to lie down, but to sit on his throne. When his eyelids fell, his head drooped and his grip loosened, the key slipped from his fingers and clattered to the stone floor to wake him with a start, bringing the siesta to an end. True or not, it confirms the rule that the siesta should not be a prolonged snooze; aficionados say that the optimum length should be no longer than half an hour. More and you are liable to wake up feeling woozy and bad-tempered. One expert even confesses to taking two siestas: one at midday, another in the early evening.

Do not be misled by skeptics who tell you that the siesta is an outmoded custom dating from when workers in the fields needed to shelter from the midday sun under trees or in the shadow of a cool patio. Midday, by the way, in Spain means not twelve noon, but the hours when the sun is hottest, that is between 2PM and 4 or 5PM. It is commonplace for officials in Madrid to return to their offices as late as 7PM, showered, crisp and cologned. Many do not resurface until the end of the afternoon, which in the summer can mean as late as 9PM. The siesta remains firmly entrenched. Indeed, in recent years it has won renewed respectability following American studies in the 1980s that point to the biological need for a midday sleep and its powers to prevent cardiovascular diseases. An enterprising Catalan businessman has set up a string of establishments throughout Spain where you can walk in off the street and buy a siesta, preceded by a soothing five-minute massage, for those, he says who live too far from work to drive home just for half an hour's snooze. It will only cause grief—even offense—if you ignore the rules and try to mold the ritual of the Spanish day to normal western practices. The servant Sancho Panza was quick to reproach his master Don Quijote when the sad knight seemed forgetful of the sacred siesta, as if his master were guilty of a shameful dereliction of duty. Cervantes is not the only Spanish author to celebrate the practice as a natural and essential component of human happiness.

But every *Madrileño* knows that within a few miles of this urban inferno are mountains where, as Ernest Hemingway observed in *For Whom the Bell Tolls*, you can be caught in snowstorms in June. Navacerrada near Segovia is now a popular ski resort, but even in early summer, when Hemingway set his tale of a doomed republican offensive during the civil war, you shiver on those harsh hillsides and often have to take shelter from snowstorms. Hemingway sums up first the incredulity, then acceptance of the inevitable, in the following dialogue that precedes a summer blizzard:

While they had spoken the sun had clouded over and as he looked back
up toward the mountains the sky was now heavy and gray.
"Sure," Pilar said to him, looking at the sky, "it will snow."
"Now? Almost in June?"

"Why not? These mountains do not know the names of the months. We are in the moon of May."

"It can't be snow," he said. "It can't snow."

"Just the same, Inglés," she said to him, "it will snow."

Robert Jordan looked up at the thick gray of the sky with the sun gone faintly yellow, and now as he watched gone completely and the gray becoming uniform so that it was soft and heavy; the gray now cutting off the tops of the mountains.

"Yes," he said. "I guess you are right."

Even in the heart of the city, protected, you might think, from the extremes of the bare mountains, many an impoverished summer tourist, lulled by the heat of July and tempted to sleep rough in the park, has shivered in nocturnal temperatures that can plunge to zero. "I have watched," wrote Hemingway in *Death in the Afternoon*, "on a July night when I could not sleep, the beggars burning newspapers in the street and crouching round the fire to keep warm. Two nights later it was too hot to sleep until the coolness that comes just before morning." Madrid, he observed, is itself a mountain city with a mountain climate: "the heat and cold come and go quickly there."

It is hardly surprising, with these bitter extremes of temperature, that *Madrileños* are not very keen on the great outdoors. That is not to say that they do not like their climate, for they praise it as healthy and invigorating, and, as Hemingway noted, they are proud of its changes. They are particularly proud of their famed sunshine and the beauty of their light, to which they attribute their characteristic *alegría* or gaiety. Conscious that the sun is their most glorious asset, they are none the less ambivalent about it, as a passage by Pedro Antonio de Alarcón in *Visitas a la Marquesa* shows:

A beautiful foreign lady, who gloriously represented her beautiful country at balls and concerts, said the other day to a Member of Parliament, I don't know if a senator or a deputy: "What sun there is in Madrid! I don't know how your excellencies can spend your afternoons in the sad atmosphere of the Cortes speaking of strange human affairs, instead of enjoying these beautiful days, looking at the infinite sky and taking in the caresses of the gentle sun." "Ah, señora!" replied the statesman, "You people from the north value these things. We Spaniards have become weary of so much sun, and there are days when we don't know what to do with it. From which, Marquesa, I conclude that if the sun were exported, we would be the leading commercial nation of Europe!"

This passage was pasted up in subway trains during one recent summer, part of an initiative by the city authorities to familiarize locals and visitors with the glories of Spanish literature.

Madrileños, almost embarrassed at the exuberance of their weather, prefer it in the background, an accompanying relish to their life, not the main course. There are few examples in Spanish culture or literature of the sort of nature celebration that became common in northern Europe from the Romantics onwards. A walk in the park has always been as much as most *Madrileños* aspire to, and then only after the fierceness of the day is safely past. Many are acutely conscious of the damaging effects of drafts, and damp. The people of Madrid are urban animals. They look to their own city for entertainment and diversion. And they regard the conquest of nature, not the celebration of it, as the mark of civilized living. Taking a country walk or enjoying winter sports have caught on in recent decades among the prosperous middle class. But most *Madrileños* look at you strangely if you rhapsodize about the call of the wild.

El campo, the countryside, has a negative, almost dangerous connotation for Castillians from the rugged hinterland surrounding the capital. The word evokes barren wind-swept fields, harsh rocky plains and *sierras*, predatory animals and backbreaking toil and poverty. It is a challenge, a threat to be subdued, not unless you are very rich a pleasure to be enjoyed. When *Madrileños* talk about going home to visit the far-flung rural backwater whence many of them came a generation or so back, they don't say, as a British or American city-dweller might, "I'm going to the country." Rather, depending on their social class, they say, "I'm going to *el pueblo* (my village) or *la finca* (my estate)." "The country" is okay if it is their own clearly defined home territory, when it is treated with the fiercest protective loyalty. But in general, apart from the odd day out, *Madrileños* are in my experience indifferent to the countryside or prefer to keep away from it.

In some Spanish regions like Galicia or the Basque country, local landscape and climate are praised in literature and art. But it is mostly regional identity that is being celebrated and the consciousness of a people; it is purely specific, and usually has to do with the main source of livelihood: the sea, the fertile fields, pasture. In Castille and La Mancha around Madrid, regional loyalties developed mainly in relation to the town: Castillian art favors the still life, controlled, domesticated and indoors, or ecclesiastical topics.

Spain's vast central plains, formerly kingdoms, of which Madrid forms the center, are unforgivingly harsh, parched and monotonous. In *Madrid Observed* Michael Jacobs quotes a nineteenth-century traveler's opinion that Madrid's surroundings formed a "hideous, grassless, treeless, colourless calcined desert." Such an impression formed by the poor traveler toiling across those barren wastes *en route* to Madrid, can still be confirmed today if you glance from your plane or train or car as you approach the capital. Those who scraped a living from such terrain did so from necessity, not choice, and were for the most part poor. Don Quijote would have been considered crazy merely to have ventured upon this unpromising land, even if he had not suffered from the delusions that drove him upon his quest. The proverbs and sayings of country folk, relished by the long-suffering Sancho Panza, emphasize the harshness of the natural world. Madrid is still summed up as "three months of winter and nine months of hell" (*tres meses de invierno y nueve meses de infierno*). The air of the city "can kill a man but not snuff out a candle."

This is not to say that *Madrileños* do not appreciate natural beauty; they do, but they prefer it cultivated and controlled, trimmed and verdant, not parched and raw. Early visitors to Madrid had ample time to take in the harshness of the surrounding countryside, because they had to traverse more than 250 miles from any direction to reach

their destination. And until the advent of the railways in the nineteenth century, the usual method was to travel by sea to ports like Vigo or Cádiz or Santander, and then take a mule train to the capital. It could take weeks.

It is hardly surprising that early travelers to Madrid expressed frustration and exasperation when they finally arrived, wearily recounting their initial disenchantment with the prospect that greeted them in their exhausted state, saddle-sore, thirsty, over-exposed to the elements that were extreme winter and summer alike. The French writer Astolphe Marquis de Custine's 1830 account is typical: "These plains do not offer the eye the richness of lands with good soil. They do not even have the grandeur of complete solitude. The traveller arrives in the capital of the kingdom feeling sad rather than annoyed. Since morning he has not seen a tree and he has only passed through dirty villages." A natural reaction would be to dive for the shady lodgings and throw oneself into a siesta. The siesta was, and remains, Madrid's best remedy for any dip of the spirit an exhausted visitor might experience on finally reaching their destination.

Unnatural Capital
Madrid did not emerge as a natural capital. It commanded no busy trade route and had no access to the sea. Dropped in the middle of a vast arid tableland, scoured by extremes of heat and cold, lacking natural resources and human improvements, the town did not seem an agreeable place to live, and was an improbable candidate to accommodate the court of the most powerful monarch in the world. It was chosen in 1561 by Felipe II as his *única corte* (single court) for pragmatic, even capricious, reasons. He seems to have been motivated primarily by considerations of power, convenience, and fun—key ingredients of *Madrileño* style—although Felipe was not by all accounts a fun-loving person. He was keen to outwit troublesome rivalries between competing regional barons. Madrid, though at the time only a modest village, not even a town really, was strategically placed between the competing power centers of Segovia and Toledo. The establishment of the court permanently in Madrid sapped the influence of these more important cities, and caused the decline of further flung metropolises like Valladolid and Seville.

Valladolid housed a tenacious clan of dukes and marquises, and had flirted with heresy, while Toledo was controlled by a powerful archbishopric that successfully prevented the building of a cathedral in Madrid until the late nineteenth century. It was not finished until 1993, when the Pope came to consecrate it. The historian Alfredo Temblo Magno believes that Felipe took exception to Toledo, the *de facto* capital, because it was too cold. The ill-developed backwater of Madrid also had the advantage of being free of pre-existing power structures that might challenge the royal will. Neither high aristocracy nor the ecclesiastical hierarchy had much weight in the town. As early as the twelfth century, writes Temblo Magno, its personality had started to emerge as "the land of gentlemen who had lost their 'raison d'être,' who had abandoned the military life and found a new source of income from local administration of trade and supplies." It was also conveniently close to the main hunting grounds enjoyed by previous Castillian monarchs who had lodged in Madrid for that reason: mainly El Pardo, Segovia Forest (Valsaín) and Aranjuez. It is often suggested that Madrid's position in the middle of the peninsula made its choice as capital bureaucratically tidy, and it was an additional advantage to be as far from and near to everywhere else, and this too may have tipped Felipe's choice.

Finally, the Alcázar, the ancient Muslim fortress, built on the town's high western ridge, provided magnificent views over the king's private hunting ground, the Casa de Campo, and the Guadarrama mountain ridge beyond, giving it a strong defensive position. It also had excellent water supplies, from underground streams within the rock, prompting the Arabs, who first settled the spot, to call it Mayrit or Magerit, "the place of many springs." The Alcázar (the Spanish absorption of the Arabic *Al Kasr*, or fortress) was not only the largest royal palace in central Spain, but also the most comfortable. Work under way on royal palaces at Segovia and Toledo was far from finished.

So Felipe became the first monarch to settle in Madrid, and from the start the entire purpose of the town was to serve the court. Although based in the Alcázar, he spent most of the time out of town, in one or other of a network of royal residences on estates dotted around the capital, In this way the medieval tradition of the itinerant court did not immediately disappear. On the contrary, it became customary for the monarch to set foot in Madrid itself hardly at all, spending the spring in leafy Aranjuez, the summer in the cool hills of Valsaín, and the autumn at El Escorial, the imposing pile whose construction became his life work and reflected his obsessive personality in every granite block. El Escorial, a combination of palace, mausoleum, monastery and seminary, was created by Felipe II as a royal pantheon and monument to the Spanish Habsburgs as defenders of the Catholic faith. He spent only a few months of winter in Madrid, with long stays at El Pardo in between. Madrid owes its origins to royal caprice in an authoritarian age.

An "apprentice stream"

Madrid's lack of an important river has prompted centuries of scornful derision. The feeble Manzanares serves no useful purpose, provides no natural focus and is not even beautiful. Only Goya, whose panoramas celebrate washerwomen hanging out their sheets and young men and women having fun along the banks on feast days, succeeds in endowing the river with any dignity. Jokes abound. Alexandre Dumas, who enjoyed Madrid, bought a glass of water, drank half of it and told the water seller he should throw the other half into the Manzanares, which probably needed it more. On his return to Paris, Dumas declared he would not write about the river because despite his best efforts he had been unable to find it. The French writer was only following a rich *Madrileño* tradition that continues to demean the city's own river. Although dignified and proud, as George Orwell noted approvingly in *Homage to Catalonia*, sometimes to the point of pomposity, Spaniards and especially *Madrileños* have a well-developed sense of irony and self-mockery. This biting irreverence runs through the satire that is the city's finest literary contribution. Francisco de Quevedo, one of Madrid's greatest satirists, called the Manzanares an "apprentice stream" where frogs and mosquitoes died of thirst. The land was moistened by the Manzanares, said another skeptic, as if by a finger tracing saliva. When Lope de Vega, the great playwright of the Golden Age and the Shakespeare of the Spanish stage, was asked what he thought of the fine new bridge that connected the town to the western side of the river and the road to Segovia, he said the authorities should either buy a river or sell the bridge. Yet the bridge, built in 1583, still serves its purpose well.

Urban Dangers

Madrid was, and largely remains, a city of outsiders, *forasteros*, a word that suggests bumbling naiveté. Most people who call themselves *Madrileños* came from somewhere else just a generation or two back. This constant influx has produced a fresh and uncomplicated view of social roots. It is still taken for granted by many that anyone coming to Madrid is in pursuit of wealth or adventure. Once the traveler—or the would-be immigrant—had braved the frightful journey, he or she would enter the unprepossessing town by one or other of its gates, say the southern Toledo gate, still the entry point for poor migrants from the south, eager to get a foothold into the life of a burgeoning community. Or from the east, down the straight road from the ancient university town of Alcalá de Henares that followed the *cañada*, or traditional drovers' path, the established route of the sheep transhumance, by which the sheep were driven south every autumn to warmer pastures, to return to their verdant northern hillsides in the spring. A few years ago the sheep-driving tradition was restored, every autumn. Every October the principal thoroughfare of Madrid is invaded by thousands of sheep, a spectacle that invariably hits the international front pages. It recalls the age when the region was renowned internationally for the production of Merino wool, one of the few crafts that was not directed exclusively at the court.

The next step for new arrivals was to head for one of the three principal hubs of the city, depending on their business: the Royal Palace for favor and influence, the Plaza Mayor for spectacle or trade, the Puerta del Sol, for gossip and perhaps shady deals. Most early foreign visitors agree that Madrid was exhausting, filthy, corrupt and frivolous, and also dangerous, with a seething predatory low life, redeemed by disappointingly few artistic or natural attributes. It also stank. With no drains of any kind, householders just threw out their household waste after 10PM with the careless cry *agua va!*—water on the way. As night falls you may still occasionally be surprised to feel splashes of cold water on your head, usually the result of someone watering, even hosing, the pot plants that flourish on almost every balcony. Perhaps in historic recollection of the former practice, watering plants after dusk is rather frowned upon as antisocial, even slightly disgusting.

A book entitled *Guide and Advice to Strangers who Come to the Court in which They are Taught to Flee the Dangers that there are in Court Life* first appeared in 1620. The author, Antonio Liñan y Verdugo, warned those from out of town who might come to do business in Madrid that "of every four things one sees, one cannot believe even two," for everything was just "fabulous appearances, dreamed up marvels, fairytale treasures and figures like actors on a stage." The handy guide also gave advice on how to avoid being robbed or attacked in the street. A later *Guide to Unwary Outsiders* of 1873 begins with the following cautionary couplet: "While in the court you must/ remember to move with care,/ for no one ventures to kiss/ without attempting to bite."

Felipe II

Felipe II's decision to settle the court in Madrid transformed the town from a sleepy backwater that possessed not a single printing press into a baroque imperial capital. But despite this achievement, he has been saddled with an exceedingly negative reputation down the centuries, which emerged even during his own lifetime as what Spaniards called "the black legend." Some historians have tried to restore the balance in recent years, and sought to brush up the king's image, but their efforts have been condemned by critics as an attempt to create a countervailing "rose-tinted legend." The argument was particularly lively in 1998 during the commemoration of the 400th anniversary of Felipe II's death. The main players in this historical debate were, as is often the case in Spanish historiography, Anglo-Saxon, with Geoffrey Parker upholding the traditional view of an austere, buttoned-up monarch, and Henry Kamen arguing that the "black legend" lacked any basis in historical fact, and was largely a figment of Protestant propaganda.

Felipe II came to the throne in 1556 as the most powerful monarch in the world. He inherited from his father the Holy Roman Emperor Carlos V, who ruled as Carlos I of Spain, an international empire that included most of Western Europe, South America, and important possessions in Asia. At the same time, Spain's aggressive foreign policy set it at war with Catholic France, Protestant England, and the Islamic Ottoman Empire. He also faced a rebellion in the Low Countries, and a revolt in his own back yard among *moriscos*, former Muslims nominally converted to Catholicism. It is hardly surprising, then, that Felipe aroused loathing at home and abroad.

But his reign coincided with the Siglo de Oro, a Golden Age of art, theater and literature that was never surpassed, and remains a vibrant component of *Madrileño* culture today. Lasting roughly between 1580 and 1680, the Golden Age was a century of artistic flowering unmatched since, except perhaps for a tentative few decades in the early twentieth century. His reign also saw the surge of intense religious activity associated primarily with the Inquisition, whose best efforts

were often turned against the most original thinkers. This, coupled with the need to entertain the volatile mass of poor and up-rooted people who flocked to the city, led the king to encourage popular participation in mass royal ceremonies, religious fiestas and theater.

As an individual Felipe was an austere, obsessive hypochondriac, a shy and piously, even fana-tically, religious man, who never shook off the influence of his father. Carlos I gave his son detailed written instructions on how he should behave as king, which included advice on how he should regulate his sex life with his future wife:

I am sure you told me the truth when you confided to me your past life and that you will continue thus until your marriage. But I must advise you from then on, since you are still young and of delicate health, and I have no other son, nor wish to have; so, much depends on you taking care of yourself. So do not give yourself straightaway or without moderation. You will not only damage your health, but weaken yourself so much that you risk not producing heirs or even dying... So I appeal to you that shortly after your marriage, you use any excuse to keep away from your wife and don't return too soon, and then only briefly... And if you, as you told me, have not yet had contact with a woman before your wife, do not let marriage provide the opportunity, because that would be sinful before God, and unworthy to your wife and the world. Keep yourself above rumors and temptations.

Prince Felipe was sixteen at the time. Carlos also urged his son not to depend too much on any single person. Felipe conscientiously took all his father's advice to heart. Unable to delegate, he confided in few, and tried in vain to administer his vast empire virtually single-handed while drowning in documents.

When everything became too much for him he sought refuge in one of his many country seats, hunting and enjoying his gardens. He tried, not without initial setbacks, to introduce the style of ornamental gardens that he had seen during his trip to the Low Countries, using imported gardeners. He gave meticulous instructions for horticultural work in Aranjuez, south of Madrid, where he installed camels in a private zoo, and in the Casa de Campo, where he introduced pheasants, and the medicinal herb gardens at El Escorial. He ordered flowers to be planted in pots, regulated by color and flowering season, and decorative trees. But such tastes, acquired in the Spanish-controlled Low Countries, were too exotic for austere Spain. When the king came back after a year away he found that the gardeners had omitted to water the plants and they had shriveled up and died. The gardeners had gone back to cultivating their fruit trees and olive groves, their almonds, mulberry trees, vegetables, and melons as they had always done. Felipe was renowned for this love of nature, but what he really liked was the *el jardín*, the garden. His compatriots preferred *la huerta*, the kitchen garden, and they still do.

Urban Pleasures

Despite the apparent grandeur of the Spanish empire and its seemingly endless cascade of wealth gushing in from South American silver mines, the foundations of the kingdom of Castille and of Madrid were economically precarious. Wars on all fronts drained the finances and forced the king to seek ever greater loans from German and Italian bankers. The result was spiraling debts that eventually even Andean silver could not cover. The defeat of the Invincible Armada in 1588 by England was the last straw that plunged Spain into crisis and an agony of self-doubt. The spirit of the age swung from heroism to disillusion or *desengaño*, creating the characteristic dualism of the Golden Age between optimism and pessimism, the dream and reality, enthusiasm and irony. The ambivalent mood is apparent in writings of Pedro Calderón de la Barca and the portraits of Diego Velázquez, and it prompted the bitter satires of Quevedo. "There are many things here that seem to exist and have their being, and yet they are nothing more than a name and an appearance," Quevedo wrote, toward the end of his life.

The economic crisis also shaped the society of the Golden Age, comprising precious few productive people, a great many idle spenders and a growing mass of what contemporaries called *marginados*—poor drifters or *pícaros*, who lived on their wits. Among them were impoverished gentry or *hidalgos*, who turned to Madrid as to a Mecca, in search of some favor or opportunity. The court acted as a great magnet, drawing to itself from all over the country the rootless, the dishonest, and the ambitious.

Legitimate business was often the last thing on visitors' minds. Madrid had little taste for manufacturing or trade, a trait still detectable today. It was, and remains, a place far more interested in consumption and patronage than in producing. In the sixteenth century the only people to know anything of commerce in Madrid were Genoese bankers. Manufacturing was confined to the production of lace, fans, leather-work, coaches and other objects for the court, crafts immortalized in the street names in the old part of town. The lack of manufacturing or any serious business activity may lie behind *Madrileños'* cheery—if apparently purposeless—vitality, observed by the Scottish writer Henry Inglis: "There is less appearance of business in the streets of Madrid than in any city I have ever seen: the population seem to have turned out to enjoy themselves. Two things contribute mainly to give that air of ease and pleasure to the pursuits of the inhabitants of Madrid, the great proportion of women of whom the street population is composed, and the extreme slowness of the movement." There is something about the extreme slowness of motion, Inglis goes on, that is "entirely opposed to business and duties; but the street population of Madrid, with few exceptions, merely saunter; and wherever you reach an open space... hundreds of gentlemen are seen standing, with no other occupation than shaking the dust from their segars."

This writer has identified another key social activity celebrated by *Madrileños* (and other Spaniards) apart from, indeed after they wake up from, the siesta. That is the *paseo*. Again, the English word "stroll" or "saunter" does little justice to this deliberate and elaborate social rite whose name became transferred to the boulevards—or *paseos*—where it was practised. The *paseo* takes place any time between the end of the siesta and nightfall, and is intended to enable the city dweller to benefit from the evening breezes that relieve the oppressive afternoon heat. Inglis earmarked the key to successfully practising the *paseo*, that it be conducted slowly, languorously and deliberately. It is this "extreme slowness of movement" that is hard for today's visitors to Madrid to get the hang of. They either stride along as if they were in any other western capital, that is, as if they were actually going somewhere, or they loll about vaguely and inelegantly as if in a daze, their casual body language considered by locals as aesthetically offensive, and a positive invitation for some passing *pícaro* to lift their bag.

The purpose of the *paseo*, and purpose it has despite its apparently random quality, is only partly to take the evening air. Mainly it is an opportunity for display, and for sizing up fellow *paseantes* or strollers. *Madrileños*, like many southern Europeans, are passionate about eye contact. Directly meeting someone's gaze is not, as it is in some cultures, considered either an aggressive act or necessarily a flirtatious one. Men will lock glances with other men, women with women, as part of the process of appraisal, sizing up, observing, checking out clothes, accessories, hair, every detail of personal style that the *Madrileño* takes so seriously. This is done openly, and to new arrivals, with a disconcertingly bare-faced impudence. But the *paseo* is also an opportunity to engage in conversation with your companions, friends or family, with whom you may walk arms linked, several abreast. The *Madrileño* man has the habit of strolling with his female companion with his hand placed around her shoulder so that his fingers caress her neck. It is a gesture that conveys both intimacy and possession. Inhabitants of the city are often brilliant at keeping up a lively exchange of conversation, rarely missing a beat of the social spectacle passing before them. Display is a crucial element in all this, the talent for which remains unsurpassed in Madrid as it has been down the centuries. Hence the instinct to dress up for the *paseo*, have your children, even your dog, perfectly orchestrated, and held in check.

As the Golden Age degenerated into the final last gasp of the twelve-year war of the Spanish Succession (1701–13), Habsburg corruption and poverty gave way to the Bourbon King Felipe V. Educated at Versailles, he launched an ambitious program of building works, including fountains, public sanitation, street lighting and the laying out of wide, tree-lined boulevards or *paseos*, where ladies and gentlemen, including royalty, would stroll, and so too would the lower classes. The *paseo* provided an opportunity for classes to interact. Madrid was for centuries a society comprised mainly of masters and servants, and relations between them were often freer than in other European capitals. The *paseo* was an informal, albeit structured, opportunity for contacts to be established, including those between classes. As the dangerous, precarious town life of the seventeenth century gave way to the more organized, safer and settled Bourbon eighteenth century, the *paseo* grew in importance to become an essential part of the *Madrileño* day, and an opportunity for women to parade openly, perhaps comparable to the spa-town pump room parades celebrated by Jane

Austen. Ramón de Mesonero Romanos describes the *paseo* in 1830 as an event: "where amorous intrigues rule the day, where the confusion, the constant social intercourse, the ceaseless civilities, the variety of clothes and faces, the noise of coaches and horses, the dust, the boys selling water and cinnamon... all combine at first to irritate foreigners, who, however, end up by loving it all."

Madrileños still appreciate the way a woman walks, the way she uses her hands, her fan, her eyes (Gautier noted that the Spanish word *ojear*, to eye or use your eyes, has no French equivalent), the way she dresses her hair, all of which show off to greater advantage when walking in the dying afternoon sun. All these attributes are closely observed. Curiously, Spaniards do not value the quality of a woman's voice, which is often loud and harsh. It is still a shock to see the most demure, elegant women of the capital shriek with all seductive allure of a blowtorch. Men, with their over-elaborate elegance, their hair slicked with *gomina*, their cologne, their too carefully matching ties or cravats and pocket handkerchief, that would look over the top, even ridiculous in the drawing room, can cut something of a dash in the sunny, leafy street.

Perhaps around this time the *piropo*, the improvised compliment hissed into a female ear by a passing male, gained currency. Spaniards, for all their fame as physical, tactile people, are not renowned for groping women in public. Such behavior, to be found in other Mediterranean cultures, is considered demeaning to Spanish male dignity. The flirtatious verbal compliment evolved into something of an art form, although in recent years it appears to have lost some of its former sophistication. "Your eyelashes are so long they could tie up my heart and bind it to you for ever" is an example of the *piropo* at its rococo best. Most women may have to make do with a murmured *guapa* (beautiful) or even the characteristic *chst* sound. Female etiquette is not clear on these occasions—some women interpret the *piropo* as outright harassment, which some of them undoubtedly are. A haughty indifference is probably in order, perhaps with a trace of a smile or a nod of appreciation if the *piropo* is particularly fine. If, however, a woman were to respond in any way to the implicit invitation, the man would probably die of shock.

The *paseo*, then, was not merely a languid affair; it could be quite hectic. Its spirit was summed up by the writer Lope de Vega in a letter to his patron the Duke of Sessa: "Madrid is still as your lordship left it, Prado, coaches, women, dust, executions, comedies, a lot of fruit—and very little money." The Prado, in this case, meant not the museum, but the shady tree-lined avenue along which the building later sprawled and whose name it assumed. The Paseo del Prado was originally a way of taming the countryside, or "prado" on the eastern fringes of the city. The smart people took over the stretch between the fountains of Cibeles and Neptune, a thoroughfare which became known as the Salón del Prado. Here they paraded on foot or in their carriages, or sat out on chairs to enjoy the spectacle that unfolded every evening between the siesta and dinnertime. "The crush is so great in this confined space," wrote Gautier,

> that you can scarcely put your hand into your pocket to take out a hand-kerchief. You have to tread on each other's heels and follow the crowd as if you were queuing for the theatre... The carriages are nothing extraordinary... But the horses are beautiful with their Andalusian saddles on which the proud young things of the city strut like peacocks. There is nothing more elegant, noble or gracious than the sight of an Andalusian stallion with its

beautiful plaited mane, its long thick tail reaching the ground... I have seen one mounted by a woman of a pink colour [the horse, obviously, not the woman] bathed in silver and of incredible beauty... The Prado is one of the liveliest spectacles you can see and it is one of the finest boulevards in the world. Not for the site, which is quite ordinary... but for the surprising numbers of people who go there every evening.

Much of Madrid can appear to some visitors, at first sight, ordinary. Hemingway said that most people who first went there didn't like it much. But when they do get to like it, what captivates them is the vibrant collective energy of the people, which is a key to understanding the culture of the city. This may be summed up as follows: unless any activity contains some element of fun, a *Madrileño* will not bother with it.

CHAPTER TWO

Puerta del Sol:
Ruffians and Royals

There remains no gateway at the Puerta del Sol, nor any image of the sun. The two big convents that once dominated this confluence of ten streets have gone, along with the church of Buen Suceso (Happy Event, an expression still used as a coy reference to an impending birth). Of the cafés and bookstores that once served as the focus for news in an age before newspapers there is little trace, nor of the benches where townsfolk gathered to exchange gossip and hatch plots. Yet, despite the aggressive incursion of vehicles, kiosks, street furniture, and other obstacles, the Puerta del Sol remains the thumping heart of Madrid. Its character was formed when it marked the eastern boundary of the town, the frontier or border post that at once separated and united those within and those without, an ambivalent haunt of teeming lowlife and a place where honorable citizens brushed shoulders with the dregs of society.

To get a taste, just cross the vast tumultuous space early in the evening, press with difficulty against the crush of lively people, or watch from the upper window of the pastry shop, La Mallorquina, one of the few establishments dating from the nineteenth century that retains its original function. In those days people remarked upon the waft of fragrant air around the Calle Mayor just where the street opens into the square. The sweet warmth still catches your nostrils today, from the ovens that reach under the square, with the scent of countless pastries bearing names like "Saint Anthony's egg yolks" or "Saint Catalina's sighs," recalling their origins in convents. But the most characteristic pastry is the light, fragrant, coiled *ensaimada*, brought in the nineteenth century from Mallorca, which gave the shop its name. But the turbulent history of the Puerta del Sol goes back long before then and has more sinister tales to tell.

Pícaros and Low Life

When in 1578 Felipe II's court favorite, Antonio Pérez, went in search of hired killers to assassinate Juan de Escobedo, the troublesome secretary of the king's half brother Don John of Austria, he sought his hitmen in the Puerta del Sol. This was a shady business that caused Pérez to flee from Spain under sentence of death. The town's eastern gateway became notorious throughout the seventeenth century as the haunt of *mal vivir*, of lowlife and of insolent scoundrels, known as *pícaros*. The *pícaros* were immortalized in a unique genre of satirical Spanish literature of the sixteenth and seventeenth centuries, the *picaresca* or picaresque. Cervantes' classic *Don Quijote*, published between 1605 and 1615, portrays the imaginary world of a knight errant, full of noble thoughts,

EL INGENIOSO
HIDALGO DON
QVIXOTE DE LA
Mancha.

*Compuesto por Miguel de Ceruantes
Saauedra.*

EM LISBOA.

*Impresso com licença do Santo Officio por Iorge
Rodriguez. Anno de 1605.*

courteous manners and altruistic quests, but it reveals, with a gentle irony, the real world of idleness, rudeness, and adventure. The *pícaro*, as depicted in Cervantes' world is both indolent and adventurous, and always on the move. Everyone is moving, and talking, coming and going on the roads and in the taverns across the country. But not once, in the whole of Cervantes' oeuvre, do you see anyone working. Work, to the sixteenth-century inhabitant of Spain's new capital, was seen not as a noble cause, but something more like the fulfillment of a penance. Minimum effort was the prevailing ethos; idleness was seen both as the ideal and as the most fertile terrain for love. Something of this atmosphere still clings to the Puerta del Sol.

It is unclear why the Sun Gate is so called. Some say that a medieval castle that bore a gilded motif of the sun once stood on the spot, others that the streets fan out from it like the sun's rays. Or even that the Comuneros in their regional revolt against the nobility and exorbitant taxation of 1520 placed a placard of the sun there. A final theory has it that you only have to stand or, if you install yourself early enough, sit in the upper window of La Mallorquina and look east across the square at sunrise to know why the most transited spot in Madrid is called Sol. "The original gate faced due east and provided entrance to the newly risen sun," writes Juan Antonio Cabezas in his classic 1950s guide. Sol marks the center of Spain, "*kilómetro cero*" the spot from which distances to all the towns of Spain are measured, the hub of the nation. But it was also originally nicknamed Pestilence Gate, and until well into the nineteenth century it frequently became waterlogged after heavy rain.

At the western end of the Puerta del Sol the Augustine monastery of San Felipe el Real was founded in 1534, whose raised terrace and cloisters became a popular meeting point and the marketplace for news and gossip. The actual "sun gate" between Calles Carretas and Montera was pulled down in 1570 to broaden what was becoming an important gateway in and out of the town. The spot, today a paradise of slot machines, became known as the "Mentidero de la Villa," the town's gossip shop. Luis Carandell in his brief but charming little guide, *Madrid*, says: "So wise must the people who frequented it have been, that it's said that news reached the Mentidero before the events themselves had taken place." And when, in 1841, the convent was pulled down and replaced by the handsome apartment building that stands today, gossip-mongers simply transferred their *mentidero* to surrounding cafés and invented the typical discussion group of Madrid, the *tertulia*. These cafés on the square are gone too, supplanted by *tertulias* in cafés elsewhere in the city. But the tradition of idle or sleazy gossip, the exchange of information of doubtful veracity, intrigue, and shady deals—still the great passion of some *Madrileños*—began here at the Puerta del Sol.

Here soldiers mustered before being marched to imperial wars, and those discharged from distant Flanders battlefields hung about in hope of better times. Landless peasants and other drifters converged to this place, looking for an opportunity to attach themselves to someone as a servant or bodyguard or a hanger-on, or seeking a chance to make a quick *real* from gambling, thieving, prostitution or just getting by on their wits. The whole purpose of Sol was to bring together a social mixture, those from high and low who might have a use for each other, or no use at all. The Italian writer Edmondo de Amicis described in 1873 how he was captivated by the Puerta del Sol:

The first days I couldn't tear myself away... I was there hours and hours, and I enjoyed myself so much that I would have liked to spend the whole day there. It is a square worthy of its fame, less for its scale and beauty than for the people, for the animation, the variety of the spectacle on offer throughout the day. It is a square like no other; at once a salon, a promenade, theatre, academy, garden, town square and market. From dawn to dusk you will see a constant multitude, and a multitude that comes and goes along the ten great streets that open on to the square. You'll find traders, demagogues, idlers, the unemployed, old retainers, elegant youths; here is trafficking, political chitchat, flirting, strolling, reading the newspapers, debt collecting, making rendezvous with friends, preparing demonstrations against the ministry, concocting false rumors that sweep through Spain, and fabricating scandalous tales of the city. On the pavements, wide enough to accommodate four carriages abreast, you have to force your way through. In the space of one paving stone you'll see a civil guardsman, a match-seller, a financier, a poor man, and a soldier. Groups of students pass by, servants, generals, ministers, respectable folk, bullfighters, ladies, beggars who whisper in your ear so as not to reveal themselves, women on the make who offer you a questioning look, light women who touch your elbow, everywhere high hats, a smile on the lips, hands seeking friendly hands, joyful greetings, shouts of tinkers laden with hardware with their shop around their neck, cries of newspaper sellers, shouts of the water sellers, hoots of buses, whips cracking, sabers rattling, guitars strumming, a blind man's songs.

Then the regiments pass with their bands, the king passes, the square is hosed with immense streams of water that cross in the air, people run with great armfuls of newspapers and supplements, an army of functionaries emerge from the ministries, the regiments pass again, shops light up, the multitude becomes denser, your elbow is touched more insistently, voices raise and the whole square is in movement. And it is not the bustle of a busy people; it is the vivacity of cheerful persons, a carnival-like joy, a restless idleness, a feverish overflow of pleasure that takes hold of you and makes you want to go round and round the square without leaving it: you are seized by a boundless curiosity and, to be honest, a desire to do nothing, to think of nothing, to eavesdrop upon conversations, to saunter and to laugh.

By the nineteenth century Sol had acquired the lightheartedly hectic buzz it has today. But it also kept the slightly disturbing edge you would expect in the vortex of any metropolis worth its salt. In centuries gone by, personal security throughout Madrid, and especially this spot, was too precarious for street life to be anything other than deadly serious, even threatening. The main brothels were clustered around here. One of them, situated between the Calle del Carmen and the Calle de la Salud, was renowned for having in its window an image of the Virgin, whose hands and head could be manipulated from behind by a special lever. The spectacle was so scandalous that a pair of religious-minded beggars denounced it for heresy. The brothel was duly closed and its managers jailed. An oratory and subsequently a convent were built on the site, later to make way for a couple of cinemas.

The area drew a seventeenth-century *demi-monde* of impoverished noblemen, *hildalgos*, "sons of somebody" who would rather starve than besmirch their honor by working, idlers and drifters, and the astute and ubiquitous *pícaros*. The mercenaries hired by the king's right-hand man, Antonio Pérez, were called *pícaros*. It was the first use of the term, according to the nineteenth-century biographer and scientist Gregorio Marañon, who gives a vivid account of Escobedo's death and a cruelly unflattering portrait of King Felipe, who, legend says, ordered the murder of his secretary. Rootless and marginalized, the poor formed an important and growing component of Madrid's fiercely unequal society in the Golden Age, as country folk flocked from all around just as the town's apparent economic prosperity, based on its gold and silver brought from the South American empire began to flag. Begging and cheating, praying and fiestas seemed to be the prospect facing many. The deserving poor had a recognized place in this bureaucratic Catholic society whose ideas and behavior were intently scrutinized by the Inquisition. They were issued with identity cards that granted them the right to beg alms from the plethora of religious foundations. This was in strict accordance with the Spanish belief—still vigorous today—that you don't exist unless you have a document to prove it. A contemporary equivalent is the sale of a newspaper for homeless people, *La Farola*, or *La Calle*. Many vendors brandish the paper as a badge, asking in a singsong whine for "a little help," to buy a hot meal or a room for the night. They may be reluctant to part with the one copy that justifies their presence on the street.

The seventeenth-century begging license, once achieved, gave the authorities absolute right to monitor its holder's every move and whip the precious document from his grasp at the hint of a transgression. The permit was valid for one year, confined the bearer within his or her parish, and renewal was dependent on devoted religious observance. In exchange for alms the licensed beggar was expected to pray for the souls of those who had given them. The genuine poor had a right to charity, but in return they had a job to do, to pray for the donors' souls. This *quid pro quo* is vividly sketched in the best known picaresque novel, *Lazarillo de Tormes* (1554), in which a blind man, assisted by our young hero, intones prayers for every conceivable misfortune in order to get money out of people:

> He knew hundreds of prayers off by heart and he said them in a low, relaxed and sonorous voice which made the church vibrate; he put on a humble and devout expression and looked very respectable... He knew prayers for lots of different things: prayers for women who couldn't have children, prayers for women who were pregnant and prayers for women who were unhappily married, to make their husbands love them... He made a lot of money from these tricks.

But however carefully the authorities sought to register the poor, and to chivvy and persecute them while at the same time granting them charity, they could do little to control the flourishing criminal underworld. This vigorous underclass was not, however, actively persecuted, and herein lies the ambivalence of the picaresque condition. Illegal acts were treated with a certain tolerance, such that *pícaros* were simultaneously outlaws and part of the social underbelly of the royal court. "The established power never considered the underworld as a threat, never saw it as an implacable enemy, but rather as an unwelcome guest impossible to get rid of: this remedy was never even suggested," says Manuel Fernández Álvarez in *Felipe II y su tiempo*. The reason for this *laissez-faire* attitude was that the criminal class was never in a position to challenge the society upon which it preyed. *Pícaros* even had their uses: they could be hired to carry out tasks that a justice system attached to the Crown could not openly touch, "a dirty war that the State could not carry out directly," observes Fernández Álvarez, with a conscious nod to political events in the 1980s, when illegal government hit squads carried out the killings of suspected Basque separatist gunmen. The sixteenth-century system was based on the exchange of favors intrinsic to court life: justice could turn a blind eye to certain wrongdoings in exchange for services rendered. Such services ranged from giving someone a fright in the dark to stabbing the same person to death, and is amply documented in the literature.

Cervantes satirized exactly such a contract killing in his picaresque novella *Rinconete y Cortadillo*, a rollicking tale of two young rogues who are initiated into a scruffy brotherhood of criminals. They are led by the astute but illiterate Monipodio, a Fagin-like character who acts as intermediary between the town's aristocrats and policemen who seek his help to settle their own scores on the quiet. In return, the authorities turn a blind eye to robberies orchestrated by Monipodio's gang of young thieves, taking their cut. It has been suggested that Cervantes's tale, published in 1613 was a direct allusion to the mysterious real murder of Escobedo in 1578, which contains all the qualities of a picaresque tale.

Cloak and Dagger

Antonio Pérez was the illegitimate son of a cleric of Jewish extraction who worked as secretary to Felipe II. When Pérez senior died, young Antonio took over the tasks of his father and became secretary of state for southern Europe. He became acquainted with Felipe's flamboyant half-brother, Don John of Austria, the illegitimate son of Carlos V. Don John yearned to be granted a kingdom of his own, an ambition echoed by the fictional Sancho Panza in *Don Quijote*. The king instructed Pérez to try to curb Don John's ambition, fearing that he planned to set up as an independent monarch in Spanish-controlled Flanders. But Pérez got on well with Don John and persuaded the king to give his brother some viceregal powers in Italy. John in return received Pérez generously at court and in his country house. Meanwhile, Pérez kept the king informed of his every move. In 1574 Pérez sacked Don John's personal secretary and replaced him with his old friend Juan de Escobedo, a relative of the king's private secretary, Ruy Gómez. When Don John negotiated a successful peace treaty with the Low Countries in 1577, he and Escobedo demanded a bigger say in the court in Madrid. In *Imperial Spain, 1469–1716*, the distinguished British historian John H. Elliott claims that Escobedo fell under Don John's spell and by the time of his return to Madrid "his devotion to Pérez had noticeably cooled." Escobedo even proposed leading an invasion of England, which the king strongly opposed, although he was to launch such an adventure some ten years later with catastrophic results.

Pérez ("vain, deceitful and sly," writes Elliott) meanwhile started to feel nervous because Escobedo ("dour and intransigent") had possession of a number of compromising letters between Pérez and Don John that referred to expectations of possible favors from the king. Escobedo became insistent, demanding royal recompense for years of service, but months went by and the king, who did not like him much, did nothing. Escobedo eventually started tightening the screw on Pérez. Perhaps he threatened to tell the king of Pérez's affair with the Princess of Eboli, the widow of Ruy Gómez who had returned to Court in 1576 after three turbulent years in a nunnery. Or perhaps he found Pérez and the princess selling state secrets to Dutch rebels. Versions vary. In any case, Pérez became so worried that he urged the king to give Escobedo an estate or a sinecure to make him back off. The king did nothing, so Pérez, realizing that Escobedo had it in his power to ruin him, resolved upon murder.

Escobedo was stabbed to death in the street by three assassins a few blocks from the Royal Palace as he was riding home on March 31, 1578. It was Pérez's fourth attempt to eliminate him. Before heading for the Puerta del Sol to recruit his contract swordsmen from *pícaros* willing to sell their services, he had vainly plied his vaunting rival with cups of poisoned wine, and on one occasion with a cream custard laced with arsenic.

But the murder that Pérez believed would save him from disaster marked the beginning of his downfall. To the amazement of observers, months passed without anybody doing anything to investigate this crime committed at the heart of the court. Geoffrey Parker, mining a rich seam of Spanish historiography in his *Philip II*, says that the reason was simple: "Escobedo was killed by order of the king and the deed was organized by Antonio Pérez." Elliott reports that the king, perhaps realizing that Pérez had tricked him into ordering the death of an innocent man, "passed through agonies of indecision." He allowed the killers to slip unharmed from Madrid. With Escobedo's family baying for justice, the king then arrested Pérez. One of the mercenaries, suborned apparently by the Escobedo camp, confessed his guilt and pointed the finger at Pérez. The king ordered Pérez to be interrogated under torture, whereupon he confessed to the killing, saying he was carrying out the king's orders. But he could not prove it. All his papers had been confiscated. He was condemned to death.

Before the execution could be carried out, Pérez escaped from prison with the complicity of his wife, Juana Cuello, who was allowed to sleep with him, and who offered a sumptuous banquet to fellow prisoners and the guards, thereby distracting their attention. Still weak from torture, he rode some 200 miles to Zaragoza, in the neighboring kingdom of Aragón, which enjoyed autonomous powers and a degree of legal immunity from Castille, where he had hidden copies of his correspondence with the king about Escobedo's death. He took refuge in a Dominican monastery amid demonstrations and popular riots in his favor, which the king's army put down at the cost of fourteen deaths. At this point the Inquisition stepped in, accusing Pérez of blasphemy, making pacts with Protestants, magic and sodomy, as well as opposing the Holy Office. In 1592 he had to undergo a ritual public confession of guilt, after which he agreed to flee to exile in France, and his effigy was publicly burned. In France, then England, he launched a campaign of defiance and intrigue against Felipe II that lasted not only until the king's death in 1598 but until his own in 1611. But the mystery remains. The historian Henry Kamen's view is that no proof exists concerning the king's involvement in Escobedo's death on a dark street in central Madrid. Parker—and most historians past and present—assume the king was behind the whole thing. Elliott believes that the king was manipulated by a cynical courtier primarily concerned to save his own skin.

The Picaresque

With unscrupulousness on such a scale characteristic of Madrid's ruling elite, it is perhaps hardly surprising that a satirical literature arose that mocked this farrago of hypocrisy and skullduggery from the vantage-point of those at the very bottom of a stratified society. The picaresque novel, generally considered to have been pioneered by *Lazarillo de Tormes*, was consolidated by the darker vision of *Guzmán de Alfarache* by Mateo Alemán in 1605, and Quevedo's subtle and sophisticated *La Vida del buscón* (1626), which is usually translated as "The Swindler." This covered the period of Spain's Golden Age from its economic and artistic splendor to its collapse and ruin.

The classic picaresque novel is an autobiographical tale whose hero, from the lowest social level with shameful family origins, is buffeted by misfortune. He makes his way in the world by tricks and deceits, driven by hunger or the desire for social advancement. The hero moves from master to master in an itinerant life whose gallery of personalities gives the narrator opportunity to observe various customs and social types with piercing shafts of sarcastic social criticism. The tales unfold as a succession of adventures and mishaps that contain stories within stories, folk tales and anecdotes, and explain the hero's final disgrace. The language is racy, colloquial, and spiced with fables and proverbs that lace modern-day Spanish, in the same way that Shakespeare's expressions have penetrated the English language so deeply that we are always surprised to discover their source. It comes as no surprise, however, to learn that the picaresque novels were all banned by the

Inquisition. The first time I read the opening words of *La Vida del buscón* was on a little poster in a subway train in Madrid as part of the city's literary classics promotion:

> *I come from Segovia. My father was called Clemente Pablo; he came from the same place, may he rest in peace! He was, as everybody knows, a barber, although his head was so much in the clouds that it annoyed him to be so-called and he said they ought to call him a reaper of cheeks and tailor of beards... As he shaved them he lifted their heads to wash their faces and my little seven-year-old brother easily stripped their pockets of every farthing they had...*

The duplicitous and precarious world of Don Pablos, *el buscón*, was created by the writer Francisco Quevedo, whose turbulent life, full of unexpected breaks and sudden reverses is another perfectly picaresque experience. Born in Madrid in 1580 and orphaned young, Quevedo was connected with the court, as his father, once a secretary to the daughter of the Holy Roman Emperor Carlos V, served the fourth wife of Felipe II and married a lady-in-waiting. He studied theology and obtained his degree at the university of Alcalá near Madrid. Quevedo was a prickly individual—a recent biographer, Pablo Jaraulde, believes that his aggressiveness derived from a basic insecurity—whose waspish humor won him many enemies. He had to lie low in Italy for a while

to escape the consequences of a duel in which he killed his opponent. But he enjoyed the protection of the Duke of Osuna, Viceroy of Sicily, who sent him to Madrid in 1615 as his personal ambassador, where on behalf of the duke, who had political ambitions, he handed out generous bribes to influential courtiers.

Intrigue caught up with him in Venice and he had to flee for his life disguised as a beggar. His fortune, together with the duke's, came crashing down and at the moment he should have been at the pinnacle of his career he was reduced to being the governor of a provincial prison. He wrote constantly: a treatise on currency, satirical poems, Greek translations, essays on philosophy. In 1621, while prison governor, he wrote a contemporary history and commentary on the death of Felipe II. He made huge efforts to ingratiate himself into court favor, but could not vanquish the enmity of powerful opponents, and was constantly engaged in bitter lawsuits. He wore curious lorgnettes with green-tinted lenses to correct his myopia and, with his shambling pigeon-toed gait, was the object of cruel scorn from his enemies. He referred to himself as *ciego y cojo* (blind and lame). Reputed to have been both a womanizer and a misogynist, he frequented brothels but married only late in life, briefly and unhappily. He railed against the corruption under Felipe III, the imperialist failures of Felipe IV and especially the vaunting power of the king's minister, Don Gaspar de Guzmán, the Count-Duke of Olivares. He harangued the count-duke in the twilight of the Habsburg monarchy under the catatonically torpid reign of Felipe IV—ill-advisedly, since the king's minister was for some two decades the most powerful man in Spain.

In a turnaround as swift and arbitrary as any picaresque tale would dictate, Quevedo was named royal secretary in 1632 and offered the post of ambassador to Genoa, which he declined. By 1639, when he was 59, Spain was in steep decline. Quevedo sums up the epoch in a couplet in one of his bitterest satirical poems, *Poderoso Caballero es Don Dinero* (A Powerful Gentleman is Mr. Money). In a neat summary of Spain's colonial history, he describes how "Don Dinero" was born honorably in the West Indies, came to die in Spain and was buried in Genoa, in settlement of debts to Italian bankers. Corruption was widespread in the ruling elite and Felipe IV did nothing about it. Condemned by Olivares for his writing, Quevedo was clapped in fetters and imprisoned in a monastery in León. It remains unclear exactly what the charges were against Spain's most brilliant and versatile writer, who had moreover often put his skills at the disposition of the regime. Probably it was because he wrote satires against the king— especially, as the years went by, against the unjust tax system that bore most heavily upon those who could least support it—and he was suspected of spying for France. He languished in jail for four years until the powerful minister's downfall in 1643. By then Quevedo was 63 and, weakened by his captivity, died two years later. When, on his deathbed, he was consulted about arrangements for music at his funeral, the sharp-tongued old satirist roused himself to say: *La música, páguela el que la oiga*—"Let those who hear the music pay for it."

His creation Pablos, the hero of *La Vida del buscón*, learns how to endure hunger, and that crime pays. The tale's translated subtitle is "An example of one who wanders the world, and the mirror of misers." Sent to study at the university with a young nobleman who has taken him up, Pablos hears that a legacy from his father—who was executed by his uncle, the public hangman—is waiting for him in Segovia. So he sets off on his own to claim it. He meets various oddballs on the way, all of whom are amusingly satirized. Pablos collects his money and moves on, making for Madrid. He meets an impoverished gentleman, who devotes himself to seeming comfortably off without working, although he is so poor that he has to walk with care to avoid revealing his bare backside beneath the cloak that he swings nonchalantly over his shoulder. The gentleman's life is all a fake, a make-believe world based on the real or imagined past glory produced by Mexican gold and Peruvian silver.

The gentleman tells Pablos what he might expect in Madrid:

The first thing you've got to know is that in Madrid you can find all types, half-wits and very sharp minds, the very rich and the very poor. The city hides criminals and a good man's qualities are not appreciated, and there are some people there, me for example, that you don't know anything about, where they came from or who they are. Some of us are gentlemen without funds, others empty-bellied, half-baked, scabby, skinny and wolfish. We live by our wits: more often than not our bellies are empty as it's very hard to get other people to feed you...

Pablos learns from his new friend's companions how to impress by ingenuity, pretense and flattery. But when the group suddenly finds itself in jail, he buys his escape, deserts them and makes his way to Seville, the richest city in Spain and the country's criminal heartland, where Cervantes' Monipodio runs his empire. On the way he joins a company of actors and makes a comfortable living as a playwright, but then falls in with a gang of cardsharps, takes up with a gambler's moll and decides to sail with her to South America, fearing his luck will eventually run out. The moral twist lies in the final sentences: "I thought things would go better in the New World and another country. But they went worse, as they always will for anybody who thinks he only has to move his dwelling without changing his life or ways."

Convents and Brothels

This irreverent satirical vision of the world developed from the po-faced, arbitrarily hierarchical society in which only aristocrats, clerics, state bureaucrats, or military officers were respected, and any attempt at criticism was ruthlessly censored on punishment of imprisonment and death. No one lifted a finger to do anything productive—work of any kind was generally frowned upon, and everyone's efforts were dedicated to trying to get into someone's service or secure a favor and escape from poverty and social indignity. The system bore heavily upon women, although women are frequently portrayed as sexually scheming and unscrupulous. Brothels, for instance were the obvious consequence of a social structure that sought—following Carlos V's advice to his son Felipe II—to banish the erotic from married life, while condemning a single woman who traded sexual favors. Many middle-class daughters whose families were too poor to provide the essential dowry faced no alternative but the convent or spinsterhood. Most nuns entered the convent with no vocation whatsoever; they were "desperate nuns" (*monjas desesperadas*). They, in turn, gave rise to a curious personality of the epoch, the *galán de monjas*, the wooer of nuns, typically a gentleman of good birth who stood close to the barred and shuttered windows of one the city's numerous convents, whispering to his chosen nun. Nestor Luján talks of the *tráfago amoroso* (amorous trade) in nunneries and the rape of nuns by clerics or lovers. Love affairs were mediated by ladies' maids, while *billets doux* were passed through the iron bars. Luján notes how brief and fleeting such affairs usually were and quotes a well-known proverb: "The love of nuns, a bush fire and wind from the backside are all the same."

Such affairs ostensibly revived the ideal of perfect platonic love, and became the subject of songs at court. They also provided picaresque writers with ample material for ribaldry. Pablos describes how he became "a barred-windows Johnny, after a bit of coif" and began to woo a nun, leaving the acting profession at her request. He started attending religious services in the courtyard of the convent and made his neck "a couple of yards longer" by craning to catch a glimpse of his nun, joining the gamut of pathetic lovers who roasted in the summer sun and "sprouted shoots and roots" in the winter's damp. This was a frustrating kind of romance: "If she speaks it's like falling in love with a caged thrush, and if she doesn't it's like falling in love with a picture... I saw I was well on my way to Hell just for indulging my sense of touch..." Eventually he wheedles some money from her and makes off.

The nuns had the reputation of being fickle and demanding, and it was widely believed that the Antichrist would come to earth born of the sacrilegious love between a monk and a nun. One convent, the Benedictine convent of San Placido, founded in 1623 by Doña Teresa Valle de la Cerda under the patronage of Felipe VI's secretary Jerónimo de Villanueva, came to enjoy a particularly scandalous reputation, due initially to rumors that numerous nuns, including Doña Teresa herself, were possessed by the devil and had to be exorcised by their confessor, Juan Francisco Garcia Calderón. Doña Teresa had been engaged to marry Don Jerónimo but when all the preparations were completed, she told him she did not want to marry as she had a religious vocation. Don Jerónimo not only accepted her decision, but agreed to fund the building of the convent, next door to his house off the Calle del Pez in the Malasaña district. It became a popular meeting point for members of the court, including the Count-Duke of Olivares and King Felipe IV himself.

A peaceful, closed community established itself until, a few years later, one of the nuns began terrorizing her spiritual sisters with strange gestures, words and actions. Despite efforts to calm her, she became more and more violent. García Calderón, the confessor, known for his virtue and his deep doctrinal knowledge, declared that she was possessed by the devil. A few days later, another nun began to display the same symptoms, and in a short time, the majority of the community, including the prioress, was, according to Don Francisco, bewitched by the devil. Three years later, the Holy Office imprisoned the confessor, the prioress and many of the nuns. The trial lasted several years, during which the facts were never fully clarified. Under torture, Calderón confessed to having engaged in sexual practices with his spiritual daughters, and was condemned to life imprisonment by the Inquisition. The nuns were separated and sent to different convents throughout Spain. Doña Teresa was banished for four years, but having good connections at court, was able to return as abbess long before her sentence was served.

Worse depravity was to come, however, a year later when Felipe IV courted one of the nuns, Margarita de la Cruz, plotting to see her with the help of Jerónimo de Villanueva, who lived next door. Villanueva had commented on her beauty to the king, who decided to see for himself. The king slipped into the convent, initially in disguise, on several occasions so that he could admire the lady anonymously. Rumors began to swell around the court about the king's actions, but, determined to win Doña Margarita, he ordered a tunnel to be dug linking his friend's house with the convent through a coal cellar, so that he could enter the convent without being seen. Wind of his plans reached Doña Teresa, who urged the count-duke and Villanueva to persuade the king to drop the idea, but they could not dissuade him from his plan to visit Margarita's chamber at night. Forewarned of his impending nocturnal visit, Doña Teresa persuaded the nun to lie on a funeral bier and pretend to be dead. She carried a crucifix and was surrounded by flowers and lighted candles.

News of the scandal reached the ears of the Inquisition and eventually the Pope, who demanded to see all the relevant documents and started proceedings against Villanueva. After two years of deliberations, Don Jerónimo was acquitted on pain of fasting and almsgiving. He was also banned from the convent and forbidden to refer to the scandal. The Count-Duke of Olivares stepped in to make sure the king's indiscretion went no further. He made the inquisitor-general Antonio de Sotomayor an offer he could not refuse: a large sum of money and retirement in Córdoba, or banishment within 24 hours. Don Fray Antonio accepted the first option, but tipped off Rome to pursue the matter. The count-duke then ordered strongmen to arrest and jail the messenger, Alfonso Paredes, whom the inquisitor had dispatched to Rome. The casket containing the incriminating evidence was swiftly returned to Madrid where, the story goes, the king and the count burned it without even looking inside. Paredes remained in prison until his death, while Felipe VI was so horrified at the outcome of his immoral scheming that he ordered the installation of a clock in the convent that rang the death knell at every hour. He also commissioned the artist Diego de Velázquez to paint his masterwork, *Christ on the Cross*, which remained in the convent until the early nineteenth century and now hangs in the Prado. Legend says that once the king realized the trick that had been played on him, he achieved his aim and continued to visit the lady.

Those women who resisted the convent in favor of spinsterhood were also prey to ladykillers, who later came to be known as Don Juans. Should they become pregnant, they had to abandon the child or disgrace the whole family. This explains the proliferation of foundlings or *niños espósitos*, who were frequently dumped at dead of night by a fountain or in a church. It was common for Madrid's bell-ringers who opened church doors in the early hours to find one or more baskets containing newborn babies who had perished in the terrible winter night. Those who survived were named after where they were found, hence the rich litany of Spanish surnames including "de la Iglesia," "de la Fuente," "de la Calle," "del Rio," and so on.

Appearances and Favors

The main social goal in picaresque society was respectability. That meant money, of course, plus the ability to make the best showing possible in a world where giving a good impression—*quedar bien*—was, and in Madrid remains, paramount. When the tearaway teenagers Rinconete and Cortadillo first meet (typically taking a siesta in the porch of a roadside inn), they introduce themselves. One confesses to be on the run from Madrid after suffering a beating for having robbed a seller of papal pardons of all his money: "I set off to do my exile so speedily I did not have chance to find a mount." The other confesses that he too made a quick getaway from Toledo after a magistrate took an interest in his thieving: "'But I... contrived not to meet him, leaving the city so swiftly that I did not have time to fit myself out with a mount, money, hired coach, nor even a cart.' 'Forget it,' said Rincon, "for now that we know each other, there's no occasion for these grand airs. Let's confess simply that we hadn't a bean, nor even any shoes.'"

These tales, to which contemporary sayings and comments in any daily newspaper in contemporary Madrid make constant reference, are an astute reflection of social conditions, especially of the sharp division between the wealthy aristocracy and the impoverished mob. There was nothing exclusively Spanish about such a gulf, but what made it unique was the lack of any social layer in between. "The uniqueness of Spain lay not so much in this contrast as in the absence of a middling group of solid respectable, hardworking bourgeois to bridge the gulf between the two extremes," writes Elliott. Seventeenth-century Madrid was polarized in a way summed up by Sancho Panza's grandmother: "There are but two families in the world, the haves and the have-nots (*el tener y el no tener*)." And the dividing line between one and the other was not rank or social position, but whether they had anything to eat. Food created its own social gradation. Every Spanish picaresque novel is obsessively preoccupied with food and recounts in minute detail the efforts to obtain food, how to eke out meager morsels and how to pretend both to yourself and to the world that you had eaten when you hadn't. Such efforts produced amazing feats of ingenuity, reflected in the common saying: *más listo que el hambre* –"smarter than hunger." Securing the next bite was the overwhelming concern of the mass of the populace, from the impoverished *hidalgo* surreptitiously pocketing crumbs at court, to the *pícaro* making a desperate raid on a market stall, in an episode in *Don Quijote*. Long weeks of emptiness passed in scheming for a square meal, which would then be wolfed down in an orgy of eating, and shortly forgotten as the pangs of hunger returned.

What drives the picaresque novel, apart from the random encounters that give it all the anarchic enchantment of its present-day descendent—the road movie—are the social transactions, the trafficking of favors between the haves and have-nots. Picaresque literature is full of examples of the very Spanish concept of *el favor*, that great lubricator of social intercourse which remains a vital element in modern Spanish society.

Lazarillo de Tormes, published anonymously in 1554, is the first picaresque novel, episodic and cheerier in tone than darker, later examples of the genre. Lazaro's father dies in war after being banished for some civil transgression. His mother, unable to support him, sends him off in the care of a blind beggar. In the service of the blind man he learns to endure hunger and cold and to shift for himself. One typical exchange shows how he learns to match the blind man's craftiness. Man and boy agree to share a bunch of grapes, each taking one at a time. But the blind man starts to take two at a time, Lazaro keeps up and they end up stuffing themselves as fast as they can:

When the bunch was stripped he sat there for a while holding the stalk; then he shook his head and said:
"Lazaro you've been doing me. By God I swear you've been taking three grapes at a time."
"I didn't you know," I said, "but what makes you think I did?"
The crafty old man replied:
"You know how I spotted you were eating three grapes at a time? Because I was eating two at a time and you didn't say anything!"

Lazaro's master's cruelty forces him to desert, after taking suitable revenge, but later he acknowledges a debt of gratitude to the old man, his only teacher. He then finds himself attached to a penniless gentlemen, and finds his ingenuity tested to the limit simply to keep from starving. The poor boy, instead of being helped is impoverished further by his master, whom he has to support by begging. The short tale again satirizes that deep-seated Spanish preoccupation: to impress and put on a brave show, attributes considered even more important than being warm or fed. This streak of vanity is caricatured by the gentleman who swaggered around town greeting his prosperous friends, even though he had not even a shirt to wear under his cloak, and had to accept bread stolen by his servant to stave off starvation. "It's a matter of honor you see," he explains, saying that he forsook his life of comfort and prosperity, fleeing his home town because a neighbor who was his social inferior refused to doff his hat first.

Lazaro gets the message: "This sort of people have an old and well-kept rule. They may not have a penny in their pocket but they've got to keep up appearances. There's nothing anybody can do about it. They're like that until they die."

The tone of *Lazarillo* is basically lighthearted, but according to the writer Ana Sanchez Salcedo in *La Picaresca*, catalogue of an exhibition mounted by the regional government of Madrid in 1999, that of the later *Guzmán de Alfarache* "already reflects the pessimistic spirit of the baroque age, it is the scornful, satirical mirror of a society in crisis. Together with Cervantes' *El Quijote*, the work of Mateo Alemán is considered to mark the birth of the modern novel."

Mateo Alemán

Alemán's own life is full of picaresque details. Born in Seville in 1547, he studied arts, technology and medicine, but abandoned his studies when his father died, and fell on hard times. He began a haphazard life, trading and sinking into debt. He got a job in with the Royal Bookkeepers, which did not improve his circumstances much. On one occasion he freed some neighbors from jail, and found himself with a prison term in Madrid as a result. Freed, he obtained the post of investigating the conditions of prisoners condemned to forced labor in the mines. He became acquainted with a homicidal friar, cattle thieves, bandits, deserters and ruffians of all sorts. Finally, Alemán decided to devote himself to literature, but despite the success of *Guzmán*, prosperity eluded him. With mounting debts he returned to prison, this time in Seville. He spent time in Lisbon, then in 1608 sailed for Mexico where he continued writing and died sometime after 1615. In a letter to a friend written in 1597, Alemán expresses his concern at the increase of the number of *pícaros* in Spanish society. He distinguishes between three types of poor: those whom nature prevents from earning a crust; the "rich poor and the poor rich;" and the fake poor, the *pícaros*, who, "being bad, lose their good qualities, sucking the substance from which the poor must subsist." Alemán wrote in a letter introducing his novel that he aimed to illustrate, by describing "some of the stratagems and tricks of the fakes," the difference between the good and bad poor.

The character Guzmán de Afarache comes from a bad family, but pretends to be from aristocratic stock. He leaves home and heads for Madrid with his character as *pícaro* already well established. His adventures begin and he carries out skillful tricks to prosper in society. He travels around serving various masters: masons, captains, the French ambassador, sometimes as a simple servant, sometimes as a jester or a pimp. At times he deceives, at others he is deceived. He tries to change his condition, but without conviction: "I resolved to be good; but I grew tired of the attempt after two steps." Finally he is sent to the galleys, from whose benches he tells the tale. Lazarillo is a clear forebear of Guzmán, but the later creation is a cynic who cheats for pleasure, not, as Lazaro does, out of hunger. The author pleads for this tale to be considered as a lesson of the bad end to which a bad life leads: hence the text contains ethical speeches about the sale of jobs, revenge, friendship and justice. Still, it is not a serious work, and seeks to raise a smile with the *pícaro*'s tricks. It is elegant, masterful satire. It was a huge success.

Picaresque episodes are so sharply drawn that it is difficult to imagine that they were not based on real life, especially the tales of desired social advancement. Luján notes that seventeenth-century literature was full of Spaniards' obsessive ambition to own a horse-drawn carriage. It was, he says, a necessity for them as an indication of social worth. Parallels are easily drawn with today's yearning for the smartest, fastest car or piece of electronic gadgetry. All this despite, or perhaps because of, fierce restrictions imposed by Felipe II; only nobles were allowed to use coaches drawn by two horses, four horses were permitted only if their masters were being driven, six-horse carriages were a prerogative of the royal family. Coaches were, in any case, heavily taxed. The aim of these rules, a relic of feudal sumptuary laws that dictated what members of each social stratum could wear, was partly to discourage the enjoyment of gratuitous luxury and partly to keep each person in their social place. Where your precise place in the social hierarchy was so clearly and minutely identified, it naturally encouraged a fierce desire to move up a notch.

The carriage rule seemed also intended to prevent the conveying of ladies to dubious rendezvous and to prevent indecent intimacies from occurring within the vehicle. Quevedo described these *navios de iniquidad* (ships of iniquity):

> You can't imagine the cycle of sin that goes on in them. A maiden steps into a carriage through the door on one side and emerges a future mother from the door on the other side... Oh, coaches, coaches, how much harm have you done to our realm! How many households have you destroyed, how many marriages have you broken, how many rich men have you impoverished, how many jealousies and resentments have you caused, how much honor have you put into question, how many families have you broken apart!

Nonetheless, throughout the seventeenth century it became the height of *Madrileño* fashion to *ruar el coche*, to go for spin, especially for women. The playwright Tirso de Molina invented a new word for the pastime—*cochizar*—and wrote the following verse in *La huerta de Juan Fernández:* "A maiden in her house/ is a plum on the tree/ who sometimes at thirty three/ has flowered and become a prune./ But in Madrid there is none/ who is what she seems, because at birth/ she's put in a coach instead of a cradle./ So that when she matures she just/ drives around [*cochizando*] day and night until in the end, maidens in a coach/ are plums in a basket." At the end of the century, the writer Quiñones de Benavente has one of his characters saying: "I would rather go by coach even if I don't eat." It sums up the *pícaro*'s philosophy.

In *La Vida del buscón*, the hero Pablos gives a snide opinion of Madrid when, answering a passing soldier who asked him if he has come from Madrid, he says he has passed through the town. "'That's the best thing you could have done, pass through it,' comes the reply, 'it's a lousy place. By god, I'd rather be somewhere in snow up to my waist, doing a manly job and chewing wood, than put up with the way they fleece an honest man.'" But typically, the soldier turns out to be a loudmouth and a charlatan. One of the Swindler's rare reverses occurs in Madrid when he meets up again with his former noble friend Don Diego, whom he had served in their student days. Don Diego finds his erstwhile servant courting a cousin of his, passing himself off as a man of wealth and property and boasting to a couple of gentlemen friends that he is going to marry a lot of money. "Don Diego didn't stay to hear any more but went straight back home. On the way he met my two latest friends (the one with the noble insignia and the jeweled chain)... and told them all about me. He told them to arm themselves and to waylay me that night in the street and knock my teeth through my head." Pablos is ferociously attacked and left bleeding in the street to be rescued by the nightwatchman. He is taken to a barber who stitches up a knife wound on his face "as long as a hand," his cover blown, his prospects for a fine marriage in ruins. The site of his ruin: the Puerta del Sol.

CHAPTER THREE

The Royal Palace: The World of Velázquez

Diego Rodríguez de Silva y Velázquez, who was born in 1599, revolutionized European painting by portraying his subjects with a realism so palpable that you feel you may bump into them on the streets of Madrid. But of his own long and productive life in the city there remains little that reveals what he was really like. This is not just because of the passage of time. It has to do with historical accidents, political upheavals, bizarre lapses of judgment by those in authority down the centuries, and the artist's own efforts to cover his tracks and project himself as something that he was not. For a man so piercingly shrewd in revealing the innermost thoughts and ambitions of his subjects, from monarch to street urchin, his own desires were remarkably convoluted and veiled.

He wanted to be honored both as a great painter and as a fine gentleman. These two ambitions drove his life's work but were in mortal contradiction in a feudal society that rated an artist as merely an artisan. Eventually, shortly before his death, he achieved both his goals, but through stealth, manipulation and single-minded dedication to self-advancement, characteristics that one would never attribute to him judging from the apparently spontaneous, intuitive brilliance of his work.

Velázquez spent his whole career juggling with the contradiction between appearance and reality. This is a very *Madrileño* preoccupation, although the artist was actually born in Seville, a grand and cosmopolitan city in those days, and came to Madrid only when he was 24. But like many of those in his adopted city, he laid paramount importance upon how things seemed: the main thing was *quedar bien*, to appear in the best possible light. In the Habsburg court he was to serve all his life, this desire for superficial appearance was far more important than the underlying reality. And yet Velázquez, more vibrantly than any artist in Europe, immortalized the reality surrounding him. He even had the nerve to impose his own ambitions upon that reality, portraying himself in his most masterly and realistic work, *Las Meninas*, wearing a noble insignia to which he aspired but to which he was not—until three years later—entitled. He lived the same contradiction between dreams and reality that many *Madrileños* experience today, and he got away with it by virtue of his talent and his skillful engagement with men in power.

Perhaps it was the clear-eyed realism of Velázquez's vision that prompted him to adopt the lifelong practice of obsequious deference. That seems duplicitous, but a good many *Madrileños* would still regard such a stratagem as perfectly consistent with the goal of achieving an ultimate ambition. At any rate, from the moment the young artist pitched up in Madrid, he played his cards close to his chest, speaking little and conducting a blameless private life, providing no cause for malicious gossip. In the seething *mentideros* or rumor mills of the city, Velázquez's name seems never to have cropped up, never even mentioned by that inveterate destroyer of reputations, the playwright Lope de Vega. Velázquez was a revolutionary so discreet that he made no impact whatsoever on the political scene that he chronicles so faithfully. He was a man so correct in his behavior that would-be rivals fell away powerless, unable to find a weapon to wield against him. He was a provincial outsider who triumphed at court and survived the downfall and death of the powerful patron who brought him to the notice of the recently crowned King Felipe IV, his fellow Andalusian, the Count-Duke of Olivares. Velázquez, low-key and uncommunicative, devoted himself entirely to work and family. Over the years he prospered under the king's protection, and a few months before he died in 1660 he finally achieved the honor he had craved. But where, one wonders, did he meet the ruffians and drinkers with their rough complexions who mock us still with their sparkling, cynical glances?

Career Painter

At the age of twelve, Velázquez was apprenticed to the Sevillian painter Francisco de Pacheco for six years, living with the family as a sort of servant. His first step toward social advancement was to marry his master's daughter Juana (apparently a common practice among shrewd apprentices), with whom he was blissfully happy all his life. Pacheco introduced him to his fellow Sevillian Don Gaspar de Guzmán, Count-Duke of Olivares, who by 1622 was installed in the court in Madrid as the indecisive young monarch's *valido* or right-hand man: the most powerful man in Spain. Through the Count-Duke's good offices, Velázquez was presented at court and commissioned to paint the king's portrait. The result was so well received that it opened the way to the royal favor that the artist enjoyed all his life. In October 1663 the king appointed Velázquez his court portraitist. Velázquez moved his wife and young daughter to Madrid, lodging initially in the Calle de la Concepción Jeronima, behind the Plaza Mayor in the heart of the Habsburg city, and embarked upon his road to triumph.

That first portrait of Felipe IV, executed at the moment when he was the most powerful monarch in the world, marked the high point of Spain's imperial glory. Velázquez captured in this painting the pinnacle of Spain's world expansion and dominance just at the moment it was to enter its decline. Perhaps even more faithfully than the brilliant writers of his time, he charted Spain's slide from elegant grandeur to decadence and ruin. As the years rolled by and portrait followed royal portrait, successive images of the monarch show his face becoming progressively older, clouded by worries, disillusioned by defeats abroad and revolts at home. Finally the point came when the king declined to sit for more paintings because he had no wish to face the portrayal of his own decline.

One of Velázquez's finest portraits is his equestrian study of Don Gaspar de Guzmán himself, painted some time in the 1630s, when the king's favorite was at the zenith of his powers. The painting brilliantly displays Velázquez's twin talents for both realism and deference. He portrays his patron as a proud nobleman in his prime astride a prancing horse, his mustaches arrogantly twirled, his body turned away to conceal his bulky midriff. He is clad in black armor and a grotesquely exaggerated billowing general's sash, his arm raised as if to lead his armies into battle. It is all theater; in reality the count-duke was slow moving, gout-ridden, and had no military ability or experience of war. His skills were rather manipulative and bureaucratic. But this magnificent portrait vibrates with energy and force. It seems real.

The Buen Retiro
The Count-Duke of Olivares held the dithering king under his thumb for more than twenty years. Around the time Velázquez painted his portrait, the count-duke sought to consolidate his influence over the king by organizing the construction of a huge palace complex to the east of Madrid that the king could use as a summer retreat. The count-duke's plan, it was said, was to build a glorious gilded pleasure palace for the king that would effectively cut the monarch off from the day-to-day running of the country, leaving his astute *valido* with a free hand. The Palace of the Buen Retiro, as it was called, formed the focus for the Botanical Gardens and the Prado park to the east, and dominated the whole area of the city that grew up in its shadow, shifting for the first time the center of gravity away from the Royal Palace on its fortress site on the city's western edge.

Only two buildings remain of the fabulous Buen Retiro: one is the former ballroom, the Casón del Buen Retiro, which faces the curlicued main gate to the Retiro park. The building, cruelly modernized, is now part of the Prado Museum, housing nineteenth-century paintings. And nearby is the second, the sole remaining wing of the palace, which contains the magnificent 100-foot long ceremonial hall of kingdoms— the Salón de Reinos built in the 1630s—whose ceiling celebrates the 24 kingdoms of the Spanish monarchy. The building currently houses the Army Museum. The Salón de Reinos, whose vaulted ceiling is a virtual

Sistine chapel of gilded escutcheons and coats of arms, is a rare example of Velázquez's art as an interior decorator that has astonishingly survived to the present day. The kingdoms illustrated include not only the ones you would expect, Aragón, Navarra and Catalonia, but also Portugal, Lombardy, Naples, Austria, Milan, Peru, Mexico, Sardinia, Sicily, Burgundy and Flanders—a dazzling testimony to the reach of Spanish power in its imperial glory days.

Velázquez painted five equestrian portraits of the royal family and his masterpiece *The Surrender of Breda*, also known as *The Lances*, specifically to decorate the Salón de Reinos. These paintings are held by the Prado Museum, which plans as part of its expansion project to return them eventually to their original setting. The fascinating hotchpotch of centuries' worth of rifles, swords, uniforms, cannon, campaign tents, suits of armor and faded scarlet-and-gold banners currently occupying the building is due to be evacuated to the Alcázar of Toledo in the teeth of opposition from the military old guard. Perhaps a lingering military yearning to recall imperial glories accounts for the survival of this extraordinary room, when so many comparable treasures have been lost. It still evokes, perhaps more than any other point of the city, Spain's confident opulence at the peak of its imperial grandeur, and it is easy to imagine the artist lovingly crafting the succession of royal heraldic devices, honoring both his art and his monarch.

At the opposite, western, side of the city lies the Royal Palace, the heart of the court where Velázquez lived and worked. The pompous pile set high on the site of the original fortress or Alcázar replaced the medieval palace that was largely destroyed by fire in 1734. The Plaza del Oriente to the east ("orient") of the palace is a product of the early nineteenth century, when the occupying French king, Joseph Bonaparte, Napoleon's brother, cleared away a clutter of churches, convents and houses to create an open view from the palace rooms. In the center of the square, recently restored as a fine pedestrian garden after a period of being invaded by traffic, is a statue of King Felipe IV astride a rearing horse. The statue, based on a sketch by Velázquez, is one of the finest in Madrid, and was executed by the Florentine sculptor Pietro Tacca in 1640.

It originally stood in the courtyard of the other palace, the Buen Retiro. Tacca created the horse's gravity-defying prance by construc-ting the hindquarters from solid bronze, appar-ently following the advice of Galileo. On the stone base is a bas-relief of the king decorating his court painter.

Apart from the statue, little remains to show the painter's link with this spot, where he spent most of his life in the king's service. The décor of the original palace, for which Velázquez was largely responsible, was destroyed in the fire. A recently erected plaque on the curved wall of the building opposite the palace that now houses the elegant Café de Oriente, next to the Teatro Real Opera house, says that Velázquez lived and worked in a building nearby attached to the palace. The truth is that the remains of that building, the royal Treasury House, a grace-and-favor dwelling granted to the artist by the king, were destroyed in 1996 to make way for an underground parking garage. The remnants of the place where Velázquez produced his most famous late works, and whose chapel was portrayed in the background of his masterwork *Las Hilanderas* (The Spinning Women) were bulldozed amid a scandal that horrified Madrid's cultural world. Entrance to the fateful parking garage is just a few steps from the commemorative plaque. Defying howls of outrage, the conservative Mayor of Madrid, José María Álvarez del Manzano, justified the decision to destroy the last vestiges of Velázquez's home by saying that Madrid was full of such buildings.

Up the hill just a few hundred yards to the south, is the Plaza Ramales, where Velázquez was buried. But this spot too has had its associations with the artist blurred over time. Until April 1999, it was a grassy little oasis at the confluence of several nineteenth-century mansions, symbolically protected from hectic circulating traffic by low iron railings of the kind that might surround a suburban bowling green. The only clue that this was the resting place of Spain's finest Golden Age painter was a pretty plinth, erected in 1961, bearing the inscription: "In this place was situated the parish church of San Juan, where the Court painter Silva y Velázquez was buried." The church was pulled down in 1809, in yet another attempt by Joseph Bonaparte to clear away ecclesiastical buildings to free up space in the clogged city. The job was hastily completed within days. In April 1998, the Madrid town hall authorities announced that they were planning to widen the roundabout. When the national heritage body found out—apparently by reading reports in the local press—it ordered a halt to any building work until efforts had been made to find Velázquez's remains. Only the church's walls had been pulled down in the rough and ready demolition job in 1809, leaving the crypt untouched. It was assumed, therefore, that Velázquez's bones lay within. Since detailed historical records remained of the artist's coffin and burial garb, there were high hopes of finding his remains. Some historians remained skeptical, however, saying that it was the custom at the time to fling all bodies into a common ossuary, and to tamp them down with the passing years to make room for more. The town hall, sensitized to public opinion after the parking garage scandal, grudgingly agreed to halt the bulldozers, but refused to pay for the work. The Culture Ministry said that it would pay the bill when it found enough money. Nearly a year later archaeologists began digging, and their search went on for months, laying open the entire square. Finally, early in 2000, experts admitted that amid all the debris and unidentified bones that were turned up, there was no way of establishing for sure whether the mortal remains of Velázquez were there or not.

High and Low

If you stroll out on to the Plaza del Oriente after a night at the Opera, you may be lucky enough to come across an electrifying performance by a one-man theatrical troupe who, against the backdrop of the Royal Palace and the flushed Madrid sunset that Velázquez immortalized, enacts the entire history of Cervantes's *Don Quijote*. The out-of-work actor Luís Hostalot wears on his head a helmet constructed of a kitchen colander spiked with forks; his old nag Rocinante is a stepladder on which he teeters precariously, brandishing an ancient sword in his right hand. With his extravagant gestures and his eccentric appearance he perfectly embodies the quest of the Knight of the Sad Countenance. Smart American tourists, bemused Japanese and stunned locals in their opera-night finery stop dead in their tracks en route to the café. With wild eyes and flailing locks, he declaims to the Madrid night this epic of Spanish literature, one of the finest novels in the world, flinging back his helmet to reveal a waxen bald pate when he switches to the character of Quijote's faithful squire Sancho Panza. He falls off his horse, becomes entangled in the arms of an invisible windmill and rails against those he thinks are keeping him from his sweetheart Dulcinea.

Your first reaction is incredulous amusement at this astonishing spectacle. Is the poor man is deranged, on drugs? But so compelling is his sincerity, his dignity amid his ridiculous clanking ironmongery, his passionate belief in his reckless venture, that the crowds linger, sit on the Opera house steps, ignore the persistent street violinist who fruitlessly shoves his bow up their nostrils. This strange man, with a battered leather waistcoat and ragged shirtsleeves simply is Quijote and his loyal servant battling against the limitations of worldly existence. Like Quijote, this enterprising actor becomes more lovable, worthier of our respect as his tale unfolds. And we find that at the end, when the actor acknowledges the showers of applause and coins, despite the preposterous fantasy he has constructed, his feet are still on the ground, he is not mad, but revealing through his art some timeless truth about human endeavor, loyalty and desire.

Cervantes died in 1615, a few years before Velázquez came to Madrid, but the writer's pioneering ability to portray with honesty and sympathy the least prepossessing characters of his time—from the lowest to the highest—was a skill Velázquez brought to painting. In addition to painting members of the royal family, dukes, princesses, popes, and cardinals, Velázquez also portrayed the stunted and handicapped dwarves, the *bufones* who lived at court as mascots and jesters, treating each one as an individual with the same respect that he showed the king. Even the dogs that slump at their royal masters' feet exude weary wisdom. His subjects are neither sentimentalized nor caricatured, but closely observed and portrayed with a benevolent neutrality unprecedented in its day. The works for which Velázquez is best loved are those of ragged street ruffians or artisans whom he portrays as gods or Greek philosophers.

The Triumph of Bacchus, also known as *Los Borrachos* (The Drunkards) and painted some time before 1629, must be the most realistic, affectionate and beautifully executed celebration of a ruffians' booze-up in the history of European painting. The artist has taken a lighthearted interpretation of a mythological figure—the Greek god capable of freeing mortals from their slavery, if only briefly, through the gift of wine. The painting, glowingly restored in recent years and hanging in the Prado Museum, came under intense critical scrutiny when Velázquez became fashionable again in the late nineteenth century after centuries of neglect. The question that critics asked was this: could the impeccably correct Velázquez be mocking the gods by portraying them amid lumpen street folk, satirizing the authorities as did contemporary writers?

"Here, our Velázquez has assembled a bunch of porters, *pícaros*, the dregs of the city, filthy, sly and moronic, and he says: come on, let's make fun of the gods...," wrote the twentieth-century writer and philosopher José Ortega y Gasset about *Los Borrachos*. Bacchus in the painting seems lost in thought, but the drunkards are looking at us, inviting us to join them in their fiesta. The central drunkard is even offering us a cup of wine, while his companions, clearly the worse for wear, makes a gesture of complicity, as if to include us in the group. It is hardly surprising that this painting has been lovingly reproduced on ceramic murals in several of the most popular bars in Madrid. Ortega y Gasset notes, however, that although the artist's eye may have been ironical, it was not scornful. His aim was realism, not a send-up. "For Velázquez, a mythological subject was the opportunity to assemble real figures in an intelligible scene. It is not mocking or parody but it does turn the myth on its head, and instead of being carried away into an imaginary world, he is brought firmly back to reality."

Other recent critics, the former Prado director Alfonso Pérez Sánchez and Jonathan Brown, perhaps the best-known Velázquez expert outside Spain, say the artist intended no irony in his portrayal, but was being perfectly straightforward and respectful. Indeed, Velázquez was even less inclined than Cervantes to cast aspersions on the rigid caste structure of his age. His paintings, for all their realism, lack the bite of the picaresque literature they accompanied. Velázquez had no desire to offend the king whose approval he was desperate to maintain, or to arouse the curiosity of the Inquisition who were already pronouncing anathema on the work of writers of the time. It was not until Goya, more than a century later, that art became a political instrument and hypocritical priests, evil witches, pimps and prostitutes became the targets of scorn and satire.

But Velázquez's achievement was to humanize his gods, to portray them for the first time in European painting as real people with red faces and calloused hands. The god Vulcan is shown as a rugged workman at his forge, the warrior Mars blank with fatigue and disillusion, Mercury and Argos vanquished by failure; and two legendary figures of Greek philosophy, Aesop and Menipo—painted as Spain was plumbing the depths of its long decline—are portrayed as a pair of tough old boys with a look of such cynical malevolence that, frankly, you wouldn't want to meet them on a dark night. "Wide as was the gulf between Court and country, it could still be bridged by an artist of the calibre of Velazquez, drawing his inspiration impartially from both," writes the distinguished chronicler of imperial Spain, John H. Elliott. The fusion of the classical and the popular that inspired the great artistic achievements of Spain's Golden Age, was overlaid in Velázquez's work by what Elliott calls an extra dimension of awareness. "For Velázquez caught in his paintings the sense of failure, the sudden emptiness of imperial splendour that had buoyed up Castile for more than a century."

Court Climber

As the decades passed and the empire foundered, Velázquez's fortunes prospered. He won the respect of the royal family for the brilliance of his work and their friendship through his discreet manners and his intelligence. His swift rise within the closed court hierarchy under the patronage of the count-duke naturally aroused the envy of lesser court painters. But Velázquez was astute enough to survive all the intrigues, even the sudden fall of his intimate friend and protector in 1643. Don Gaspar was destroyed by the machinations of his enemies who pinned upon him responsibility for the monarchy's military and financial ruin. Velázquez meanwhile maneuvered himself skillfully at court, unobtrusively destroying any potential challenger to his supremacy. He surrounded himself with submissive underlings, and made no effort to foster a school of disciples or encourage anyone who might rise up in competition. The only painter ever to receive favors from Velázquez was his son-in-law Juan Bautista Martínez de Mazo, who married his daughter Francisca, and only to the extent that his own position was unthreatened.

Throughout his early years at court he was constantly pleading for money and advancement, and made it clear his ultimate ambition was to be ennobled. Counting on the king's protection, he was swiftly made a court usher and given lodgings in the palace compound. He spent a fruitful year or so in Rome and, on his return to Madrid, was given a studio in the palace where the king used to visit him almost every day to sit and watch his protégé at work. Velázquez continued to press for advancement throughout the 1630s, becoming chamber painter, accumulating court functions and income, and badgering for the military honor of the Order of Santiago. He eventually succeeded in becoming a custodian of the Royal Palace, and was granted the key. In 1643, as his patron the count-duke fell from grace, Velázquez was put in charge of redecorating the royal salons. From that date his production of paintings dropped off sharply. He became lazy and slow and for years went without completing a single work. In 1652 he applied to become palace *aposentador*, a coveted post as general supervisor. There were four other applicants, and none of those responsible for making the appointment wanted Velázquez to obtain the job. But the king appointed him anyway. The painter's sloth, which had become remarked upon, suddenly vanished and he flung himself with relish into his new responsibilities. So it was that one of Europe's finest painters, placed in charge of an army of functionaries and servants, devoted himself to ensuring the supply of firewood for heating the mini-city of the palace, providing clean sheets, and determining the order of ceremonies or the disposition of furniture and statues.

It was at this point that Velázquez's twin ambitions entered more sharply into conflict. In order to be admitted to the noble Order of Santiago, he had to undergo a long and detailed vetting process revealing of the preoccupations of the age. His family tree was minutely scrutinized to establish his *limpieza de sangre* or purity of bloodline: confirmation essential for entry to the Order that he was free of any taint of Jewish or Moorish blood. The other precondition was that he should be of noble status, which meant that he had to establish that neither he nor his forebears had ever sullied their hands with work or trade. Recent historical research suggests that Velázquez was of mercantile stock—his grandfather was a maker of gentlemen's breeches—and that his family was very likely of Jewish origin. Yet, having got so far in his tireless quest for a title, Velázquez lied through his teeth about his roots and mobilized his friends to back him up in fabricating bogus testimonies. His family hailed from Seville and were of Portuguese origin, suspected of indicating Jewish descent. So it would have been logical to conduct investigations in the southern and central border region between Portugal and Spain where many Portuguese *conversos*—Jews converted to Christianity—fled in the late sixteenth century to escape an Inquisition even crueler than the Spanish one. The name Silva had already become what it remains today, a common Portuguese name among those of Jewish extraction. But, using the excuse of the war with Portugal, the artist requested that testimonies be sought neither from Lisbon or Porto. He sent investigators instead on a wild goose chase to the remote northern border towns of Monterrey, Verin, Pazos, Vigo and Tuy, where not surprisingly no one had heard of him or had anything negative to report.

He was also fortunate in the testimonies concerning his supposedly noble origins. Countless fellow artists, including Zurbarán, Alonso Cano and even his father-in-law Francisco Pacheco, whose studio he had entered at the age of twelve, swore that he had never plied his trade as painter. They unanimously testified that the artist had only ever conducted himself with the decorous idleness proper to the nobility, and insisted he had never sold a painting for money. His artistic abilities were simply a divine gift, in no way a means to earn a living. One favorably disposed noble even pointed out as a proof of merit that the artist was an accomplished horseman. Alonso Cano declared that "in all the time he had known Velázquez he had never heard it said that he had a trade or a shop or an office or had ever sold paintings, that he had carried out the work only for his own pleasure and in obedience to Your Majesty for the adornment of the Royal Palace." Cano added that neither the artist nor his parents had engaged in "vile, low or mechanical trade." This was all nonsense: everyone knew that their friend derived his entire income from painting. The evidence simply did not stand up. The Order of Santiago continued to resist because there was no proof that he was a *hidalgo*, gentry, the son of

somebody, and anyway his maternal grandparents were commoners. In the end the king had to ennoble his favorite artist himself, on November 28, 1659, in recognition of his genius.

The curious thing is that Velázquez had completed his definitive masterwork *Las Meninas* (The Maids of Honor) three years earlier, in 1656. A year before that the king had granted him the privilege of a spacious apartment in the Treasury House, an annex to the Royal Palace reserved for royal functionaries, where he had easy access to the king's apartments. (This was the final home that was sacrificed for a parking garage.) *Las Meninas* is undoubtedly Velázquez's greatest work and probably the finest painting in Spain. In it the artist portrays himself wearing the tunic and insignia of the scarlet sword of the noble Order of Santiago. This honor entitles him to install himself prominently in the foreground of this most intimate of palace paintings, in a condition of equality with the royal subjects. Goya, by contrast, a man of humble origins who never sought or received a title, paints himself well in the background of his 1800 masterpiece *Portrait of the Family of Charles IV* in somber tones and with indistinct brushwork. But Velázquez's proud flourish was three years premature. It showed not so much the reality that he had ascended from his plebeian station to the nobility, but rather the intensity of his desire for such an advancement. This suggests an answer to the centuries-old question of what exactly is the subject of *Las Meninas*: it is the artist, his ambitions, his desires, and his portrayal of a brilliant fabrication presented as the purest, informal realism. He wanted simultaneously to ennoble his art and himself.

Some have suggested the Santiago cross was added later—by the king after the artist's death, according to some versions—but examination of the canvas after it was cleaned in 1984 "seems to show that the painting of the cross is uniform with the rest," writes the distinguished Velázquez expert, Jonathan Brown. Others suggest that Velázquez added it himself, but the composition of the work, with the artist portrayed on terms of intimate equality with his royal patrons, indicates that he deliberately assumed he was already knighted.

Velázquez enjoyed his title for less than a year. He died in Madrid in August 1660, followed a week later by his sweet-natured wife, Juana de Miranda. His work fell from popularity for centuries, to be reclaimed by critics in the nineteenth century. The German art historian, Carl Justi, whose 1888 work was reprinted in Madrid in 1999 as *Velázquez y su siglo* on the eve of the artist's fourth centenary, wrote: "He was the painter who best knew how to penetrate the Spanish soul, who found the form and expression that suited the spirit of his people... He painted with such finesse and sharpness, with such simplicity and representative force, that the greatest masters who contemplate his work feel tempted to break their brushes." Velázquez was given a sumptuous funeral in the parish church of San Juan Bautista near the Royal Palace on the site of the Plaza Ramales. Dressed in his tunic with the coveted scarlet Dagger of Santiago on his chest, he was laid out in public view for a day with his hat, sword, boots and spurs, as befitted a nobleman of the court. He was then placed in a coffin lined with fine black velvet surrounded with golden railings, and adorned with a cross, with gold fastenings and hinges, and two keys. After a mass performed by musicians of the royal chapel, the coffin was lowered into the crypt.

When, as we have seen, the church was swept away in 1809 on the orders of Spain's occupying French ruler Joseph Bonaparte, the crypt was undisturbed, but with the intervening centuries Velázquez's bones have now been given up as lost. Some years back a small statue was commissioned to adorn the Plaza Ramales, to give it more prominence as the master's presumed final resting place. It shows him painting—as he did to dazzling effect—the city's magnificent evening sky, of which the square on its raised knoll offers a fine perspective. But in the interest of some local electoral advantage, the statue was placed instead on the roadside in the middle of the nineteenth-century Salamanca district (admittedly in a street bearing Velázquez's name) at the other end of town in a quarter that did not exist until centuries after the artist's death. Furthermore, this small-scale figure designed to top a delicate monumental plinth is mounted on low granite blocks that critics condemn as ridiculous. It seems that even after his death this genius of European painting, involuntarily helped by the indifference or clumsiness of successive Spanish authorities, has succeeded in covering his tracks.

CHAPTER FOUR

Plaza Mayor: Blood and Theater

Walk to the center of the arcaded Plaza Mayor. Go diagonally across the vast cobbled square that is surprisingly quiet in this raucous city, until you reach the magnificent equestrian statue of Felipe III, created by Giambologna and then by Pietro Tacca after the former's death in 1608. Unless it is a Sunday morning, when the square is filled with stamp and coin enthusiasts, you may notice that few of those around you appear to be locals. Trying to avoid squinting into the sun, look up at the horse's face, and then turn to walk in the direction of the animal's left nostril. Your steps will take you to the little Calle Felipe III, and on the left, at number 4, impossible to overlook, is Moore's, one of the best loved of Madrid's legion of Irish pubs. Beneath its cheery wood-cladded bar are dark dank rooms once used as torture chambers for the Spanish Inquisition. Those accused of sorcery, heresy, Judaism, bigamy and other heinous crimes languished in those underground stone chambers before being brought out in shackles, clad in penitents' yellow cassocks and tall pointed paper hats, or a crown of flames. They were then forced to parade in the Plaza Mayor in front of thousands of eager spectators, before being garroted or burned at the stake in an opulent spectacle that lasted from dawn to dusk.

The Plaza Mayor, still one of the biggest enclosed spaces in the heart of the city, started off as a lake, then was cleared as an open space outside the city walls opposite the Guadalajara gate of the old settlement of Madrid. It was known as the Plaza del Arrabal, (of the Outskirts) or sometimes "La Plaza de la Pestilencia." It burned down three times in its history: the fire of 1631 lasted three days and killed thirteen people. Twenty-seven houses were destroyed and another 24 badly damaged. While firemen tried to quench the blaze, King Felipe IV and his right hand man, the Count-Duke of Olivares, hastened to the square and ordered that the body of the city's patron saint, San Isidro, be brought to the scene, along with images of the Virgin from five nearby churches. They raised an altar in the square, and installed others in surrounding balconies. They then gave permission for residents to salvage what they could from their houses. Street porters, with their handcarts and their reputation as *pícaros*, wanted to shift wooden doors, windows and other remnants scavenged from the handsome buildings, but the operation was kept under control and large-scale pillage apparently avoided.

On its completion in 1619, the plaza had become the great focus of Madrid, a vast arena capable of holding a third of the city's population, the scene of spectacles of all kinds: state ceremonies, bullfights, public executions, *autos-da-fé*—the ritual condemnation of heretics—mock battles and tournaments, circus acts and carnival fiestas. It also functioned as a market. In 1620 the square witnessed eight days of processions and popular fiestas for the beatification of San Isidro, who was to become patron saint of the town following the miracle of the well. This miracle had reportedly occurred when the laborer Isidro prayed that the waters of the well in question would rise and deliver his son who had fallen into its depths. His prayers were answered. The following year, royal fiestas were held here in honor of Felipe IV, and later the same year crowds gathered for the public execution of Rodrigo Calderón, Marquis of Sieteiglesias. There followed in 1622 the simultaneous canonization of five saints: San Isidro, San Ignacio de Loyola, San Francisco Javier, Santa Teresa of Jesus and San Felipe Neri. To celebrate the occasion there were bullfights, fireworks and even a play by finest playwright of his epoch, Lope de Vega, in the open air.

Lavish entertainments were laid on in 1623 for the Prince of Wales, England's future Charles I, who arrived in Holy Week under the alias Tom Smith seeking to negotiate a marriage with the sister of Felipe IV.

Hundreds of friars from the order of Santa Barbara, as well as Augustines, Capuchines and Trinitarians with crucifixes and skulls in their hands, their heads covered with ashes and crowned with thorns that made blood run down their foreheads, beat their breasts with stones and made extravagant gestures of penitence, in a procession that crisscrossed the Plaza Mayor before the astonished gaze of the visiting foreign prince. A tournament was organized in his honor, with ranks of horsemen bearing lances and 500 horses taking part. Haggling over the royal nuptials foundered over the religious question, but Charles was none the less thought to have harbored genuine feelings for the Infanta, watching her during the ceremonies "as a cat does a mouse," according to the beady-eyed Count-Duke of Olivares. For the six months that the prince remained in Madrid, until his departure for England on September 9, "there was an uninterrupted series of astonishing festivities," in the words of Ramón de Mesonero Romanos, one of Madrid's best-known nineteenth-century chroniclers.

The Inquisition

Dating from 1478, the Inquisition was at its most influential around the early seventeenth century. Felipe II was terrified of heresy, and the Crown used the holy office as a means of control, ostensibly to protect Catholic orthodoxy against heretics, but in practice the dreaded institution reached deep into the political fabric of his realm and the most intimate corners of his subjects' personal life. "Because of its formidable power and national range, it was inevitable that the Inquisition also acquired political functions, especially in such a confessional state in which the religious and the political were so interlinked," writes Manuel Fernández Álvarez in *Felipe II y su tiempo*. But there was more. The Inquisition took over all matters related to sex, not just bigamy, but other practices forbidden by Christian morality—homosexuality, lesbianism and bestiality—which it considered destructive of the sacrament of marriage and even the work of the devil. Fernández Álvarez claims that "having responsibility for sexual repression gave a particular bias to the mentality of that society, with such force that it could be said that something of that has remained to the present day." The Spanish

Inquisition ceased, in other words, to be merely a religious institution under the control of Rome, to become the most powerful political instrument of the Habsburg kings.

Not until 1808 did the French king Joseph Bonaparte abolish it, and even then halfhearted attempts were made to revive it during the Bourbon restoration after 1814. As late as 1799, the German traveler Wilhelm von Humboldt, in the diary of his visit to Spain that year, writes:

> *The Inquisition is still very active and causes a lot of damage to enlightened thinking due to the efficiency with which it obstructs literary communication with abroad. In addition, even today they continue to carry out house to house searches in search of books, and if they do not succeed in destroying them, try by other methods, like prison, etc., to annihilate entire families. Two years ago they carried out an authentic "auto da fé" and the criminal was led to the public square. Given that he had recanted, he was not tried, but despite everything, the ceremony took place...*

The first *auto-da-fé* took place on January 21, 1624, when Benito Ferrer was burned alive for pretending to be a priest, and another such ritual was celebrated in the Plaza Mayor in 1632 against 33 heretics, heralded in advance by court town criers. General Padilla and the Marquis de la Vega were both executed here in 1648 for conspiring against the king. Other notable *autos-da-fé* included that of 1680 against 118 prisoners, including 80 Jews of whom 21 were burned alive. The proceedings started at 7am and it was already dark by the time the swearing in, the sermon, the reading of the charges, the sentences, and the procession of the prisoners had taken place. Throughout, King Carlos II and Queen María Luisa remained on the royal balcony of the turreted Casa de la Panadería, once the central market for regulating and distributing bread throughout the city, an essential operation for the maintenance of popular order. It is still the handsomest building in the square, and the underground torture chambers reach deep under its foundations.

Here is an example of a sentence meted out to one unfortunate victim of the Inquisition, condemned for one of the commonest sins, practicing Judaism:

Manuel Díaz, also known as Manuel Enríquez, also known as Antonio Correa, from the town of Estremoz, Portugal... aged 30, Judaist, servant, swindler of Portuguese, came to the trial as a penitent, wearing his penitent's cassock: he admitted his errors and was appropriately reconciled, with the confiscation of his possessions (of which he had none) and life imprisonment without remission, and forbidden to have contact with Portuguese and was sent as an oarsman in His Majesty's galleys for five years without pay, then imprisoned and clad in a hair shirt to complete the rest of his sentence. No greater punishment was imposed because he had already been condemned by the king's justice to 200 lashes (which were carried out) and ten years in the galleys.

He was one of the lucky ones, spared the bonfire, or the garrote.

Historians who have sought in recent years to restore the blackened reputation of Felipe II have attempted to do the same with the Spanish Inquisition, pointing out that the deaths and tortures were exaggerated, and in no way disproportionate to the practices of civil courts throughout Europe at the time. As Madrid started to establish itself as capital, the intermingling of Christians, Jews and Moors created a bubbling cauldron of religious and racial complexity over which the Inquisition kept a particularly vigilant watch, keen to impose orthodoxy and severe religious dogmatism. In his classic study, *Imperial Spain, 1469–1716*, John H. Elliott writes: "The Spanish Inqusition, operating in a land where heterodox views abounded and where the new heresies might therefore easily take root, was naturally terrified at the least hint of subversive practices, and dared not tolerate even the slightest deviation from the most rigid orthodoxy, in the fear that even the slightest deviation would open the way to greater heresies." The whole operation worked on the basis of fear, secrecy, denunciation and torture, a terrible machine that escaped the control of its creators to take on a life of its own, Elliott says. Its great success was to persuade the people to fear heresy even more than the institution designed to extirpate it. One of the main causes of fear of the Inquisition was its right to confiscate the property of those who were found guilty. "Reconciliation" meant economic as well as social ruin, not just for the accused but their descendants too. Naturally, with the proliferation of tens of thousands of spies and informers throughout the country, debate was checked and the vigorous range of Spanish life was narrowed, "forcing a rich and vital society into a straitjacket of conformity."

One extraordinary episode revealed the zeal with which the Inquisition, at the behest of Felipe II, pursued its crusade against heretics, even to the point of arousing the hostility of Rome. Cardinal Bartolomé de Carranza, Archbishop of Toledo and Primate of Spain, was arrested for heresy in 1559 within months of his appointment by the king. For seventeen years, first in Spain—perhaps near the cellars of Moore's—then in Rome, Carranza remained a prisoner, condemned, stripped of his office and with his writings inscribed in the Inquisition's index of banned books. He emerged in 1576, a broken man of 73, to die a few days later. This was a cleric who had earned a great reputation as a theologian and was a distinguished delegate to the Council of Trent. He accompanied Felipe II to England in 1554 and became religious adviser to Mary Tudor and a ruthless suppressor of English Protestantism. This was around the time that Thomas Cranmer was burned at the stake. In 1559 Carranza went to Flanders to investigate the clandestine trade in heretical literature with Spain.

One would have thought he was the perfect candidate for Primate of Spain. But Dr. Carranza had powerful enemies, partly because of his poor—albeit *hidalgo*—origins; he had antagonized a number of disappointed aristocrats who had each eyed the rich see of Toledo with greedy anticipation. Fatally, he had aroused their *envidia*, their envy, a corrosively powerful vice to which Spaniards are said to be particularly prone. In addition, his travels with the king had, in critics' eyes, tainted him with Lutherism, the heretical Christianity of northern Europe. Even a cravenly apologetic recent book on the Spanish Inquisition concedes that Carranza's trial was "unjust." Carranza escaped burning by his skill in argument, by his good standing in Rome, and by the express wish of the king. The 21 bundles of documents concerning the trial, held in Madrid's Royal Academy of History, show quite clearly that the basis of the case against Carranza was not the unorthodox nature of his views, but the bitter personal enmity he had aroused among his rivals. He even agreed to rewrite a book on the catechism that was considered heretical, but by then the Inquisitors no longer wanted to know.

Religion and Spectacle

The public trials and executions in the Plaza Mayor provided great theater. They surely inspired what successive visitors to Madrid have observed: that *Madrileños* have an enormous interest in—some would say obsession with—death, suffering and the celebration of mourning. The Plaza Mayor was used not just for mass trials and burnings. It became the focus of all kinds of festivities and lavish displays of popular celebration, patronized and orchestrated by the authorities in the name of the king, and usually with a strong religious inspiration. The deep religious foundation of the most humble of popular Spanish festivals is something difficult for the outsider without a Catholic background to grasp. But wild all-night sessions of singing, dancing, drinking, bullfighting, pilgrimages and all kinds of extravagant celebrations are firmly attached to religious festivals, saints' days and important dates in the ecclesiastical calendar.

This inseparable intermingling of often bloody fiestas and the Church, typical of Madrid's festivities, dates from the devout Felipe II's personal interpretation of the counterreformation movement that culminated in the Council of Trent, reasserting Catholic doctrine throughout Europe. "The Catholic Church must promote ceremonies, lights and godly ornaments to excite the spirit of the faithful by means of visible signs of piety and religiosity," the king decreed early in his reign. Obviously these ceremonies played a vital part in offering an impoverished people the opportunity—or the illusion—of participation. Protestants used to a more solemn and austere Christian tradition still boggle at such extravagant displays of apparently religious devotion, which to the non-Catholic eye can display excesses more often associated with pagan or non-Christian rituals, but which the Catholic authorities encouraged with shrewdly judged effect. The passionate anti-Catholic Richard Ford wrote waspishly in his mid-nineteenth century "Handbook for Travellers in Spain" of the May festival honoring Madrid's patron saint San Isidro:

By these and other melodramas, given gratis in a poor land, where amusements are rare, the church maintained its popularity: labour was gladdened by a holiday which while it refreshed the body combined religious consolation for the soul. But Christianity was thereby dwarfed into a superstition and Paganism was virtually revived, for it might be the festival of Bacchus or Venus: but the stock in trade of the old firm was soon taken by the early Popes and by these pilgrimages of piety and fun the infallible Vatican rendered as acts of devotion sources of enjoyment… And their flocks, wedded to festivals which suited themselves and their climate, will long prefer them to the dreary Sundays of our purer Protestantism, which has no machinery for canonising whitebait.

Not everyone was so skeptical. The atheist French author Prosper Mérimée, later to create in the factory girl Carmen the quintessential image of seductive Spanish womanhood, was captivated: "The truth is I love these Catholic ceremonies and I wish I could believe." Nonetheless, the most magnificent of all the processions were at that time organized by the Inquisition.

Hence, in spite of the king's austere and dour personality, "in Madrid they celebrated everything," remarks the historian Pedro Montoliú Camps, from the birth of a prince to carnival masquerades, sessions of the court, pilgrimages and bullfights. The king defied Rome on another occasion, this time over the question of bullfighting when in 1566, the Holy See ordered the practice to be stopped on pain of excommunication for organizers, bullfighters and spectators. The arguments used by clerics and moralists against bullfighting were similar to those still used by opponents of the practice today:

Those who with manifest danger put themselves upon the horns of bull venture or lose their body and soul. And… if what is spent on these spectacles were applied instead to jousts and tournaments, to test young people in skills, prowess and agility, to contests with horsemen and other such exercises, obtaining more fruitful entertainment, we would avoid the atrocity of seeing human blood and Spanish blood shed for fun, wild beasts fighting each other as they did in Rome and not cruel beasts against man, whom God created to be lord and master of them all.

But the king, aware of the huge public appetite for the gore and glory of bullfighting, ignored the papal order; as far as he was concerned, the only valid reason for stopping a bullfight was to mark the death of a member of the royal family.

Less frequently heard were complaints about the cruelty inflicted on the bulls or the losses suffered by cattle-breeders, although the writer and satirist Quevedo sounded off about this in a speech entitled "Against the present customs of the Castillians." To meet such criticisms, measures were proposed that improved the security of the bullrings, like tying up the bulls, and limiting access by the elderly, women, children and the lame. In general, bullfighting on horseback was considered less risky than fighting on foot. After strenuous pressure, Felipe II obtained a new papal ruling that annulled excommunications decreed against lay people and soldiers in bull festivals. He argued that this kind of spectacle encouraged the virile courage—*bravura*—that was considered innate to the Spanish character. By the seventeenth century, *corridas*—translated into English as "bullfights"—had become one of the most popular festivals among both the public and the court.

Those early *corridas*, in the enclosed expanse of the Plaza Mayor, and elsewhere in the town, took on the form that bullfights broadly maintain today. Their characteristically elaborate organization rested firmly in the hands of the local authorities, ultimately the state, at that time obviously the royal court. Today, bullfights are still a matter

of state, scrupulously regulated by a special tauromachy department of the Ministry of the Interior. The town hall nominated committees to organize the details of the *corrida*. They were responsible for buying the animals, hiring the bullfighters and the musical accompaniment—four drummers and one or two trumpeters—plus arranging the construction of stands and terraces for the public, decorating and fencing off the square, covering the granite cobbles with sand, and spraying the arena with water before each kill. In addition they had to prepare the arms used in each stage of the contest: the *garrocha* (goad), the lance, the sword, and the darts. The committees also hired the mules that would drag the slaughtered bull from the ring and arranged the food that would be offered to the assembled authorities during the spectacle.

Members of the public, who attended bullfights *en masse*, were grouped in strict social and economic hierarchy, ranging from the balconies and windows that overlooked the square, the wooden scaffolding with graded platforms around the area and the barrier that defined the bullring. Prices varied accordingly, and as to whether or not you sat or stood in the sun (*sol*) or shade (*sombra*). Despite efforts and threats of hefty fines, it was difficult to prevent people sneaking on to the makeshift framework of platforms without paying. First-floor windows were commandeered for the use of legal and administrative officials, high nobles and secretaries of the king, ambassadors and other official foreign visitors, and other representatives of the court and the kingdom of Castille.

Bullfighting remains popular, though decreasingly so as decades pass, and from spring to autumn the fortunes of top matadors and upcoming stars are detailed every day in the culture section of all newspapers. Highlights, especially gorings, are replayed in slow-motion on television with the same relish as goals in football matches. The bullring at Las Ventas, a mock Arabic-inspired pile built in 1929 to the east of the city, is regarded as the La Scala of the taurine art. *Corridas* at Madrid's San Isidro festival in mid-May are the pinnacle of the bullfighting season. Every afternoon for two weeks, the finest matadors dispatch Spain's finest bulls. Bullfighting remains a passport to wealth and fame for thousands of poor boys, and a handful of girls, and there is no shortage of applicants to Madrid's bullfighting school in the Casa de Campo.

But despite widespread publicity, bullfighting remains a minority enthusiasm, its prestige eroded by a seemingly unstoppable deterioration in the quality of bulls—some of whom can barely stand up in the ring—and abuses such as horn-shaving, designed to make them less deadly. Animal rights campaigners have curbed some barbaric local customs, such as tying flaming brands to bulls' horns and chasing them through village streets. But the *fiesta nacional,* as bullfighting is traditionally called, seems as immune to accusations of cruelty as it was 500 years ago. Some believe the tradition responds to Spaniards' desire to prove themselves in the face of mortal danger, and satisfies their obsession with death and suffering, as the British writer Gerald Brenan observed:

> *A mysterious change comes over some Spaniards in the presence of death and suffering. These things seem to draw out of them some deep approval, as if their own death-instincts had been unloosed and given vicarious satisfaction. It is not sadism or love of cruelty, but a sort of fascinated absorption in what they regarded as the culminating moment of existence. They unite themselves to it as the voyeur may do to the spectacle of another person's orgasm.*

Golden Age Drama

Another popular form of entertainment was the theater, and portable stages were rigged up in the Plaza Mayor. Popular drama flourished in the 1570s under Felipe IV, who liberalized the whole business from regulations imposed by his predecessors. He also introduced novelties such as places where *tertulias* or discussion groups could be held, and where clerics were allowed to attend. He gave permission to sell sweets, chestnuts, pine nuts, aniseed cordial and wine among theatergoers. Women were admitted, in a special section of the theater reserved for them called the *cazuela* or cauldron, where a man was specially employed to press them in and to squeeze their bone crinolines so that more could be accommodated.

Many of the plays by Lope de Vega, Pedro Calderón de la Barca, Tirso de Molina and others of the seventeenth-century Golden Age of

Spanish theater have never been bettered and are still performed in Madrid today to huge acclaim. Theater originated as a haphazard entertainment in the open-air courtyards or *corralas* between building, particularly around the Plaza Santa Ana and the nearby area where budding writers and satirists lived. During the early years of Madrid's newly established court, the art developed under the influence of a brilliant clutch of writers into a sophisticated, though popular, form with rules, coherent plots and characters, and a poetic vigor that remains unsurpassed centuries later. The themes were often amorous intrigues between ladies and gentlemen of the court, mirrored in liaisons between their servants, and interwoven with power struggles drawn from episodes of Spanish history and legend. The works range from tragedy to farce, delineating in fine detail the hierarchical society of seventeenth-century Spain, and portraying its rich variety of personalities.

Lope de Vega's best-known play, *Fuente Ovejuna*, written between 1611 and 1618, was based on events in a small Castillian village. It tells of how villagers rose up against a cruel feudal ruler who persecuted his serfs and raped their women. One intended victim, Laurencia, resists, prompting the community to turn against their tormentor and kill him. When the Catholic kings seek out those responsible, the villagers, even under torture, blamed only *Fuente Ovejuna*. Because of their sufferings, they are forgiven for taking justice into their own hands, and the village is placed beneath the control of the Crown to prevent similar abuses, a solution to which all submit. The work follows a pattern perfected by Lope: a bloody struggle of honor between nobles and commoners, mediated via a love affair and resolved by the Crown.

The work of Lope's near contemporary, Calderón de la Barca, explores philosophical conflicts. Calderón's best-known play, *La Vida es sueño* (Life is a Dream) celebrates a rich variety of characters with vibrancy and brio, while examining the fleeting nature of their life and their struggle between survival and personal liberty. The pessimistic tone perfectly reflects the creeping uncertainty of an empire in decline and a society in decadence. Perhaps the popularity of Madrid's Golden Age theater owed much to its promise of momentary escape from a collapsing world.

Theater then was a lively affair, and Quevedo devotes a chapter in his picaresque novel, *La Vida del buscón*, to an episode in which the hero Pablos joins a band of traveling players. He takes to the profession most successfully, making the most of his deep voice, but after being pelted "with rotten quinces, cabbage roots and water melons" because a particular play is so poor, he decides to try to write one himself: "I spent my time doing this, acting, and making love to the actress." The hero makes a name for himself, writing plays, poems and even prayers, charging for each literary effort. The enterprise makes him rich, but the company breaks up when the manager is jailed for debt. Although Pablos is pressed by his colleagues to set up a company of his own, he confesses that "I had no real interest in the profession and had only taken it up to tide me over a difficult patch. I had money now and was well set up and so all I thought of was having a good time. I said goodbye…" He then moves on to his next adventure, with a nun.

Lope de Vega

When Félix Lope de Vega y Carpio was born in 1562, Madrid scarcely existed. In the course of his 72 years, Spain's greatest playwright, the creator of Spanish theater, observed how this tiny town became transformed into a flamboyant royal court and the heart of a world empire. Lope lived in a part of town that was from the start associated with writers and poets, near a *mentidero* or gossip center similar to the one near the Puerta del Sol. But the so-called "Representatives" *mentidero*, situated on Calle León and the corner of the Calle del Prado was less concerned than others with striking shady deals or seeking dubious advantage at court through bureaucratic trickery; it was devoted above all to the

theater. Regulars included playwrights, actors, poets and impresarios of high and low social status. Here were discussed the hits and flops among new plays—or *comedias*, as they were called—the money problems suffered by actors without contract and the scandalous lives of many actresses. It was a scenario comparable to the precarious and rollicking shenanigans that Shakespeare had to contend with in London. In Madrid's theatrical gossip-house, complaints were raised against ecclesiastical censorship and, invariably, the latest details of Lope's successes, on stage and in bed.

Lope bought his handsome three-story house in what is now Calle Cervantes in 1610 and lived and worked there until his death in 1635. The house, and his beloved garden behind it, which he described in detail in a poem within a letter—"My garden, smaller than a kite,/ has only two trees, ten flowers/ two vines, an orange tree, a white musk-rose"—has been lovingly restored. It gives an intimate impression of the writer's personal life and of the intellectual spirit of the seventeenth-century city that he adored. It is perhaps Madrid's most evocative reconstruction of that moment. Even the well and the orange tree in the garden that he mentions in his writings seem unchanged from his loving descriptions. He wrote lyrically to his son Carlos Félix: "I trapped for you the new-born fledglings/ with their varied colors and songs/ wanting to please you; I planted the vigorous shoots/ of the green trees; and flowers too." Elsewhere in his poems he talks of his rose borders, and his clambering jasmines and honeysuckle, of lilies "with leaves like swords, violets, carnations, hyacinths, narcissus." A translator friend in Antwerp used to send him tulips every spring. Those who care for Lope's garden today have no lack of information about how it should look.

Lope's secluded garden behind his house was, and still is, a delight in spring, and a respite from torrid summer days. Once, the writer cheerily greeted a friend who arrived early one morning to pick up an urgently commissioned play; the friend recalled: "he had finished the first act, had time to eat some breakfast and had watered his garden." One winter Lope expressed concern that some of his plants had frozen to death. Shortly after he moved in, Lope pestered his patron the Duke of Sessa for money to dig a well: "I need one in my garden," he complained, "because it is parched through lack of water."

When Lope moved here, he had to deal with one of the most perverse and hated legacies of the court of Felipe II: the *Regalia de Aposento* or lodgings rule. This forced owners of properties of more than one floor to give up half of that floor to a servant or official of the court who would take possession and rarely show any sign of leaving. As a result, many *Madrileños* built only single-story dwellings, or houses that had a second story set back from the street and concealed from view, which came to be known as *casas de malicia*—malice houses, deliberately designed to avoid this enforced hospitality. However, even for owners of multi-story houses, like Lope, there were, inevitably, ways round the rules. They made elaborate efforts to show that their homes were *de incómoda repartición*—inconveniently divided up—and could not therefore be shared with anybody. The aim was to hoodwink the authorities when they came to examine the houses by arranging the ground floor as stables and the top floor as a granary or storage area, unsuitable for family life. The home-owner would then assure the visiting official that the middle floor was the only area used by the family, who naturally took up all the available space, and could not spare room for anyone else.

However, by the early seventeenth century, *casas de malicia* had so proliferated throughout the town that the authorities took the matter in hand. They resolved the situation by imposing a tax on owners of multi-story houses, which exempted them from having to share their homes with anyone. This was how Lope enjoyed his simple but spacious house, to his great relief. "My little house, my tranquillity, my little plot, my study," he wrote shortly after he moved in, and he continued to produce his astonishing output in that house for the rest of his life.

Lope de Vega had an extraordinary personality that combined both erotic sensuality and religious spirituality. He had at least eleven children, five from his two wives and five—whom he recognized—from one of his many mistresses. In later life he entered the priesthood, then produced another child, and created a scandal when the child's mother, a widow, moved into this house. This heady mixture seemed prefigured by the circumstances of his own birth in 1562. His mother Francisca and his father Félix settled in the austere Castillian regional capital of Valladolid, where they produced two children. But within a few years, Félix—despite his intense religious piety—decided to move to Madrid in pursuit, it seems, of a woman with whom he maintained an amorous relation. Francisca promptly followed him to Madrid where a reconciliation evidently occurred and Lope de Vega was born.

Young Lope was born and grew up in the lively area around the northwest corner of the Plaza Mayor, a neighborhood of traders and artisans. He could read Spanish and Latin at the age of five—although, as he could not yet write, he dictated to his friends the verses he composed—and he wrote his first play when he was twelve. As a teenager he may have studied at the university before enlisting briefly in the navy. On his return, he began distributing his first writings, and embarked upon his first big love affair, with Elena Osorio ("Filis" or "La Dorotea" of one of his most important works, a thinly disguised memoir written years later that recalled those turbulent years of young love). Elena was an actress from a distinguished family of comics, and was married to Cristóbal Calderón. Lope conducted a passionate romance with Elena for more than five years, and reacted violently against her parents when they expressed their disapproval. He learned with fury of a new relation between Elena and a rich nephew of a prominent cardinal, and fired off a fusillade of wounding and libelous poems, which were read throughout Madrid's theatrical world, accusing Elena's parents of pimping their beautiful daughter for money. They sued for defamation and he was clapped into the court jail in the Santa Cruz Palace—today the Ministry of Foreign Affairs—and banished from Madrid for eight years and from Castille for two.

Despite the banning order, Lope made numerous clandestine incursions into the city, where he began a new amorous adventure, with Isabel de Urbina ("Belisa," daughter of the court painter Diego de Urbina). They married in 1588 and set up home in the Mediterranean city of Valencia, where Lope's first theatrical works began to win him the popularity he would enjoy for the rest of his life. Meanwhile, in Madrid the theatrical impresario Gaspar Porres tried to negotiate Lope's return, and installed him in the household of the Duke of Alba, near Toledo, where as part of his duties the young writer traveled the western part of Spain, bordering Portugal, visiting the duke's properties. But in the autumn of 1594, Isabel died after producing their second daughter. The child died soon afterwards, as had their first daughter Antonia who had been born in Valencia.

Between 1596 and 1598, Lope met the beautiful Micaela Luján, immortalised in his work as Camila Lucinda and began an affair with her that lasted more than ten years. But he also courted Juana Guardo who, though neither beautiful nor particularly well-bred, was rich, and he married her in April 1598. The two relationships ran in parallel for many years, and included additional passing affairs in the meantime. Lope had three daughters and a son with Juana, while of the seven children borne by Micaela Luján, he recognized five after their relationship ended in 1608. The two youngest, Marcela and Lope Félix, he brought into his family house in Calle Cervantes, with Juana's agreement. Around this time he became secretary to the young and agreeable Duke of Sessa, an association that was to support Lope financially for the rest of his life. The playwright never stopped pestering his patron for money, complaining of endless penury, although his phenomenal output must have made him rich, while the hours spent at his desk cannot have left him much time or opportunity for reckless spending. But in 1612 Carlos Félix, Lope's only legitimate son and his favorite child, died, prompting one of the most beautiful elegies in Spanish literature. And Juana, who had been poorly since the birth of their last daughter, died the following year.

Shortly afterwards, Lope developed an intense religious spirituality and decided to enter the priesthood. He obtained permission to celebrate mass in the pretty chapel in his house, which he could see from a little iron-grilled window in his bedroom. In later years, this enabled Lope, like Felipe II in El Escorial, to attend religious services in his own house from his own bedroom without getting up. His health began to fail. Nonetheless, his output remained prodigious and he produced 448 dramatic works by 1618. He was 53 and was settling down to a tranquil clerical life when he fell passionately in love again. Marta Nevares Santoyo, 26, in addition to being very beautiful, was the best-educated woman he had ever loved, but she was married to a trader. Romantic poems began to pour from his pen, as his amorous feelings resurfaced as vigorously as they had in his youth, but this time in the clear knowledge that this would be his last grand passion.

Rumors flew, egged on by Lope's literary rivals, and he mocked his loved one's husband to the point of scandal until, in an unexpected twist of fate, Roque Hernández, the husband, suddenly died. With Marta he had his last daughter, who came to live with her father. A brief period of peace prevailed until scandal broke out afresh when the widowed Marta moved in to live with him.

Throughout all this emotional turmoil, Lope continued to write inexhaustibly, winning not only national but international fame when his work began to be performed in France. In 1627 he made a detailed inventory of all his possessions, enabling the curators of what was is today his museum to fill his home with objects that, even if they did not originally belong to him, were of the same period and similar to those that he had. This has contributed to the extraordinarily convincing calm intimacy of his house today. You long to move in yourself. But after years of happiness and productive work, Lope began to suffer a series of blows. In 1620, his sweet-natured daughter Marcela left home to join a convent. Marta his wife became ill, blind, and eventually mad until she died in 1630. Two years later his daughter Feliciana left home to get married, and a year after that his beloved son Lope Félix died while diving for pearls off the coast of Venezuela. The final blow occurred in 1634 when Antonica, his daughter by Marta, was seduced and subsequently abandoned by Cristóbal Tenorio, a *protégé* of the powerful Count-Duke of Olivares. One morning, when he went as usual to awaken his daughter, he found the disordered evidence of her hasty secret flight, and suffered the worst grief of his life. He nonetheless continued to write and write... until his own death a year later. The whole city turned out for his funeral. But through the indifference of his patron the Duke of Sessa Lope's body was flung into a common grave and all trace of it lost.

The house obeys the logic dictated by the extremes of Madrid's climate; the bedrooms, and within them the beds shrouded in heavy cloths, are hidden deep within the recesses of the building, to escape the sun in summer and to keep warm in winter. It gives them a certain claustrophobic coziness still favored in many Spanish households, in contrast to the austere, rather chilly feel of the more public rooms.

The most fascinating part of the house is the little anteroom before Lope's enclosed bedroom alcove, where the women of the household assembled to sew and chat. It has no chairs, just a low platform covered with velvet, with crimson silken cushions placed round a brass brazier, giving it a Moorish, almost harem-like intimacy. This is separated from the main study by a gorgeous draped Flemish tapestry. The study itself, the finest room in the house and with the most authentic feeling, is spacious and welcoming, with a sturdy wooden table covered with a thick woolen cloth, and leather and wood chairs grouped in an endearingly functional austerity. Heaped upon rough wooden shelves are some 1,500 giant-sized books from the sixteenth and seventeenth centuries, an extraordinary sight, propped up informally, just waiting to be lifted out and read, perhaps in the scented seclusion of that lovely garden.

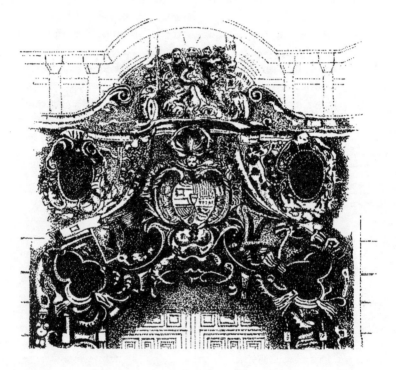

CHAPTER FIVE

The Buenavista:
Goya and the Duchess

The Plaza Antón Martín in the heart of old Madrid marks the dividing line between the bohemian intellectuals' quarter frequented by artists and writers and the seedier, poorer neighborhoods down the hill to the south. In 1766 the square was the scene of a revolt of an unprecedented kind; the so-called "Mutiny of Squillace" was a protest against an order by King Carlos III's unpopular Italian minister to ban the traditional full-length Spanish cape and the broad-brimmed Spanish hat.

The ostensible purpose of the Marquis of Squillace's curious and provocative decree was to cut street crime. He argued that robbers were able to secrete their weapons in the cape's voluminous folds and hide their face beneath the broad-brimmed *chambergo* hat. If you ever get the opportunity to try one of these stylish and mysterious capes—and you can still buy them at Seseña's, a traditional tailors more than one hundred years old in the Calle la Cruz, near Sol—you will find that by swinging the circular cloth around over one shoulder and back in front of you over the other, the cloth stands up around the lower half of your face, effortlessly covering it. With a hat pulled over your forehead, only your eyes would show. Your appearance inevitably calls up the expression "cloak and dagger." The Spanish word *embozado*, which means muffled or disguised, refers specifically to the action of throwing a cape around to cover the face. In an effort to discourage the wearing of the cape, Squillace apparently ordered tailors to be stationed in doorways to cut off the extra cloth of those who defied his ruling.

But the authorities failed to appreciate the importance of the cape and the broad hat as symbols of male pride and authentically Spanish dress– which was being swiftly eroded under pressure from the supposedly more modish French. The cape, with its characteristic shorter over-cape (or, for women, capacious hood) is thought to have evolved originally from the Roman toga. The garment was adopted by the Church, then the monarchy and eventually by the people. It was for centuries a classless garment that managed, as it gradually disappeared elsewhere in Europe, to survive only in Spain. Squillace's ban sparked off history's first fashion revolt—although discontent had been brewing anyway, and the fact that he introduced such an arbitrary and draconian measure suggests that the spirit of revolt was already in the air. An enraged mob—caped, one assumes—marched from the Plaza Antón Martín on the Royal Palace. The king took fright, sacked Squillace and sent him packing, and swiftly withdrew the decree. The uprising reflected a wider resentment of the pervasion of French habits felt both by the popular and the educated classes. The ill-feeling also caused a backlash against all things French. Those who wore French clothes—typically the full-skirted coat and the three-cornered hat— were often attacked in the street.

In 1777 Goya painted a vibrant street scene—*La maja y los embozados* (The Woman and the Muffled Men)—which shows a finely dressed young working woman (or, more likely an aristocratic lady dressing up as someone more plebeian) surrounded by a pair of mysterious, threatening figures whose identities are completely concealed behind their wound-round capes and pulled-down hats. The image confirms the worst fears of those who wanted to do away with this enveloping Spanish male attire. But it also shows its dashing allure; the cape was popular among bohemians, intellectuals and politicians until about the 1920s and 1930s, when it virtually disappeared in favor of the overcoat. But in recent decades, like the lace mantilla or the embroidered silk shawl—the *mantón de Manila*— the cape has regained a certain popularity as a statement of Spanish artistic style and identity.

The defeat of Squillace prompted a fashion among the well-to-do of celebrating the traditional *Madrileño* style of dress of the popular classes—the so-called *majos* and *majas*. *Majo* is a noun or an adjective meaning a "fine" or "beautiful" person, and is still used as a compliment. Fashionable ladies and gentlemen in eighteenth-century Madrid took to copying the cocky elegance, the flamboyant and distinctive fashion adopted by capital's laboring and artisan classes: the coachmen, seamstresses, cigarette makers or market traders mostly from the working-class area of Lavapiés just down the hill from Antón Martín. In an era when ordinary people throughout Europe were becoming increasingly similar in appearance, with tricorn hats, breeches and mob-caps, the *majos* of Madrid gloried in their colorful and distinctive traditional costume, indifferent to—even defiant of—French fashion. A *majo* wore embroidered shirts and a short jacket with many buttons, his hair held in a heavy bobbled net, and he carried a knife in his belt. *Majas* wore mid-calf-length skirts with a mass of petticoats, pearly white stockings, tight embroidered bodices, and had intricately braided hair topped by a dramatic lace mantilla. These women were renowned for their voluble wit, sassiness, and cheek, for brazenly talking back to their superiors. Madrid was still largely a city of servants, but servants who were renowned for talking back and deferring to nobody. Their readiness to take up a quarrel was indicated by the sheathed poniard the *maja* traditionally carried in the garter of her left stocking.

Aristocratic *Maja*

One aristocratic lady who admired and copied this provocative style was the young and beautiful Duchess of Alba, who became renowned as one of the richest and most charismatic members of late eighteenth-century Madrid's enlightened society. The duchess, named Cayetana, loved to wear the *maja* costume, in which she was often painted by Goya, and she liked to mingle with the popular classes of her city. Some art critics believe that she is the model for the woman approached in the street by the cloaked and hatted men, a suggestion, says the Prado's Goya catalogue warily, "that cannot be discarded." The duchess was only four when the Squillace revolt occurred. But she came to share the proud nationalist spirit that rejected French influences and sought to keep hold of traditional *Madrileño* style. In her defiance of social conventions, however, the duchess was often almost as bold as the rebels who marched upon the palace in defense of their long cape and broad hat.

There is an engaging tale of how the young duchess, a high-spirited teenager bound at the age of thirteen in a marriage of convenience, stepped out one afternoon from the family Buenavista Palace. The palace had been recently built in Calle de Alcalá on the corner of Paseo de Recoletos near the newly installed Cibeles fountain. Still in its leafy grounds and with its high walls and iron gates, the building is today the army headquarters, and the spot is a hub of smart Madrid. But at that time it bordered the eastern limits of the city, beyond which was open countryside that the authorities sought to tame by establishing tree-lined boulevards. The story goes that Cayetana, accompanied by a maid, strolled out informally dressed, wanting to pass as a simple woman of the people. Her beauty and elegance caught the eye of a young theology student who was walking nearby, reading a book. He approached and engaged the duchess in conversation. Thinking he was heading for a conquest, he invited her for a drink at a nearby refreshment stall. The duchess promptly started ordering everything in sight, and the young man began to realize with a fright that he would be unable to meet the enormous bill that she was running up. His flirtatiousness changed into an appalled silence. Cayetana took no notice and kept on ordering, and murmured to the barman—who recognized her—"until he has to leave his breeches."

When the bill was finally presented, he did indeed have to leave his breeches in part settlement, and covered his bare legs with—as it happens—a large Spanish cloak. The young man was mortified with shame and humiliation, while Cayetana laughed heartily. She cheered him up and asked him about his life and ambitions, then invited him to call on her next day with the promise that she would introduce him to someone who would help him. The young theology student accordingly turned up at the imposing Buenavista Palace gates next morning, expecting to be shown to the quarters of a maid, only to find that the object of his gallantry was the lady of the house. Cayetana was in animated discussion with a number of friends who found her exploit hilarious. The student felt ridiculous at the joke played upon him, but was rewarded with gifts and help for his future advancement. The anecdote illustrates the young duchess's complex character: extrovert, impulsive and manipulative, kindly or malicious at whim.

Cayetana de Silva Álvarez de Toledo, thirteenth Duchess of Alba, one of the grandest grandees of Spain, became the star of Madrid's social firmament during a rare moment of peace and stability in Spanish politics, during the reign of the Bourbon kings Carlos III and Carlos IV. It was a period of reform and prosperity that lasted from the banishment of Squillace in 1766 to the invasion by Napoleon's French troops in 1808. Even isolated and culturally backward Spain experienced some of the spirit of the Enlightenment that was sweeping the rest of Europe. Ideas of rationalism and education abounded, even though these never implied in this deeply feudal society any improvements of the conditions of the poorest classes: the nobility to which the duchess belonged clung to, and frivolously enjoyed, all their privileges. But great architects, sculptors and painters flourished and brought a touch of flamboyant modernity to the provincial little capital. Among them was Francisco de Goya, the court painter who became the Duchess's *protégé* and intimate friend. The depth of their intimacy remains a mystery but it is widely believed that it developed into a passionate affair.

Cayetana was born in 1762, the only daughter of parents who pretty much left her to her own devices. She was effectively brought up by her grandfather, Fernando de Silva, the Duke of Alba, a friend of the French Enlightenment philosopher Jean-Jacques Rousseau. The duke subscribed to the philosopher's belief in the innate freedom and innocence of the individual, and applied his ideas to the education of his granddaughter. Before the family moved to the Buenavista Palace, Cayetana grew up in the family home in the center of Madrid, a handsome mansion in Calle Duque de Alba, just by the Rastro flea market. You can still see the house, set back in Plaza Duque de Alba. (It is no longer in the family and for many years now has been neglected and occupied by squatters.) At eleven, Cayetana was betrothed to a decent but uninspiring nobleman chosen by her parents, José Álvarez de Toledo y Gonzaga, whom she married two years later, when he was sixteen. There was affection but no love between them, and the marriage, held together by convention and the need to keep up appearances, was emotionally a failure. Her adolescence was marked by a succession of deaths of dearly loved family members, each of which grieved her, while simultaneously adding to her fortune and string of titles. Deliberately or not, she never had children, a choice taken by many aristocratic women of the time, the better to enjoy their entertaining lives. Rumors suggested that she had a number of abortions.

The young lady was short and slender in build. Her crowning glory was a luxurious mane of thick black frizzy hair that reached to her waist. She had a gracious way of walking, a mannered swaying gait that was produced by a slight dislocation of her spine. According to her biographer, Dolores Arroyo, she had narrow lips, large expressive eyes that could express sour dissatisfaction as often as affectionate spontaneity. Elegantly brought up as befits someone of her class, Cayetana was at ease both in the salons of the Royal Palace and among the popular classes in whose fiestas, songs and dances she enthusiastically participated. She enjoyed a hectic social life in a set

whose primary purpose in life was to dispel boredom. When the duchess in due course inherited the opulent Buenavista Palace in Cibeles, she threw lavish balls that lasted from early evening until well into the next morning. Flitting from the townhouse to a retreat in the *sierra* or to the family estate at Sanlúcar de Barrameda in Andalusia, she enjoyed discussions of art, music, poetry, bullfights, and political and amorous intrigues.

As a married noblewoman, Cayetana enjoyed enormous personal liberty denied to single ladies living in the paternal home. Her husband, as custom demanded, accepted her free and easy ways. She particularly delighted in adopting the manners, customs, expressions and dress of the street traders, the *majos, manolas* and the so-called *chisperos*—blacksmiths, renowned at this time for their skillful ironwork, who represented a cheerily scruffy social sector of the city around the Calle Barquillo, behind the Buenavista Palace. Cayetana gloried in celebrating what was authentic to Madrid, which implied a rejection of foreign—that is, French—influences. In true Spanish style she was an enthusiast of bullfights, which there was a tendency at the time to disdain as barbaric and backward. And she enjoyed the theater, even performing to great acclaim in plays performed in private theaters for her noble friends.

Francisco de Goya y Lucientes, the painter of humble origins from Fuendetodos in Aragón, settled in Madrid in 1775, recently married to Josefa Bayeu. Through his former protector in Aragón who knew the Alba family, the artist was introduced to the duchess at a ball. She was thirteen, also newly married, and he was thirty. They did not meet again for ten years, during which time Goya had become a distinguished society painter on the point of becoming chief painter to the court. The two coincided at the Capricho country palace just outside Madrid—now recently re-opened, not far from the airport—belonging to the duchess's friend, the Duchess of Osuna. Goya was commissioned to paint six pictures illustrating the joys of country life, to adorn the palace rooms. These included scenes of noblemen and women dressed as *majos* and *majas*, playing on a swing or riding on donkeys, in which Goya painted Cayetana for the first time. It was at this moment that his passion for her is said to have begun.

Their relationship continues to be a fascinating mystery for Spaniards, who have produced many films, plays and musicals about the celebrated pair. Josefa, Goya's wife, a goodhearted provincial middle-class woman who could read and write, was constantly pregnant. When Goya mentioned her in letters to his friend Martin Zapatér, it was only to recount her births and miscarriages.

She apparently gave birth twenty times, but only one son, Javier, survived to adulthood and outlived his father. Josefa did not participate at all in the social life that her husband craved in his desire to chronicle his epoch, although their marriage was apparently happy. Cayetana decided to make the ambitious and talented artist her *protégé*. She invited him to her home, gave him commissions, flattered him with attention and encouragement and was generous to his family. She gave Josefa magnificent gifts and was affectionate to their children. The Goyas spent the summer of 1786 at the Albas' country house north west of Madrid, where he painted his lyrical portrayals of spring, summer, autumn and winter that are now, along with most of his best works, in the Prado.

The painter, it seems, fell deeply in love with the duchess, but there is no evidence that the duchess responded initially with more than friendship. Some attribute the artist's deep depressions of the early 1790s to the frustration and jealousy stemming from his unrequited love. In 1796, at the age of 39, the Duke of Alba died. Cayetana was 34, still beautiful and at the peak of her social success. In the spring of 1797 she retired to the family estate in Sanlúcar de Barrameda on the Coto Doñana near Cádiz and invited Goya to join her. He stayed as the duchess's guest from July until he returned to Madrid in March the following year. From this period date the artist's most intimate portraits of the duchess, collected in the so-called Sanlúcar Album. They include informal ink and wash sketches of the duchess and her closest servants, reflecting "a piquant but always tender realism," according to a recent catalogue that accompanied a Goya exhibition. She is shown taking a siesta, combing her hair, cuddling her adopted black daughter María de la Luz, teasing her old maid. In addition, Goya painted a splendid formal portrait set against the southern countryside. She is dressed as a *maja* in full finery: golden lace jacket, scarlet sash, and heavy black mantilla. She wears two rings each bearing the names Alba and Goya, and points with her forefinger to the artist's signature at the bottom of the painting.

Many of the sketches of the duchess reappear in his engravings of his fears and fantasies, the *Caprichos*, where Goya portrays her as a figure of frivolity, inconstancy, deception and a source of anxiety and mental torment. But, one of the big unanswered questions of European painting remains: did the duchess pose for two of Goya's greatest works, "The Naked Maja" and "The Clothed Maja" (*La maja desnuda* and *La maja vestida*)? These splendid paintings, created some time between 1797 and 1800, scandalized the religious authorities and aroused the unwelcome scrutiny of the Inquisition, which denounced them as obscene. Referring to the offending paintings, the Secret Chamber of the Inquisition in Madrid on March 16, 1815 ordered "that the said Goya should appear before this court to recognize and declare as his own work, and explain the motive for producing [the paintings], for whom and with what purpose." Nearly two centuries later, despite copious research, even these basic questions remain unanswered.

The two paintings, although matching, were painted at different times and the brushwork on each is quite distinct. In *La maja vestida*, Goya used a freer style, broad brushwork and bold colors; in the naked version, the brushwork is careful and glossy, producing a sensuously gleaming and velvety finish. *La maja desnuda* was painted first, between 1797 and 1800, and its clothed partner perhaps between 1800 and 1803. The dates remain vague; a Prado publication of 1995 dates the naked portrait "around 1795 or a year or two before." Arroyo's recent biography of the duchess sums up the widely held view:

> It has always been thought that the duchess was the model, and that Goya painted her in her palace in the Coto Doñana. Together, remote from prying eyes and with all the surrounding conditions in their favor, it was logical for a sentimental relationship to develop between them. It is to be supposed that confidence dispelled Cayetana's reluctance to be painted naked. Or perhaps she proposed the idea and the painter joyfully agreed. It seems that the proportions correspond to those of Cayetana, her medium height, dark frizzy hair, the color of her skin, the shape of her breasts, the length of her arms, although perhaps he idealized her body a little... What really happened only Cayetano de Alba and Francisco de Goya know.

The twin canvases were held in a private room in the collection of Count Manuel de Godoy, the king's devious minister, where an ingenious mechanism could superimpose one painting over the other. The pair of paintings was thus reputed to form an erotic game, whereby the clothed one could be removed to reveal the secret naked version beneath. The naked version, a closely observed work, offers the first example of female pubic hair in the history of painting. The paintings have always been considered extremely provocative, not just for the nakedness, but for the daring sensuality of the pose with the hands behind the head, the full-on gaze, and the clear understanding— still rare at this time—that they are not intended to represent an allegorical figure of a goddess, but are the portraits of a real sensuous woman. Even today in Spain, the gesture of putting one's hands behind one's head is considered extremely informal and familiar if done by a man, and almost unacceptably suggestive if done by a woman. Many connoisseurs think the clothed version is the more seductive.

Whether or not the duchess was the model remains a matter of heated debate. The Prado Museum produced a publication in 1984 that conceded that Goya and the duchess had a "powerful and stormy sentimental relationship." But it dismisses the idea that the duchess sat for the twin portraits, saying that the duchess—who died in 1802— would have been around forty when the works were painted, if they had been executed around 1800—"which would not seem to coincide with the youthful beauty of the majas." A later catalogue, published in 1996 to coincide with the artist's 250th anniversary points out that the facial features depicted bear no resemblance to those of the duchess. But many argue that Goya deliberately put an unknown, inexpressive mask of a face upon the duchess's vibrantly sensuous body in order to protect her identity.

Nonetheless, it appears that the relationship subsequently cooled. After their idyll in Coto Doñana, Goya rarely painted the duchess again in the five years until her death. But he sketched a plan for her tomb, showing three hooded figures laying her to rest.

The legend persisted to such a point that in November 1945 the Duke of Alba exhumed his ancestor's bones, ostensibly to establish the causes of her death. It was widely rumored that she had been poisoned by Queen María Luisa, jealous because Cayetana had caught the interest of her favorite, Count Godoy. But it was thought the real purpose of the exhumation was to examine her physical features in order to rule out the perceived slur that she had modeled for the two majas. The legend survives today, although it seems the cause of death was identified as meningitis.

The Prado catalogue asserts loftily—if ambiguously—that "nowadays, the identification of the majas with the Duchess of Alba is almost unanimously discarded." But it then examines in detail "the possible influence that the relationship between them had upon the conception of these works." While visiting the vivacious duchess at Sanlúcar de Barrameda, Goya made a number of sketches, "whose style, the ideal of erotic womanhood could be considered precursors to the majas." The *maja desnuda* illustrates just the kind of beauty embodied by the duchess, "with slender bones, tiny stature and generous and separated breasts." Further, the *maja vestida* displays the broad sash that appears frequently in Goya's portraits of the duchess, and the subject of the portrait is, like the duchess, an upper-class lady with plebeian tastes. Though dressed as a commoner—with a little jacket but no cap, mantilla or topskirt—she wears the tiny pointed shoes embroidered in gold similar to those that Goya frequently portrayed on the feet of various aristocratic ladies throughout the eighteenth and early nineteenth century, including Queen María Luisa.

In 1808 the works were confiscated by the king when Count Godoy fell from favor. In December 1813 they were seized by the Inquisition who kept them until 1836, when they entered the Royal Academy of San Fernando: the clothed one on view, the naked one hidden in a dark room closed to public scrutiny. In 1910 they were brought to the Prado, where they hang today, side by side, in a room of their own.

Goya's paintings of *majos* and *majas* portrayed, perhaps idealized, a colorful and pleasure-seeking world that did not survive the turn of the century. After the French Revolution everything to do with the aristocratic world was to turn a shade darker, a process reflected in Goya's increasingly somber paintings.

CHAPTER SIX

Plaza Dos de Mayo: Goya and National Heroes

Spring in Madrid, though usually short, a brief parenthesis between two extreme seasons, is glorious. The sun is radiant without being too intense, the sky luminous without being oppressive. The city's best popular festivals take place in the spring and early summer, especially that of May 15, celebrating Madrid's patron saint, San Isidro. Goya most vividly captures those carefree days of fiesta, when trees are putting out fluffy leaves, birds sing after their long winter's absence, and men and women of all classes—especially lower-middle downwards—dress in their finest to sprawl upon the green hills just south of the city across the river, to dance, picnic, and flirt, and to pay homage at the chapel of their saint. Goya's twin paintings of that day are the best known, but the scene is one of the most popular among Spanish artists.

The day of San Isidro is celebrated with a pilgrimage across the river by the western Segovia bridge or the southern Toledo bridge, a gorgeous baroque construction flanked by statues of San Isidro, with his son saved from the well on the right as you head south, and opposite him his wife, Santa María. On this feast day the two statues are decked with bouquets of scarlet carnations. The banks of the

Manzanares, where once the underwear of the city flapped after being washed by an army of washerwomen, are now thoroughly covered in concrete and roads, and the whole scene is dominated by the Vicente Calderón stadium—to your right as you head south—home of Atlético de Madrid football club. But on the feast day of the city's patron saint, Madrid's popular classes—the event is above all a working-class celebration—flock down the hill from the city center, and from outlying suburbs, to make their pilgrimage to the hermitage on the spot where the laborer Isidro ploughed his master's fields. It is a part of the city, and an occasion, where you are unlikely to see the smart set.

The scene displays the best of Madrid's ability to mount a jolly show. The route to the hermitage—Paseo Quince de Mayo, "May 15 Boulevard"—is lined with stall-holders selling knocked-off cassette tapes, ice cream, slices of coconut, balloons, sunflower seeds, sausage sandwiches, special pastries to mark the occasion (it is difficult to go anywhere in this city without being presented with the opportunity to buy food or drink), clay pots, herbal remedies, cheesecloth shirts, plastic windmills, cheeses, sausages, vast bread loaves: in short, all the produce you would expect on market day in a small country town. Surprisingly large numbers still wear the dress of the *chulapas* and *chulapos*—the nineteenth-century version of the traditional *majas* and *majos*. The men's outfit consists of a check waistcoat and flat cap, while women wear a tight full-length dress with puffed sleeves and flared at the knee, with a white head scarf and a scarlet carnation. Nowadays, it is mostly the children who are decked out in traditional costume, the little boys armed with a rake, symbol of Isidro's work in the fields. But you are likely to see a cheery, well-upholstered foursome in full fig, two couples strolling arm in arm, their traditional image updated by gilt sunglasses and mobile phones. Some of the fairground stalls with their blaring music have little squares of dance floor tucked beside them, where mature couples in full regalia solemnly twist and twirl in the *chotis*, a wobbling three-step, apparently derived from "Scottish" dancing.

As you mount the slope toward the hermitage, the crowd becomes thicker, and once the pretty building comes into view, you spot signs of holy devotion mixed with the fairground jollity. The faithful attend

mass, often in the company of local politicians who conspicuously participate in this popular celebration, then kiss the relics of the saint at the altar. Then they join a long queue to collect water from the holy fountain in the patio next to the hermitage. Traditionally, this was collected in a *botijo* or closed clay water vessel with a little hole at the top and a handle for carrying. And you will suddenly notice a proliferation of stalls selling souvenir versions of these vessels, decorated with the saint's name. But most of those patiently waiting are carrying plastic water bottles. Tradition dictates that they recite the couplet: "Beautiful San Isidro/ patron of Madrid/ who brought forth water/ from the rock." Then they find a shady spot on the grassy slopes, spread their cloths, unpack their tortilla and bottles of wine and laze the day away, enjoying the spring air and admiring what remains of the view of the capital glimpsed between the high-rise buildings. Modern architecture notwithstanding, the scene is very much as Goya and other eighteenth- and nineteenth-century artists portrayed it.

Humble Saint

San Isidro was born in Madrid on April 4, 1082, married a local girl, María, and worked as a well-digger and laborer who in 1119 was hired by the nobleman Iván de Vargas to tend his fields. The couple had a son Illán, and they seemed an ordinary working family. But Isidro, unusually generous and religious, had a knack for finding springs of water, a valuable gift in this parched land, and his actions produced the miracles that earned him sainthood. He gave to the birds part of the grain he was taking to the mill, and God multiplied the quantity of flour. He gave food to a poor neighbor, and the man's cooking pot filled and refilled. When Isidro's son fell into his well, he prayed until the waters rose, carrying the infant safely to the surface. In addition, both Isidro and his wife frequently crossed rivers using no more than "faith and a mantilla." His best-known miracle was produced when Isidro spent in prayer the hours he should have been ploughing his master's land. Vargas, who came one day to the fields to observe how work was progressing, was astonished to see two white angels ploughing back and forth, accomplishing the work that Isidro abandoned while he was praying.

He died on November 30, 1172, and for centuries thereafter miraculous events continued to be attributed to him, including success in various battles by Christians fighting against the advancing Moors. His body was dug up, put in a gilded casket and installed in a chapel in the church of San Andrés in the heart of the old town. Numerous members of the royal family visited his miraculously uncorrupted corpse down the centuries. Legend has it that Queen Isabel the Catholic, while thanking the saint for having cured her from a serious illness, took the opportunity to break off a toe from his left foot. But she returned it when she saw that the mules that drew her carriage refused to cross the Manzanares, despite the water level being very low. The custom arose of bringing out the body in a procession to intercede with God when rain was scarce or the king was sick, and there were constant demonstrations of the healing qualities of water from the wells he had opened on Vargas's lands. The miraculous water was even said to have cured Felipe II's scarlet fever.

The first hermitage was built in 1528 next to the spring that Isidro struck on Vargas's land on the hillside southwest of the city across the river. And the custom arose for *Madrileños* to make a pilgrimage to the spot. The pilgrims drank the water from the well and brought picnics to eat on the grass. But Isidro was not yet canonized, so the authorities strove to keep the festivities and acts honoring him from being too solemnly observed. On June 14, 1619 Pope Paul V declared Isidro a saint, whose festive day would be May 15. In November that year, King Felipe III became gravely ill in the village of Casarrubios, and by popular initiative, the casket containing the remains of San Isidro was brought to the king's bedside. He rallied and kissed the relics, but relapsed when the saint was returned to Madrid. So the casket was brought back again, and the king recovered sufficiently to continue his journey home.

The celebration of San Isidro's beatification took place in the Plaza Mayor on May 15, 1620 and lasted eight days. According to Pedro Montoliú Camps, "a total of 156 standards and 78 crosses participated in the procession, which was preceded by masquerades, dances and firework displays." The silversmiths' guild built a special silver casket for the saint, and henceforth, May 15 became a local holiday in Madrid. On that day in 1623, the English baronet Richard Wynn, who was accompanying the Prince of Wales on his visit to Spain, attended the procession in honor of San Isidro, and reported that he achieved countless miracles "because you only had to touch the urn that contained his body to be cured." Wynn reported that in the procession that year were 700 or 800 friars of different orders, in addition to dancers, actors and trumpeters.

A new hermitage, the one that remains today, was built in 1724. And behind it stretched the famous Pradera—or meadow—of San Isidro, whose green slopes extended until recent decades down to the riverbank. This was the view that Goya painted, as if from life, in 1788. That painting, and its companion, a view of the hermitage on the day of the fiesta, were commissioned as sketches for tapestries that were to be hung on the bedroom of the Infantas in the summer palace of El Pardo, part of a series depicting amusements in the open air. Although a subject often portrayed by Goya, this was the first time he alluded to a particular time and place, making a closely observed description of the city and its people. The two paintings represent the twin facets of the fiesta—the devotion and the diversion—and the artist is said to have indicated in this charming portrayal of both aspects the ideal of how popular religious fiestas should be celebrated. The vision is idealized as well as ideal, with its harmonious melange of social classes enjoying themselves under the benevolently watchful eye of the royal guards.

The popular celebration of religious fiestas became very controversial around this time, a subject of heated debate among intellectuals and writers of the day, many fearing the uncontrolled behavior of the popular masses. One writer, Jovellanos, thought that the fiesta that followed a holy pilgrimage was a "respectable" prolongation of the stimulus of piety. Another, Meléndez Valdés, was convinced that such events just led to trouble and disorder utterly at odds with the religious purpose of the gathering. Idealized they may have been, for there were many complaints around this time concerning the "profanation" of religious festivals by rowdy celebrations that got out of hand, producing riots and fist-fights that were quelled by the forces of public order. Nonetheless, this tension is still characteristic of Madrid's fiestas today: a fierce multitude of revelers discreetly marshaled by security guards in an atmosphere that rarely erupts beyond the boisterous desire to have a good time. And all in the name of the saint.

Goya was keen to portray the "respectable" side in this royal commission, while at the same time emphasizing the easy communication of all those enjoying a day out in an atmosphere of social harmony. It was the last time Goya was to paint a social setting from which conflict was absent. Goya's engaging portrayal of *La Pradera de San Isidro* was completed in 1788, a year before the French Revolution.

Popular Pilgrimages

Twenty years on, the pretty little chapel was stripped by the occupying French of numerous precious objects donated by Spain's royal family. But the locals soon resumed their tradition of making a pilgrimage to the spot every May, and, in true *Madrileño* style, turning it into a party. They bought the special little ring-like cakes or *rosquillas; rosquillas listas* (smart cakes) were dipped in sugar and *tontas* ("stupid ones") were not. And they laid out their picnics on the grass. A nineteenth-century couplet indicates the vast quantities of food that were brought: "I've been to San Isidro/ and I've had lunch;/ more than four people wanted/ what was left over./ There was roast lamb and meat pies,/ a capon and four eggs/ and three tortillas." It was customary, until the middle of the nineteenth century, for the royal family to receive a jug of water from the holy fountain on the feast day of San Isidro.

With the arrival of the first railways after 1851, pilgrims came from all over Spain, prompting Richard Ford to observe in 1855 that on the pilgrimage you could see costumes and dances from numerous provinces throughout the country. It must have been quite rowdy. The artist Fernández de los Ríos described it in 1876 as "bacchanalia disguised as pilgrimage." He deplored the fact that the meadow was covered with food and drink stalls, that people drank poisonous liquors rather than water from the holy fountain, that they danced and sang in the dust and trudged home on foot, laden with bells and whistles. Benito Pérez Galdós observed that in days preceding the festival, it was often difficult to buy food in the town because everything had been taken to the *pradera*.

The last time the body of San Isidro was taken from its casket was in 1896, during a prolonged drought that afflicted the whole region. The Queen Regent María Cristina and her son Alfonso XIII prayed for rain as the body of the saint was taken in a procession around the streets of the capital. Reports tell us that rain fell as soon as the ceremony was completed. Newspapers of the time emphasized the state of mummification of the body and noted that it still preserved the eyes beneath the lids. In 1922 the remains were examined again, during the celebration of the 300th anniversary of the canonization of the saint. The body remained uncorrupted, although the lips and nose were worn away and most of the toes and teeth were missing, along with a chunk of flesh from the left calf. The lack of fingers and toes was attributed to "indiscreet devotions."

Heroic Dates

The once modest, until recently quite sleazy, Malasaña district is rapidly becoming smartly bohemian. Block by block, the handsome late eighteenth-century apartment houses where workers and humble functionaries once lived, and which until just a few years back were occupied by squatters and drug dealers, are being spruced up, their facades washed in creamy ochre tones, their wrought-iron balconies decked with pots of geraniums. Early on Saturday and Sunday mornings the square is awash with a stinking chaos of cans and bottles abandoned by revelers from the night before. But after the municipal dust-carts and hoses have cleared the space, old people emerge into the sunshine, and children play on the climbing frames in the little playground. At the heart of this engaging part of town lies the Plaza Dos de Mayo, dominated by a curious brick archway topped with a red-tiled roof. Beneath the arch is a statue of two soldiers backed against a cannon, each wielding a sword in battle against an unseen enemy. The heroic effect is somewhat marred by the loss of the two blades—the warriors brandish only the truncated handles. And the statue does not identify the two men, who are grasping each other with their free hands, but a plaque dated 1908 on the nearby washed wall of the church of Maravillas—the old name for the neighborhood—tells the tale: "To the popular heroes of May 2, 1808, who came to the aid of the soldiers of the immortal Daoiz and Velarde and fought here for the Independence of the Fatherland against the forces of Napoleon." This was the first and only popular uprising by the people of Madrid against a foreign invader, and it was brutally crushed after just one day. The two fateful dates, the uprising on May 2 (Dos de Mayo) and the carnage of the day after (Tres de Mayo), are memorably captured in two of Goya's best-known works.

The events have acquired a romantic patina by the force of the two Goya canvases—even the city's most loyal chroniclers concede that the uprising was less spontaneous than subsequent legend came to suggest. "But," says Montoliú Camps, "it did arouse the Spanish people from their dangerous lethargy, considered by the French troops of the emperor Napoleon as the best possible signal of submission." The fiesta that Madrid celebrates every May 2 is the only one that has no religious component. But to compensate for the absent spiritual vertebra that sustains every other fiesta in Spain, the occasion is overwhelmingly stiffened by military parades in period costume.

May 2, 1808 was a Monday, and a fine day by all accounts. Some 175,000 people lived in Madrid at the time—about the same number who live today in the old center that formed the entire city in those days. French troops had entered the city on March 23 under the command of Joaquín Murat, Napoleon's brother-in-law and his lieutenant in Spain. Of some 55,000 French soldiers, around 10,000 established themselves in strategic points throughout the city, with the rest around the outskirts and in the nearby towns of Aranjuez, Toledo, El Escorial, and toward the Guadarrama mountains. Lazy and feeble King Carlos IV, whose roly-poly features are captured by Goya in his 1801 portrait of the royal family, had done nothing to prevent the French military takeover of his capital; indeed, his government had done everything they could to cooperate with the occupying army. "Know that the army of my dear ally the Emperor of the French crosses my kingdom with ideas of peace and friendship," the king wrote to his subjects from Aranjuez on March 16. "Spaniards be calm... and you will see within a few days peace restored." Aranjuez promptly revolted, and three days later Carlos abdicated in favor of Fernando VII— equally unprepossessing, to judge from Goya's later portraits. There followed weeks of confused power play between an enfeebled Spanish monarch, a *de facto* government committee and the French who were marching upon Madrid. Feverish negotiations with the French sought to spirit the royal family out of harm's way, while rumblings of discontent mounted among the people and a few officers. Murat was whistled as he passed through the Puerta del Sol, and one version of events recounts that someone threw a stone that hit the commander's horse on the head. Murat warned that he would brook no opposition or he would treat Spain as a conquered land. The puppet government pondered whether to issue arms to the people, since Madrid's own troops numbered fewer than 9,000.

Early on the morning of May 2, a carriage slipped away from the Royal Palace containing members of the royal family fleeing to safety. Another one, containing royal servants, was preparing to leave. At about 9AM, a master locksmith, José Blas Molina Soriano, saw the coach, strode into the palace and after a moment or two ran out, shouting: "Treason! Treason! They've taken the king and they want to take all the royal household. Death to the French!" Within minutes, hundreds came running and the coach's traces were cut. The crowd swelled to 2,000. Murat's aide-de-camp, Auguste Legrange, ordered the protesters to disperse, then brought up artillery pieces and fired into the crowd, who fought back with fists and knives. Within half an hour clashes broke out between *Madrileños* and French soldiers throughout the city. French mounted troops poured into the Puerta del Sol from their surrounding barracks. They were confronted by women from the poorer parts of town, who set upon them with knives and scissors in what Montoliu calls "a mortal and unequal struggle." With 20,000 French soldiers expertly deployed by Murat, it is not hard to see why the uprising was so quickly crushed.

The only serious resistance from Spanish soldiers came from the artillery barracks of the Monteleón Palace in the Maravillas district. The palace formerly belonged to descendants of the *conquistador* of Mexico, Hernán Cortés, the Marquises of the Valley of Oaxaca, Dukes of Monteleón and Terranova, who had moved to Italy. It was converted into an army barracks in 1807 and contained 37 cannons of bronze and iron, siege, field and naval gun-carriages, numerous small muskets, rifles, shotguns, pistols, swords, sabers and bayonets, as well as copious ammunition. But the palace and its grounds, designated an artillery base only months before, had no defensive walls or ditches and was not really a military barracks at all. A crowd hammered upon the door demanding arms.

At this point—it was still barely 10AM—Artillery Captain Luîs Daoiz, a 41-year-old Sevillian, showed up. Captain Daoiz was an experienced artilleryman, having seen service in Algeria and South America. Another captain, Pedro Velarde, arrived on the scene, seeking reinforcements from among the State Volunteers, quartered in nearby Calle San Bernardo. Captain Velarde was only able to convince the colonel of the barracks to let him have the troops by promising not to attack the French. Although the 33-strong company was supposed only to protect the Monteleón Palace, Velarde led his men into the park that surrounded the palace, "prepared to put them at the disposal of the uprising." The next step was to convince Daoiz to open the palace and hand arms to the crowds banging on the doors. After some hesitation,

Daoiz agreed and distributed muskets, swords, sabers, and bayonets to about 300 people. They were soon joined by a group who had come from the palace, crying "To arms! Death to the French!" as they made their way through the streets, mobilizing residents and passersby. Some, once armed, went in search of French patrols. Others were organized into a rough-and-ready defense of the palace, with further men installed in houses round about. And another group brought out five cannons and trained them toward the access roads, ready for combat.

The French spread around the city to crush the revolt, firing into open windows, entering houses and killing those who had attacked them. Clashes continued all morning in streets throughout the city. Prisoners in the court prison, the handsome arcaded building on the Plaza Santa Cruz (now the Foreign Ministry), asked to be able to join the defense of the city, promising to return once their duty was done. Of the 94 prisoners, 56 were allowed to leave and join the battle. They seized a French cannon in the Plaza Mayor, beneath the arch that leads to Calle Toledo, and fired it three times. In the hours that followed, 51 returned to prison, four were apparently killed or wounded, and only one fled to freedom. The bloodiest fighting was in the Puerta del Sol, where hundreds of *Madrileños* stuck knives, or their fingers, into the horses of Napoleon's elite Egyptian troop of Mamelukes. But by noon the townsfolk fled, leaving a battlefield covered with blood, bodies and wounded horses. Among the fighters who fell wounded in the clashes at the Puerta del Sol was the painter León Ortega y Vila, aged eighteen, a pupil of Francisco de Goya. The young man appears in the foreground of Goya's famous work *The 2nd of May in Madrid: the Struggle against the Mamelukes*. Legend says Goya based this painting, executed years later, upon a sketch he drew at the time from the window of a house apparently belonging to his son on the Puerta del Sol. Other versions suggest that it was Ortega who made a sketch of the events, and that this formed the basis of Goya's dramatic painting.

But Monteleón continued to resist, aided by the artillery pieces that held the French troops at bay, and by a number of citizens whose bravery has gone down in history. Among them was Lt. Jacinto Ruíz Mendoza, leader of the volunteers, who fought on despite being wounded in the arm until he was gravely wounded in the chest.

Another popular hero was Clara del Rey, 47, who fought alongside her husband and three sons. While she was loading one of the cannons, she was hit in the head by a cannonball shell. She was taken to the hospital in nearby Calle Silva, where she died two months later.

The most famous heroine, after whom this barrio is named, was Mañuela Malasaña Oñero, a seamstress who was shot dead in the temple by a French bullet as she was helping her father Juan Malasaña load his rifle. Other versions of events relate that she was shot for defending herself with a concealed weapon—her scissors—or for carrying ammunition to Spanish troops. The official version is inscribed beneath a 1943 portrait of a simpering and extremely mature-looking fifteen-year-old in a hidden-away corner of the Army Museum near the Retiro Park. Her heroic stand is described there as follows: "At dusk on May 2, 1808 she left her seamstresses' workshop and was hurrying home, when she was seized by a pair of French soldiers who tried to search her, but she resisted. They promised to set her free if she went with them, but without a second thought she took from her bag the scissors she was carrying, and warned the two men not to come near her. They dared not do so, but the French soldiers shot her there and then." In the painting she is leaning with lumpish coquetry upon a wall, an embroidered handkerchief trailing from her fingers, with the arched and tiled doorway of the Monteleón barracks in the background.

Countless other names are recorded of women who fought heroically and were among those who throughout the morning were carried into the Maravillas church next door. The church formed part of a convent where nuns offered first aid in what they swiftly transformed into an improvised hospital. The church today still boasts a fabulous baroque retable and a dazzling white-clad virgin with gilded rays blazing from her head. Much restored, it exudes a shabby grandeur. Tweeting swallows and cries from the playground can be clearly heard from within. Among a number of side chapels inhabited by lugubrious statues from various centuries, all renovated at one time or another, is one chapel dedicated to the victims of May 2, 1808. It contains an agonizingly expressive gothic Christ on the cross, and claims to commemorate the first assembly of the Spanish Red Cross.

A red cross forms part of the stonework, and some say the nuns' succor to the battle victims that day was the origin of the international humanitarian organization.

Daoiz was wounded in the leg as he tried to fire the cannon. Velarde was shot dead in the chest. Daoiz, immobilized, leaned against the cannon and waited, sword in hand. He received a deep bayonet wound in the shoulder. At 1PM, the Monteleón surrendered. The French troops took a dozen or so prisoners, but others hid in the vicinity, or sneaked out from the back of the building. Daoiz was taken to his house in a street nearby, but died hours later. Another account says that Daoiz was betrayed by the French and mortally wounded when he went to negotiate a surrender. According to this version, Velarde was killed as he tried to help his comrade. The two bodies were taken to the convent of San Martín, near the Plaza de las Descalzas. By lunchtime it was all over, and the reprisals began. Executions continued until the early hours of May 3—the aftermath caught unforgettably by Goya's second painting of the pair commemorating the tragedy. In the following days hundreds were buried in the cemetery of la Florida, near the banks of the Manzanares. The little chapel nearby contains the tomb of Goya, and is, incongruously perhaps, illustrated by some of the artist's most jaunty frescoes. Historians in the years immediately after the uprising estimated that 409 Spaniards, including 60 women and 13 children, died on May 3, and that 171 were wounded. Perhaps the French lost another 500.

The two famous works that Goya painted in 1814 to mark the event—*El dos de mayo de 1808* and *El tres de mayo 1808*—sought, in his own words to the prince regent, to whom he proposed the project, to "perpetuate through the means of the paintbrush the most notable and heroic actions or scenes of our glorious insurrection against the tyrant of Europe." Despite their dramatic intensity and emotional immediacy, experts do not believe they represent any particular scene or indicate that Goya personally saw any of the action he portrayed so vividly some six years after the event. The white-clad figure of the terrified rebel who faces the firing squad with outstretched arms is often likened to a Christ-like personification of the martyr. He even has a mark of the stigmata on his right hand. But unlike conventional portrayals of Christ's martyrdom, Goya's painting transformed the customary light source; usually depicted as emanating from God, in Goya's vision the light is on the side of the assassins who illuminate their pursuit and massacre of the rebels. Out of a religious tradition, Goya produces a new creation, the fighter for liberty, an image that recurs in European art up to the present day. The two paintings are among the artist's finest late works, imbued with despair and political disappointment. They hang, amid the world's biggest collection of Goyas, in the Prado Museum.

The Prado

It is difficult to overstate the importance of the Prado Museum in Madrid's cultural development, not just for the treasures it contains— one of the finest collections of art in the world—but for the controversial history of the institution itself, a saga of woes that shows little sign of ending. Described recently by the distinguished writer and social commentator Manuel Vicent as "perhaps the only really solid Spanish institution," the museum's history amounts to nearly two centuries of accidents and misfortunes. Even its foundation had a quality of random eccentricity to it, according to Vicent's ironic account that was prompted in 1999 by a leak of rainwater into the room containing Velázquez masterworks.

The Prado comprises the Royal Collection of Paintings, Vicent writes, plus those from the vaults of the Museo de la Trinidad, which had been set up in the 1830s to house artworks requisitioned from convents and monasteries following the disentailment of religious property, and acquisitions after 1856. The Royal Collection had some 3,000 works distributed around the various palaces. These paintings were assembled in a museum, not because King Fernando VII sought to develop public artistic awareness—a sentiment entirely absent from the Spanish monarchs—but because they were removed from the walls of the royal salons, so that they could be papered in accordance with the latest French fashion. Queen Isabel of Braganza, it seems, thought it was a pity to leave them abandoned to the elements and liable to being stolen from the corridors and garrets where they were pushed out of the way. The fine neoclassical building by Juan de Villanueva, built in the 1780s and intended as a national history museum, was in ruins after the occupying French troops had stripped the roof of lead to make bullets. To house the Royal Collection, the building—which took on the name of the Prado boulevard along which it sprawled—was repaired at His Majesty's expense. But this gesture was apparently for the sole pleasure of his wife the queen, and not for the love of art, since this monarch was, in the words of the English traveler John Murray, "the most anti-aesthetic Goth of any who has smoked tobacco."

"That the original lead from the museum roof was destined to make bullets to fire against Spaniards and that the Prado owes its very creation to the French fashion for putting paper on the walls of palace salons—adornments of flowers and little castles being preferred to the paintings of Velázquez—perhaps illustrates the curse that has always accompanied Villanueva's building," Vicent observes. He goes further, attributing this malevolence to Spain's national psyche:

In fact, the Prado's leaks mark the historical bisector of our cultural misery. The rooms of a museum of painting are an ideal space for the creation of the most terrible curses. Around great works of art, the curators, critics, restorers and guards can produce morbid passions that can end in assassination. To kill or die for Velázquez would be a supreme category of the soul, but that this curse of the Prado is reduced to a few miserable leaks that drip ceaselessly into a washing-up bowl as if it were a miserable "pensión" marks the mousetrap level to which we have descended.

This extravagant polemic is typical of the self-indulgent breast-beating among many Spanish intellectuals and critics who lament the ignorant neglect to which their artistic heritage is supposedly subjected. But the rackety history of the city's most famous, and most visited, tourist attraction does give force to Vicent's scornful words.

The building was set in train by the Bourbon King Carlos III's architect Juan de Villanueva in 1785, above what legend insists—and old maps confirm—is an underground river flowing from the nearby Retiro park. Superstitious souls attribute the museum's agitated life to the subterranean currents flowing beneath it, creating disturbances and tensions among all those who live and work above. The museum suffered its first indignity in the Peninsular Wars (which Spaniards call the Wars of Independence), when Napoleon's troops commandeered the building as a cavalry barracks and gunpowder store. When peace came in 1814 further damage was inflicted by *Madrileños* who plundered wood and stone to repair their ravaged homes. In the Civil War from 1936 to 1939 it was sandbagged, and paintings were removed to the ground floor and the cellar to protect them from bombardment. Artworks were even brought from outside Madrid to be given refuge, since the Prado was somehow thought to have moral immunity. It was bombed anyway, but the paintings—detached from the walls at the start of the bombardment and stowed in the cellar to protect them from the cold entering the broken windows—were undamaged. Some 500 of the most precious works, including Velázquez's *Las Meninas* and Titian's *Carlos V*, were carefully packed up and taken by a convoy of lorries to Valencia in December 1936.

The Prado was first extended in 1918 by adding a few rooms at the back. The second extension, in the 1950s, added more rooms, and the third, in the 1960s, consisted of closing the courtyards between the existing extensions to make more rooms. Since then, the only solution to a growing collection and an explosion of visitors—prior to the present expansion, which is set to continue until well into the millennium—has been to decant the most recent, i.e. nineteenth-century, works into the Casón del Buen Retiro, a nearby former seventeenth-century palace ballroom, restored in 1971.

Neglected and starved of resources in the 1960s and 1970s, when comparable museums in London and Paris were boldly expanding to meet insatiable public demand, paralyzed in the 1980s and early 1990s by political infighting and bureaucratic bungling, the Prado suffered a succession of gaffes and scandals that brought it to the point of crisis. The depths were plumbed in October 1993, when the authorities discovered to their horror that the old roof tiles had deteriorated so much that rainwater was coursing down the walls into the room containing Velázquez masterworks, including *Las Meninas*, the jewel of the entire collection. This was not the disaster satirized by Manuel Vicent; he was referring to a similar mishap six years later when long-delayed repairs to the fabric of the building were almost completed. So shocking was the blow in 1993 that the director, Felipe Vicente Garín, resigned on the spot and parliament, in a rare spasm of cross-party harmony, approved an emergency repair program, which, notwithstanding the urgency, took three years before lumbering into action. The crisis prompted the socialist Minister of Culture, Carmen Alborch, to propose an international competition to produce a plan for expansion—a grand gesture that bit the dust in September 1996 when an international jury of architects failed to select from among 550 proposals a single project that was up to the task. Ms. Alborch's conservative successor, Esperanza Aguirre, annulled the competition, saying that none of the projects solved the problems presented by the museum's historic building and its sensitive site. She ordered the ten finalists back to the drawing board with the message that "prudence" was the watchword: there were to be no pyramids comparable to the Louvre in Paris, no obelisks, no frivolities. Late in 1998 a vastly scaled down expansion plan quietly slipped into operation, the first since 1956 and a modest but coherent proposal that suddenly seemed more in tune with the times than previous flamboyant schemes. "We are recuperating the buildings where our finest paintings were originally hung, putting them in their historical and architectural context. They are within comfortable walking distance in an urban neighborhood of great historical importance and beauty. We must respect this area and treat it with dignity. It needs gentle intervention, not a bold gesture," said the museum's director Fernando Checa late in 1998.

Fernando Checa had become director in May 1996, committed to sorting out the museum's Kafkaesque internal bureaucracy and to increasing the number of curators. The Prado has always had very few curators by international standards; for many years it did not have one for Spanish art, its strongest suit. Mr. Checa's debut was inauspicious. Within months, a sensation-seeker super-glued a painting of his own to the wall of a room containing Flemish masters, including the Prado's only Rembrandt—and nobody noticed for five days. Mr. Checa quietly invited a security director to resign and, for the first time in years, things started to calm down. He was the fifth government-appointed director in six years, a staggering turnover that contributed greatly to a saga of embarrassing mishaps. His immediate predecessor, José María Luzón, was swept from office in April 1996 after wrongly hailing as a newly discovered Goya a religious painting uncovered during the restoration of Franco's former torture chambers in the Puerta del Sol. The work, described as "a cracker of a Goya" by Mr. Luzón, turned out to be by Salvador Maella, a lesser contemporary. The work was registered as Maella's in Madrid's local government archives and a preliminary sketch was even registered in the Prado's own records. Mr. Luzón's hasty endorsement could not have been more ill-timed, on the eve of a blockbuster exhibition celebrating the 250th anniversary of Goya's birth.

The blunder revealed the damage caused by treating the museum as a political football. Mr. Luzón, an archaeologist with no specialist knowledge of Goya, was a gray placeman for the previous socialist government. At least Mr. Checa is an art historian and specialist in the sixteenth- and seventeenth-century royal collections that lie at the museum's heart. Mr. Luzón's predecessor, Francisco Calvo Serailler, had to quit in 1994 after his wife, editor of a style magazine, set up a photo-feature in which designer chairs marched across the Prado's marble flags, with Velázquez masters figuring as a mere backdrop. Another director, Alfonso Pérez Sánchez was sacked in 1991 for signing a declaration opposing Spain's participation in the Gulf War.

The chaos persisted while Villanueva's classical pile was whipped into an orgy of repair work throughout the late 1990s. Visitors had to pick their way around scaffolding, stop their ears to drilling so loud the paintings trembled, pee in rickety cubicles, eat in stuffy, crepuscular gloom and ask in vain where shifting masterworks were being hung that week. But they were undeterred, and continued to pour through the handsome neoclassical doors in ever increasing numbers.

The attractions are obvious. Villanueva's building lounges along the grandest boulevard in Madrid and contains the finest collection of Goya, Velázquez and El Greco in the world. It is bursting at the seams: of its 7,000 paintings, only 2,500 are on view. The aim is to make room for at least 500 more—another mile of art. But within those constraints, fine renovation work is emerging. Twelve refurbished rooms on its principal floor displaying more than 160 Flemish masters—including the world's biggest and finest Rubens collection—more than half of them restored to dazzling splendor and twenty never exhibited before. An entire floor was created by raising the attic roof, clearing out workshops and offices to reclaim the space for hanging paintings. The new rooms are silk-lined and naturally lit. Dim paintings once lined up in chilly ranks are glowingly restored and grouped thematically as if adorning a palace salon. Discreet informative labels replace tags formerly cryptic to the point of incomprehensibility.

While the polemic gradually died down, the museum quietly made piecemeal decisions, limiting scope for the architectural imagination to fly. It acquired two buildings behind the main gallery: an office block and a ruined seventeenth-century cloister. The cloister deal was clinched only after protracted haggling with the Church, and with the agreement of the Pope. The museum decanted its administrative activities and library into the office block and decided to revamp the cloister site, which is higher than the main building, by gouging out subterranean space for workshops, storerooms, gift shops, temporary exhibitions, cafés and meeting rooms, hence freeing up Villanueva's building for the permanent collection. The nearby Army Museum, housed in a seventeenth-century former Royal Palace was commandeered, and its military contents destined for the Alcázar in Toledo. The former palace ballroom, the Casón del Buen Retiro, containing the museum's nineteenth-century collection, will be deepened by three floors. Henceforth, the museum will comprise five separate buildings. As a result, architects were asked to do little more than design a multi-story catacomb beneath a ruined cloister and link it to the main building by a tunnel. "We want to create an intellectually rigorous and enjoyable experience that will help people understand the history of our country, and something that is economically, politically and administratively manageable. Our idea might be mistaken, but at least it's coherent," Mr. Checa says. The distinguished architect Rafael Moneo, responsible for such jewels of sensitive restoration as the Atocha railway station and the Villahermosa palace that houses the Thyssen-Bornemisza collection, was put in charge.

All seemed set fair. Chaos still reigned, but it marked the throes of recovery and renewal rather than decadence and drift. Then suddenly in June 1999, just when it looked as though the museum might be awakening in time to greet the new millennium, the nightmare returned. Rainwater leaked once more into the building, trickling around priceless Velázquez masterworks. This was what prompted Vicent's outburst. With the massive repair program almost completed, it seems that the basic fault remained. Heavy storms sent rivulets trickling down the walls of the new Velázquez room, splashing *Los Borrachos*, the artist's splendid tribute to Bacchus. The rain that poured through the new roof, specially designed to permit the entry of natural light, also approached *Las Meninas*, Velázquez's complex portrayal of the royal family, and dripped down the central stair well. The drops splashed on to the marble floor of the room where the best Velázquez works are grouped, near to *Los Borrachos*, which is hung low to permit close viewing. It was all cleared up, but hours later a film of condensation formed on the glass ceiling and on the wall near *Los Borrachos*. Humidity had plagued the new roof for weeks. And water seeped through the window of the recently opened room containing Goya's two great works on the 1808 uprising. One possible explanation for the havoc was that rainwater had been trapped in old drainpipes blocked by the new building work.

It seemed that the dark swirling chaos of Goya's Black Paintings, with their portrayals of mortals tormented by ghosts and evil monsters, was a cruel commentary upon the history of the building that houses them. Latterly, it has become fashionable to attribute the gloomy, sometimes horrific, visions of Goya's later work to the artist's cycles of psychological depression. But Goya was intensely political, and his bitter *Caprichos, Disparates,* and Images of War inspired by the battlefields themselves seem less the expressions of a manic depressive than a despairing comment on political realities, reactionary clerics, ignorance and superstition, and the futile brutality of war. Goya began his career as a faithful chronicler of a peaceful, confident and happy realm in the Age of the Enlightenment, but in his later years he illustrated in stark photographic images of chaos and decadence, the aftermath of war and occupation that drove him into exile in France, where he died. Like Velázquez, Goya portrayed the convulsions of a society transformed, its confidence shaken. Curiously, the pilgrimage to San Isidro, portrayed so cheerily in 1777, is reprised in a terrible shadowy "black" work dated between 1820 and 1823. In place of an ordered, innocent celebration, he shows what one expert calls "a Saturnalian orgy" of a people bitter and traumatized.

But, like the building in which his life's work can be enjoyed, the truth is in the whole. As part of its renovation, the Prado recently brought out some of Goya's finest "black" engravings of men tormented by evil spirits. It acquired a fine little masterpiece that it had coveted for years, showing a figure stumbling through darkness, shrouded by a sheet, while above his head frolic a clutch of horrible ghouls in obscene and malevolent disarray. The *Vuelo de Brujas* ("Witches' Flight") is one of a series in which the artist explores his vision of nightmares, ignorance and witchcraft, and it provides a cruelly faithful image of the chaos that has for years tormented the home of one of the world's finest art collections. Wanting to refresh my memory of the *Vuelo de Brujas*, I found the painting gone from where I'd seen it amid a collection of Goya sketches liberated from the vaults, but so fragile they are shown for only two months a year. Was it hanging elsewhere in the gallery, or had it been put in storage? They weren't sure. Nonetheless, today's chaos augurs well. Prado-lovers are confident that those unquiet spirits will soon be lain to rest, the flapping ghouls dispersed. The Goya that best symbolizes the Prado's renaissance may instead be its most recent acquisition, the last great Goya masterpiece in private hands, sold to the nation by the Ruspoli family in 2000. It is of the sweet and enigmatic Countess of Chinchón, a painting of a young and innocent woman in the early stages of pregnancy. This lovely portrait was for centuries tossed from pillar to post, subject to crises and narrow escapes from destruction. Now it has ended up safely in public hands, adored and treasured beyond price.

CHAPTER SEVEN

Lavapiés:
The Melting Pot

Lavapiés, one of the most authentic—they say *castizo*—of Madrid's working-class squares, is undergoing a facelift, and the square, actually a long triangle that points downhill toward the river, has been re-paved and dotted with scores of wooden benches. Within days of their installation, these benches were taken over by locals as if they had been there forever. Young Spanish boys called out compliments to passing women, elderly ladies held raucous conversations that entailed much body-shaking laughter. Solemn Africans in bright flowing robes stood or glided elegantly upon the cobbles. Lavapiés hosts more seats than town planners might find aesthetically pleasing. And they are grouped in a haphazard manner, as though the locals had demanded more and more benches. But there still aren't enough. On a warm summer evening, those who cannot find a seat bring out their own chairs, or lean up against a lamppost, hang around in a knot by the ice cream kiosk or the lottery seller.

Arabs or Berbers from Morocco or other Maghreb countries clack their worry beads, exchange comments with scurrying Chinese traders who, perhaps because they are the most recent arrivals, do not seem to spend much time sitting on the benches or chatting in the square. Chinese-owned supermarkets and wholesale handbag warehouses up and down the hill are still trading after most shops hereabouts have pulled down their shutters for the evening.

The streets that converge upon Lavapiés may resound to the triumph of Catholicism—Faith, Jesus and Mary, Ave Maria, Calvary—but this is the home of the most confessionally and racially mixed population you will find in the whole city. Despite the lived-in feel to the place—it is one of the spots in Madrid where you imagine traditions go back furthest—few living here today can trace their roots back more than one or two generations. Lavapiés, recently a depressed and rundown sink of inner-city decay, is undergoing a revival thanks to adventurous youngsters moving into cheap rented housing, and local authority funding. It always has been something of melting pot. Rather like London's Brick Lane or New York's Lower East Side, Lavapiés is an early staging post for successive waves of immigrants to the city, whose turbulent history has produced some of the richest, most colorful and characteristically *Madrileño* personalities. A sure sign of an immigrant community is the proliferation of *locutorios*, or telephone cabins for making long-distance calls—and there are plenty in this neighborhood. The intermingling seems mostly peaceful enough, although bitter turf wars between those whom locals call *Los Moros* and *Los Chinos* give rise to much comment and complaint among older Spanish residents. Energetic Chinese—or Korean—incomers are stepping on the heels of established Moroccan businesses and wholesale traders. But significantly, representatives of both communities jointly stress that trouble, if there is any, is caused by a small minority, and that the communities themselves are eager to coexist harmoniously.

The name Lavapiés sounds as though it should have something to do with washing the feet (*lavar pies*), but might also have originated from the Hebrew *aba-puest*, meaning "place of Jews." For this is the old Jewish quarter; the synagogue used to be on the southeast corner of the square where the experimental Teatro Olimpia stands. Following their expulsion from Spain by the Catholic monarchs in 1492, Jews who converted to Christianity, known as *conversos*, occupied the Lavapiés area. Perhaps this lies behind the vehement Catholicism of the street names. It was the custom for these new Christians to call their first son Manuel, so Lavapiés became known as the *barrio de los Manolos*. Over the years the *manolos* and *manolas* intermingled with migrants from all over Spain and melded to produce the archetypal Madrid working-class character that you're likely to meet in any bar or taxi: street-wise, sharp-tongued and haughty. The *manolos* were renowned for always looking neat and dapper. In the nineteenth century, the term *chulo* (from the Arabic *chaul*, meaning "lad") also became popular as a term to describe these characters. These terms are still widely used today, and to describe someone as *chulo* is to suggest that they have a certain rakish charm. Latin Americans use the word with a stronger, more derogatory meaning, but in Madrid it is only mildly disrespectful to call someone *chulo*, and some would take it a compliment.

You head downhill to Lavapiés, a descent that is both social and geographical. Lavapiés is at the heart of what are called *los barrios bajos*, Madrid's low quarters, meaning both those down toward the river, and those inhabited by the social underclass. But it also marked the spot to which new arrivals aspired, a foothold in the city. Arturo Barea writes:

> It was the lowest rung in the social ladder that began at the Plaza de Oriente in the Royal Palace with its gates open to plumed helmets and diamond-spangled décolletés, and ended in Avapiés, which then spewed out the last dregs and deposited them in the other world, in the Americas and the New World… Thus El Avapiés was the pointer of the scales, the crucial point between existence and non-existence. One came to El Avapiés from above or from below. Whoever came from above had stepped down the last step left to him before the final and absolute fall. Whoever came from below had scaled the first step upwards, which might lead to anywhere and anything. Millionaires have passed through El Avapiés before crossing the outer belt of the Rondas and turning into drunken beggars. Ragpickers, collectors of cigarette stubs and waste paper, filthy from spittle and trampling feet, have climbed the step of El Avapiés and come to be millionaires. In El Avapiés, all the prides exist side by side, the pride of having been everything and no longer wanting to be anything, and the pride of having been nothing and wanting to be everything… The two waves never break against each other. Between them lies a firm, calm beach which absorbs the impact of both and converts them into currents which ebb and flow: all Avapiés works.

The urban guts—*las vísceras urbanas*—is how Juan Antonio Cabezas describes Lavapiés. Guts provide an apt metaphor, for the area was originally the slaughterhouse and abattoir for the city, and Barea recalls the pervasive stench of rotting flesh. The nearby Rastro is named after the street down which the slaughtered animals were dragged, leaving a bloodstained trail or *rastro*. The main street is called the Ribera de Curtidores, or Tanners' Alley, testimony to the rough and stinking trades that arose in and around the urban guts. Here the social dregs of the city, or those aspiring to move upscale, met to barter pieces of junk in the hurly-burly of the wholesale meat market. No one knows quite when the tradition began, but street trading on this spot was already mentioned by writers like Lope de Vega, Quevedo and Cervantes. And "wholesale meat market" is clearly marked on the spot in Pedro de Teixera's famous map of the city of 1656.

By the eighteenth century the market was well established as a focus for exchanging second-hand goods, although the slaughtering activities began gradually to disappear. People hoping to make a small sum would come with a few bits and pieces wrapped in a cloth, which they would unfold and spread on the ground, keeping a constant eye out for the police. This came to be the typical image of the Rastro and one you can still see any weekend, when a couple of burly guards converge upon a down-at-heel individual squatting by the roadside who complains he is only trying to make an honest living. But street trading is now carefully regulated, and however persuasive the plea, the would-be trader gathers his pieces of bric-a-brac and shambles off. Stalls began to appear in the 1870s up and down the Ribera de Curtidores, which continues to be the main spine of the extensive and vaguely defined Rastro, devoted to old clothes and household effects. The deceptively scruffy but astute antique and furniture dealers did not move in until early in the twentieth century. They form a sort of aristocracy of the area, covering their tracks somewhat by displaying their wares on the street at weekends in a typically higgledy-piggledy manner that suggests a more informal trade than is actually the case. These shopkeepers do not care to haggle, although the street traders expect it. The Rastro is perhaps the only spot in Spain where haggling is conducted with any kind of elegance or respect for the art. Spaniards are not a trading nation, and *Madrileños* the least of all. But here, perhaps, the original Arab and Jewish trading roots still exist, and it is sometimes possible to engage in this stimulating practice without either party losing their dignity. Just remember that this is not, despite appearances, a place for bargains.

The *Corralas*

Around Lavapiés and the Rastro the street formations and in some cases the houses themselves go back centuries. These are the astonishingly cramped and noisy quarters evoked in the literature of the nineteenth century and whose final traces are only now being cleared away, or in rare cases, preserved. Benito Pérez Galdós describes the interlocking rabbit warrens of dark and insalubrious tenements, overrun by filthy scabby children and screaming weary women, their men largely drunk, idle or insane. The *corrala*, based around the communal courtyard, where water had to be brought from the fountain in an earthenware jar, has all but gone now. You can still buy the jars cheaply in the market, although it is difficult sometimes to distinguish the really old ones that have been lying on their side for decades, wheedled perhaps from an old country widow by passing gypsies, from those made the other day and dirtied up.

A *corrala* on Calle Miguel Servet, between Mesón de Paredes and Espino down by the old cigar factory, has been preserved. The building, dating from 1790 and described by its inhabitants as "an immense warren," was taken over in 1981 by the local authorities who started to rehabilitate it in 1984. At that time, the *corrala* comprised 104 ruined dwellings, many of which didn't even have a toilet. It is perhaps just as well that a municipal bathhouse is just across the street, where you can still get a shower for 25 pesetas. The *corrala* was reborn after extensive renovation in 1985, but just a year after the work was finished, cracks and damp spots started to appear. Thirteen years later, with the residents on the warpath, the authorities agreed to a second rehabilitation that was to repair the problems that arose from the first. But the workers started to walk off the site while residents complained that much remained to be done. The authorities insisted they would put things right. Not much remains of the original fabric of the building, except the dark gnarled banisters and balcony frames. But even the new wash of color, a warm earthy tone, and new floors cannot conceal the painfully tiny proportions and the thin walls, through which float sounds of a guitar strumming and scents of lunch in preparation. Downstairs on the street is a Lebanese tea-shop with tiled and mosaic-covered walls, a confident young man posed in the doorway. A rich racial assortment of Lebanese, North African and Chinese hurry up and down the steep streets. An occasional elderly Spanish resident walks slowly and with effort along the cobbles, with the aid of a stick, or watches from a tiny—often sparklingly renovated—balcony. The streets are being dug up and re-paved as part of the local authorities' attempt to salvage this decayed area, and a mechanical digger churns up the surface of one little lane as if it were a cake-mix, adding to the overall clatter and the area's sense of improvised anarchy.

A century ago, the locals from the *corrala* would probably have worked mostly in the cigar factory at the bottom of the street. The austerely handsome, unadorned Royal Tobacco Factory, as its old stone plaque proudly announces, was originally built in 1790 as a distillery, but modified in 1809 when 800 women were hired to produce cigars, cigarettes and snuff. In 1872 the women's jobs were threatened when the management tried to introduce a cigarette rolling machine, so they came out on strike and destroyed the offending piece of machinery. With its peeling russet paint-work and its blind dusty windows, the factory looks today as though it has been long abandoned. But from a side door you can enter a barely functioning operation that no longer makes cigars, but cigarette filters. In the wide corridors with high vaulted ceilings the 200-year old whiff of tobacco still seems to linger, but it could just be the musty smell of big bales of paper used to make the filters. This is the last dying throw of a once mighty state monopoly now just haggling over terms before closing down forever. In the central courtyard a neat, if dusty, geometric garden still survives, with dried up laurel trees and a long disused granite fountain that must have provided refreshment for generations of exhausted workers during their break.

The factory once employed some 3,000 *Madrileños*, or rather *Madrileñas*: the cigar-makers were overwhelmingly female. Hardworking, loyal, tough and independent, the *cigarreras* formed about one-fifth of Madrid's working population by the end of the nineteenth century. Like their counterparts in Seville, they inspired the image of Carmen, the feisty, flirtatious and formidable Spanish *señorita*. Madrid legend says that the *cigarreras* were the most beautiful and forward women of the whole city. They banded together into a powerful trade union and, as pioneers in the working-class struggle, won the establishment of schools, nurseries and improved working conditions, benefits hitherto undreamed of. It has often been said that Pablo Iglesias, the founder of Spanish socialism, whose mother was a washerwoman upon the banks of the Manzanares at the bottom of the hill, was prompted to form his Socialist Workers' Union after seeing the collective action of the *cigarreras*. A commentator wrote in July 1877: "Cigar-workers' strike in Embajadores: the arm these rowdy demonstrators use with greatest skill is their tongue. Four or five thousand women insulting and overwhelming their opponents. The mutiny has already lasted ten days. All speak at once. The *cigarreras* are like that."

To be recruited as a *cigarrera* a young woman had to be over the age of twelve and under thirty, and her age and good behavior had to be confirmed in writing by the local priest. Apprentices brought with them all the tools of their trade: the twin-handled basket, a chair, scissors, and a *tarugo*, the round wooden plug around which they rolled the cigars. Young men would wait patiently at the factory gate for these spirited young women to come off their shift at the end of the afternoon, to head for the shops and bars, carrying with them the scent of sweat and tobacco. The last intake was in the 1920s, after which increasing mechanization caused a gradual decline in the need for nimble female fingers. It still paid the employers, however, to hire elderly women whom locals still remember making their way painfully with the aid of a stick to carry out the menial task of removing the central vein of the tobacco leaf. Across the road there was even a refuge for women who had grown old and frail in the service of cigarette making and had nowhere to go. This was a noble, highly regarded profession, as illustrated in the following typical if melodramatic exchange in a *zarzuela* between a gentleman and an old lady on the street:

> "*What ails you my good woman?*"
> "*I trail through life begging a morsel of bread. I sleep in the street and lie sick on the frosty sidewalk.*"
> "*And your family?*"

"Ah, my family, sir! My husband died so long ago that I've forgotten when, run over by a carriage. My children? My son went bad and is in prison for God knows how long. My daughter. Don't ask me about her..."

"Have you nowhere to go?"

"No-one's going to shut me up in a home... Ah! to think of what I was and what I have become."

"Were you rich, señora, a marquise or perhaps an artist?"

"Pah! I was much more, señor. I was a cigarrera!"

You'll see no sultry *señoritas* pouring from those factory gates today, nor bent crones reminiscing of their glory days. A few men in blue overalls—with a cigarette between their lips, naturally—might trickle on to the street at lunchtime. But they are just as likely as their female forebears to greet you with an impudent quip.

More than two-thirds of the *cigarreras* lived in the surrounding *corralas*, which was another reason for their tenacious solidarity. Another *corrala* just up the street from the old factory has been restored and preserved, and its courtyard is used as a theater in the summer where the *zarzuela*, the traditional dramatic genre of proletarian Madrid, is performed. But so squeaky clean is this preserved version, so like a film-set, that it is difficult to believe that it bears much resemblance to the real thing. Only the shrieks of the neighbors during the open-air performance, oblivious to the play going on beneath their balconies, convey a whiff of authenticity.

The *Zarzuela*

The *zarzuela* itself is a boisterous mixture of opera and music hall, originally an entertainment laid on for Felipe IV in his Zarzuela hunting lodge north of the city. But today's version developed in the early nineteenth century when it reached the peak of popularity. It idealizes characters and situations typical of Madrid at the time, celebrating the typical small-time characters of the neighborhood. There is the *manola*, who despite her air of gentility, is often little more than a prostitute; the dull, corrupt policeman; the inquisitive *sereno* or nightwatchman; the feckless husband; the put-upon wife, vigilantly aware of the constant competition offered by lighter, lovelier, girls for the affections of her companion, the would-be *chulo*.

The women are always vulnerable to exploitation by predatory males of doubtful respectability, or those in positions of authority. But they use their coquettish ways and their superior wit to wrest the advantage, or simply to keep out of trouble. And the action usually takes place in the street. Hence, the drama revolves around a constant battle of the sexes, and schemes to outwit authority, schemes which never, however, remotely challenge the system. Their aim is simply to get a laugh from it.

The *zarzuela*, in other words, celebrates a romanticized vision of the lower of the two social currents described by Barea, a community that by the late eighteenth century had acquired the characteristics now regarded as typically *Madrileño*. The rich and piquant mixture is summed up by Ramón de Mesonero Romanos in his book *El antiguo Madrid*: "arrogant and loyal, fearful and indolent, sarcastic and even aggressive toward authority, disdainful of fortune and disgrace, a mixture of Arab fatalism, pride and bravery, and Castilian inertia." This spicy cocktail typified the *manolo* and *manola*, who even in Mesonero Romanos's day were a disappearing breed. He goes on:

> the haughty and independent character of these classes, of both sexes, their animosity toward the unknown, their indomitable arrogance and their lack of education linked to all the vices and dissipation associated with big cities made these neighbourhoods of our city, the area that comprises Lava-piés, Salitre, Tres Peces, Inclusa, el Rastro and Embajadores made the people there seem a separate community, isolated, hostile and terrible in the eyes of the rest of the city.

The social historian expresses his hope that, with education and government vigilance, the people of this untamed quarter might improve their love of work, acquire more civilized tastes and cease to present "an impenetrable barrier to decent persons."

Théophile Gautier, also writing toward the middle of the nineteenth century, took a more romantic view, even penetrating these insalubrious alleys in the hope of catching sight of a true *manola* before they vanished forever:

> I looked for an authentic pure-blooded manola in all the corners of Madrid but I never found her. Once, as I was walking through the Rastro, and after passing many beggars who were sleeping on the ground wrapped

in frightful rags, I found myself in a deserted alleyway and there I saw, for the first and last time, the manola I was seeking. She was a handsome girl, about 24, the maximum age for a manola—like the grisettes or modillistas in Paris. She had a dark complexion, a glance that was steady and sad, slightly full lips and with something African about her features. Her long plait of hair was so black as to be almost blue, plaited like the reeds of a basket wound round her head and held with a comb. A cluster of coral hung from her ears. A necklace of the same material adorned her tawny neck. Framing her face and shoulders a mantilla of black velvet. Her dress, as short as that worn by the Swiss women of Berne, was made with embroidered cloth and revealed a slender pair of legs in tight black silk stockings. Her shoes were of satin, in the old style. A red fan trembled like a scarlet butterfly in her fingers that were laden with silver rings. The last of the manolas turned the corner and disappeared from view, leaving me in wonderment at seeing in the real world a costume that could have come from the opera.

The last *manolas* may have gone, except for those resurrected for fiestas, but Madrid women's love of elaborate dress, fussy adornments and colorful mixtures—even for the purpose of going to the corner shop to buy a loaf of bread—is still widespread throughout the city. Many *Madrileñas* still dress and act as though every little walk through the streets of their *barrio*, or to the benches of their local square, is cause for celebration.

CHAPTER EIGHT

The Comercial and the Gijón: Café Society

The Comercial is one of Madrid's oldest and best-loved cafés. It is on the handsome Bilbao *glorieta*, or roundabout, dominated by traffic and soaring fountains. The glass in the heavy swing door that you push to enter from the street reveals the activity within, but shrouds the details. When you enter, you face to your right a curved marble bar where waiters greet you in a manner that is at once welcoming and non-committal. This makes you feel both at home and at the same time under no obligation: the sensation gives you a soothing sense of self-worth and independence, particularly on your first visit. You can stop here, have a beer or a coffee with no further commitment, or move forward and to your left through another glazed, brass-handled portal into the inner room, a vast, high-ceilinged, pillared salon filled with veined black marble tables and dark wooden chairs, and lined by fake leather benches that face inward, offering those seated there full command of the spectacle before them.

The chamber buzzes with conversation, shrouded in smoke from obligatory cigarettes and cigars, or, depending on the time of day or the season, hushed, cool and almost deserted. At each stage of your short voyage of discovery, the waiters unfussily convey their dual message of invitation and indifference. You, yourself, are the one who takes the decisions. You are absorbed into the café community, or you remain aloof, just as you please. The ambiance is as relaxed and easy as if you were in your own front room, but suggests all the stimulating opportunities that the capital may offer. This is the charm of Madrid's café society.

The Café Comercial is popular among young foreign residents in Madrid, students or language teachers, as well as visitors, young *Madrileños* and crumbling slender figures whose delicate intellectual air recalls a bygone age, as they sit sipping a goblet of cognac or *pacharán*, the sweet Navarrese liqueur made from rosehips, popular throughout Spain as a *digestif*. Within the twin doors, the roar of the outside traffic is muffled, but the magnificent pearly light sweeps into the farthest corner, to a table where perhaps a tousled young man is reading the newspaper or writing in a notebook. The light is augmented by dozens of feeble bulbs perched on grand *fin-de-siècle* chandeliers, and toward the rear of the room a piano sits shrouded in black oilcloth. The vision cannot be much changed since the café opened in 1870, the first of many such establishments that became the most fashionable and influential haunts of the city.

The Comercial became something of an intellectual refuge during the Franco era; before that it was popular with impoverished writers and discreet members of the bourgeoisie. It retains its bohemian air of the haunt of dissidents looking for a cheap and warming dish of the day, a plate of lentils or a savory stew of meaty ribs and potatoes, a cheerier alternative than they might improvise in their drab little apartment. This is in marked contrast to cafés in the more fashionable center of the city that many ambitious habitués see—or saw—as a launch-pad from which to make their name or ingratiate themselves with political and artistic figures of importance. Run by the Contreras family since 1909, the Comercial has survived almost all the city's great cafés, perpetuating their tranquil glories after their time has apparently passed.

Up the angled marble steps flanked by massive brass banisters, the light that filters through the shutters on the first floor is even more splendid and the views across the square more magnificent, but the ceiling is lower, the décor more austere, the scale more intimate. Here is the characteristic melange of old and new that infuses the best of Madrid's surviving cafés, each spiked with a streak of idiosyncrasy that brings you constantly back to one, rather than to another. A large overhead fan circulates above a group of decrepit old men playing chess on one of the square green tables upstairs, padded at the edges to prevent the pieces from slipping to the floor. In a large side room, dedicated youngsters are positioned in front of a dozen computer screens, plugged into the Internet. A roughly printed notice advises customers that they may log on for 500 pesetas an hour, and indicates a button that enables you to summon the barman to serve you breakfast or an aperitif, while you cybersurf. It is the most vivid example of how an ancient institution is adapting to modern demands. Chat lines may link these solitary keyboarders to a wider community, connecting them with others sharing their interest, but a notice downstairs, posted alongside the simple menu of the day and notice of tournaments of the card game *mus*, suggests that the Comercial is updating a quintessentially Spanish tradition that gave Madrid's first cafés their charm and *raison d'être*. The notice announces the times, and subjects, of a *tertulia*.

The *Tertulia*

The *tertulia* or discussion group is defined by Mariano Tudela in one of many books devoted to this art form as "the gathering of people who meet regularly to converse or amuse themselves." This simple definition includes the three cardinal rules of the *tertulia*: that it should have no other purpose than the pure pleasure of conversation; that it meet at fixed, regular intervals; and that it comprise roughly the same people each time. Tudela believes it to be the natural pastime of Latin peoples with a an oral, market-place culture, and an oversupply of shouters, whose insomnia or vaguely defined work commitments allow them to devote hours to their favorite activity, that of good conversation. Luis Carandell, a Catalan from Barcelona, who nonetheless writes extensively and affectionately about his adopted city, Madrid, casts a more skeptical eye. The *tertulia*, "an immemorial Spanish institution which always had Madrid as its headquarters," is simply "a gathering of men with no purpose or aim whatsoever." When a group of people meets to achieve something concrete, the result might be a political party, a business transaction or a sports or recreation association, Carandell reflects. "When they get together to do absolutely nothing at all, that is a tertulia."

Discussions obviously take place in many countries, but Spain claims to be the home of those devoted specifically to literary and artistic matters. And within Spain, the provincial *tertulia* is held—by *Madrileños* naturally—to be but a pale imitation of the finest *tertulias* of all, those celebrated in the capital. At any rate, the *tertulia* in Madrid came to embody many of the qualities now held as defining characteristics of the genre. And the theater of this art form was the café. "Spaniards are the most talkative creatures on earth," notes Benito Pérez Galdós:

when they have no subject of conversation, they talk about themselves, and naturally they're always negative. In our cafés, anything under the sun is fair game for conversation. Gross banalities as well as ingenious, discreet and pertinent ideas may be heard in these places, for they are frequented not only by rakes and swearers; enlightened people with good habits go to cafés too... Men with great assimilatory powers can reveal a considerable wealth of knowledge without ever having opened a book and it is because they have appropriated ideas poured into these nocturnal circles in these pleasant and fraternal tertulias. Scholars go to cafés too; one may hear eloquent observations and pithy expositions of complex doctrines. It's not all frivolity, stale anecdotes and lies. The café is like a grand fair where countless products of the human mind are bought and sold. Naturally there are more trinkets than anything else; but in their midst, and some-times going unnoticed, there are priceless gems.

The cafés originated in the *botillerías*, the liquor stores that blossomed after Joseph Bonaparte removed the crippling taxes from alcohol after he came to the throne in 1808. It became the custom, even for ladies, to stop and consume a glass of wine or spirit at the counter of a *botillería* before continuing their *paseo*. Then seats were provided inside and soon the café was born. It flourished until its age of splendor in the late nineteenth century, after which began its gradual decline. The café was somewhere people looked into to check who was there, lingered for a greater or shorter time to scoop up the gossip,

before moving on to the next spot, to make sure they did not miss anything that was going on. The cafés were largely male preserves, and *tertulias* were—and many of those that survive still are—fiercely misogynist. The conversation produced in the *tertulia* was, according to a recent critic writing in *El País* newspaper, little more than a mixed oral production by men: "The clubs, the cafés the taverns or casinos, were centers of conversation amidst cognac, burps, tobacco, swearing and bicarbonate." Women, if they were interested in literary, artistic, scientific or political discussions, convened their own *tertulias* in their private salons, some of which became renowned, rather than participate in this male-dominated milieu.

The *tertulia* may have been intolerant of women, but it was tolerant of cranks, who are known in Spain with some affection as *espontáneos*. A tale is told of a person in a café in the Puerta del Sol who made a name for himself by jumping from table to table and *tertulia* to *tertulia* without a pause for breath from three o'clock in the afternoon until the early hours of the morning. No one knew who he was, and no one particularly cared. But one day he disappeared never to be seen again in any of the cafés that he had frequented so regularly. The *tertulianos* became worried and even wondered whether to hold some sort of wake for him, certain that he must have died. But months later, someone reported they had seen him in a coastal town in the north, and that he was well and in a comfortable position. The news was extremely disconcerting for the *tertulia* regulars, convinced that only death could break the bond between a man and his discussion group.

Actually, the *espontáneo* or crank was more than just a light adornment of the *tertulia*: eccentric or nonconformist members of Spain's anarchist tradition came to form the backbone of many *tertulias*. The incorruptible writer, the chemically pure artist are caricatures of Spanish literature, but they have a root in reality. Their participation meant that the *tertulias* never became purely academic or theoretical discussions, and always had a strong contact with day-to-day reality, even if participants only observed, rather than shaped it. Madrid's rigid social, professional and intellectual structure made the streak of non-conformity inevitable. Bohemians I suppose they considered themselves, fighting for a place in a hostile world, seeking refuge from Madrid's bitter winters and stifling conventions. Many dozed off in the cafés, resorting to a public bench when the long-suffering proprietors finally upended the seats upon the tables.

Pérez Galdós devotes a chapter to the café in his finest social portrait of the city, *Fortunata y Jacinta*, written in 1887, the heyday of the café. He is actually describing the Café Zaragoza nearer the old center of the city, but his sketch captures the very essence of café life in Madrid: "Full of people, the atmosphere was thick and suffocating, you could chew it, and there was a deafening noise like a beehive; the Madrileños happily put up with this racket and ambiance, just as blacksmiths put up with the heat and din of a forge." Galdós describes with great energy and relish how the addictive charm of the café works on one individual:

> *Juan Pablo Rubin didn't feel alive unless he spent half the day or almost all of it at the café... He spent part of the time alone meditating on serious political, religious or philosophical problems and gazing absently at the plaster moulding, the smoke-stained painting on the ceiling, and other such decorative details... The café gave him the feeling of privacy that usually comes from one's own home. When he entered, all the objects smiled as if they belonged to him. He fancied that the people he saw there constantly—the waiters, the headwaiter, certain regular customers—were closely related to him by family ties.*

Despite such bonds of loyalty, it took only a flicker of discontent, one unhappy experience for habitués to flounce out of one café and decamp to another, a phenomenon that Galdós indulgently calls "certain inexplicable emigration currents common in the society of lazy men." Sometimes one of their number would get lost in the waves of emigration, but someone new would invariably pop up to take his place, adding zest to the group. Every movement in the ritual of serving and drinking coffee had its significance, every seat of the patrons indicated their position in the tertulian hierarchy. Galdós also celebrates one particularly popular café near the Puerta del Sol, which was the original hub of Madrid's café society. This establishment had "a tertulia of journalists dubbed the ' anteroom of the Saladero' because the members used to go to the prison of that name with pitiful frequency."

The seductive appeal of the café is evoked by Spain's Nobel Prize-winning novelist Camilo José Cela in the opening paragraph of his 1953 novella *Café de Artistas*, which describes the closed, gloomy world of the Franco years. Cela hails from the northern province of Galicia, but much of his early work, for which he is best known and which won him the Nobel, is set in Madrid and captures the suffocating monochrome post-war spirit against which humble folk strove to realize their desires. I do not know whether Cela had the Comercial in mind, but this poetic description, full of meticulously observed detail, could be of any café:

> The revolving door swings about its axis. The revolving door, swinging about its axis, makes a caressing, almost amorous sound. In the revolving door there are four sections, four compartments; if the poets are thin and spiritual, you could even accommodate two in each section. The compartments of the revolving door take the form of portions of cream cheese, of soft pale reconstituted cheese, a cheese for lactating mothers. The revolving door has a little brush at the edges, from top to bottom, to keep out the chill of the street. The revolving door is a beautiful simile, something like a metaphor from which can be extracted much meaning. The Café de Artistas is full of beautiful similes.

The short story tells of failures, disappointed love affairs, of frustrated ambitions, of a poignant death, of small favors, flirtations and gestures of kindness. The café is the stage for a small-scale human drama. Toward the end of the tale, Cela almost repeats his description of the café's entrance. But subtly, everything is darkened by the little tragedy that has unfolded. The direction of the movement no longer, as in the opening paragraph, presses in from the street with anticipation and promise, but erupts from the inside outwards, with surprises and strange personalities fighting to escape the claustrophobia of the café into the cool of the street:

> The swing door of the Café de Artistas turns on its axis. The swing door of the Café de Artistas, turning and turning on its axis, makes a caressing, amorous, painful noise. In the swing door of the Café de Artistas there are four sections, four seasons; if the poets are slender and spiritual, you could fit two in each bitter well, in each waterwheel's compartment. But if from the Café de Artistas you had to remove a dead poet, a poet with his feet first, you would have to fold back the swing door like a fan. The swing door of the Café de Artistas has a little brush along the side, from bottom to top, so that evil thoughts should not escape into the cold of the street...

This short novella evokes both the welcoming and the claustrophobic side of café society. It concludes on a note that is melancholic, almost sinister, but deeply atmospheric.

Larra: Romantic Cynic

Mariano José de Larra, pioneer of Spanish journalism, hero of café society, satirist and romantic, took his pistol and on February 12, 1837 shot himself in the head in an excess of despair. He was only 28. It was Shrove Tuesday and the shot rang out in the midst of Madrid's carnival revelries at No. 3 Santa Clara, a corner house in a side street a couple of hundred yards from the Royal Palace. High on the wall, on the corner with Calle Amnistía, a white marble plaque with a bas-relief of Larra, flanked with black olive and oak branches and somber swags, marks the spot. Tucked amid handsome apartment houses, in the heart of what was centuries ago the Arab center of the old city, this remains a quietly prosperous part of town. The midday hush is broken not by traffic, but by an elderly lady's ricocheting greeting to her neighbor as she brings home a bag of long loaves.

Larra was famous for his newspaper column, which he signed with the pseudonym "Figaro" and in which he scorned and ridiculed the absurdities of Madrid society and revealed his own black moods.

His flashing wit, misanthropy and linguistic brilliance poured into a sustained rant against the way of life in the capital, which he none the less hoped to reform. Larra was evidently a depressive, whose deep and incurable melancholia was supposedly caused by his disturbed childhood and adolescence. He grew up in France, during the exile of his father, who had been a doctor in the French army. On his return to Spain, in 1818, he recovered his Spanish, which he had forgotten in France, and studied mathematics, Greek, Italian and English. He began first a career in medicine, then law, before abandoning them both. Before he was twenty he fell passionately in love with a woman of great beauty, only to discover—so the story goes—that she was in fact the lover of his father. This bitter blow cast a shadow over his life and henceforth his affairs were doomed; his marriage was unhappy and his subsequent great love, fatal.

It is widely supposed that Larra ended his life because his lover Dolores (Lolita) Armijo had tired of him. But in one popular anthology of Larra's work, the anonymous author of the introductory essay says robustly: "A suicide victim by vocation, like [Goethe's hero] Werther, rejection by his loved one was not the cause of his suicide, but the best opportunity that he found to take his life, which is what he really wanted." In a recent novel about Larra's death, *Flores de Plomo* (Flowers of Lead), the writer Juan Eduardo Zuñiga tries to navigate between these two poles. "It is well known that no one kills himself for one reason alone, but because of a chain of events that produce the inability to survive," Zuñiga comments. Larra, he

continues, was wearied and disoriented by the insecure and unpredictable quality of Spanish society at the time, and found Madrid hard-faced and inhospitable. This, despite the fact that Larra was a successful and prosperous writer, a handsome man who enjoyed success with women and a reputation as a natty dresser. Nonetheless, he was not only politically disillusioned, but was personally unhappy. After marrying in 1829 ("young and badly," as he put it), he entered a stormy relationship with Lolita, who visited his house on the day of his death, in the company of a woman friend, to put an end to their scandalous affair. She demanded the return of her letters to him. Larra shot himself that evening, shortly after Dolores had left.

Larra's mordant demolition of every ill of Spanish society was also probably determined by his erratic background and education. Pan-European in outlook and deeply influenced by French literature, he remained an outsider who was never fully to integrate himself into Spanish society. Madrid's closed little intellectual and political world enraged him and seemed to constitute a personal affront, provoking him to paroxysms of exasperation. "A corrosive mixture that turned more and more against himself, because what pained Larra more than anything else was Larra, and so Larra ended up by killing Larra," concludes the introduction to the anthology. Nevertheless, in the course of his 28 years, Larra single-handedly developed the formerly minor literary genre of journalism into a form as well-regarded as drama and fiction.

He targets all the personalities of the city: corrupt policemen, concierges, petty officials, rude waiters, rich idlers. Larra is best remembered today for his biting piece written in 1833 called *Vuelva Usted Mañana* (Come Back Tomorrow), which no one who has ever lived in Madrid can read today without a painful stab of recognition. He describes how he has met a foreigner, M. Sans-Delai, who has just arrived in Madrid to sort out a family inheritance and to propose a project of great mutual benefit to the Spanish government. He expects to do all this in fifteen days. Larra promises to buy him lunch in fifteen months, as he is bound to still be in town. They first visit a genealogist—contacted via the acquaintance of a friend of a friend— who, astonished by their haste, urges them to return in a few days:

Three days passed: we returned.

"Come back tomorrow," said the servant, "because the señor is not up yet."

"Come back tomorrow," she said the next day, "because my master has just gone out."

"Come back tomorrow," she said the day after, "because the master is sleeping the siesta."

"Come back tomorrow," she told us the following Monday, "because he has gone to the bullfight."

What day, at what time do you see a Spaniard?

We saw him eventually, and "Come back tomorrow," he said, "because it slipped my mind. Come back tomorrow because I haven't made the final draft."

A fortnight later, the two of them return to find that their genealogist had mistaken the name, so they have to start again. And so it goes on. M. Sans-Delai finally gives up and leaves after six months, having achieved nothing. Wherever he goes he is fobbed off with excuses and urged to come back tomorrow. His grand scheme is passed round various ministries, and finally vanishes without trace: one ministry insists it sent it on, while the other denies ever having received it.

The tale reflected the reality of Spain's bureaucracy, which, with each change of government and constitution, became ever more extensive and hierarchical as the seventeenth-century Habsburgs gave way to the eighteenth-century Bourbons. But the bureaucratic frustrations and procrastination Larra lampoons still flourish. The nineteenth-century constitutional government introduced public examinations, which, if passed, guaranteed a job in the civil service for life. To obtain such security of employment became a major preoccupation of middle- and lower middle-class life in the nineteenth century and is vividly portrayed in the novels of the time, particularly those of Benito Pérez Galdós. An ever denser network of immutable procedures, intricate formalities, rituals and routines determined the structure and aspirations of middle-class life, particularly burdensome in a city invented for the purpose of administering the state. Implacable rules and officials' slippery evasion of responsibility still, exasperatingly, hold sway here, as any resident or visitor brought to tears of fury and despair by boot-faced functionaries can confirm.

Another victim of Spanish bureaucracy around this time was the eccentric English adventurer George Borrow, who spent three years in Madrid seeking to sell bibles, a brave and hazardous mission in this Catholic society. Borrow, like Larra, was given the run-around by government functionaries, "by whom the most solemn of promises are habitually broken," he complained. Unlike the fictional M. Sans-Delai, however, Borrow did finally obtain permission to sell his Bibles.

Larra hated all this. "To write in Madrid is to weep," he said in one of his last and most famous articles. With this sentiment, he inspired a succession of grumbling, bitter polemicists and intellectuals who to this day pour criticism upon the perceived degeneracy of their country. This skepticism remains vigorous among Spanish writers and journalists, although as a breed they enjoy less prestige now than in earlier decades. Many pick upon individuals of their own circle rather than general social ills, to the bafflement of the wider public. All the same, Larra is the spiritual father of Madrid's succession of often savagely polemical intellectuals, and has much in common with romantic authors like Goethe and Victor Hugo.

Romanticism, a self-reflective, sometimes self-indulgent, artistic and literary individualism that fought against academic constraints, flowered in Madrid in the 1830s, encouraged by a brief three-year Liberal constitutional interlude between 1820 and 1823. But, says Juan Antonio Cabezas, "Spanish romanticism contains more blood than ink." Larra, unlike his European counterparts, "exchanged the quill for the pistol to make himself the protagonist of his own melodrama." For Larra, Cabezas goes on:

> *romanticism is not the unleashing of individual emotions as it was for Goethe, nor a school of literature as it was for Victor Hugo. For Larra, the true descendent of [Goethe's romantic hero] Werther, his romanticism— not literary but human—has the characteristics of violence of every Spaniard. He does not drown his passions in printer's ink, attributing them to fictional characters. He suffers them, struggles with his own internal demons. And when he finds no solution to the tragedy, he reaches for*

his pistol, at the moment when the reality and the fiction of his life inter-sect, on the threshold of eternity.

Few of Larra's successors went to such lengths, but this passage reveals something of the frustrated passion that fires many of Madrid's literary figures.

After the fatal shooting, Larra's body was taken to the Santiago church in Calle Vergara, just around the corner of his house in Santa Clara, where his shocked friends from the Café Parnasillo, home of one of the most successful *tertulias* of the time, rushed in disbelief. Those who had spoken to him that very morning saw the body in the vault before it was removed for burial in the cemetery of San Justo near Fuencarral, north of the city. Stricken by the loss of a talent so young, a later generation of Spanish writers, known as the "Generation of '98" strew violets upon his grave on February 13, 1901 and read a speech celebrating him as "the guiding light of today's youth." An empty seat was always kept for him at the *tertulias* organized by Ramón Gómez de la Serna in the celebrated Café Pombo in the 1920s and 1930s. The fateful pistol is on display at the Romantic Museum in Calle San Mateo in Chueca.

Larra, brilliant, *déraciné*, tragic, is a quintessential hero of café society. In one of his first articles, written in 1828 when he was only nineteen, he casts a prematurely jaundiced eye upon its attractions and its *engaño*—a ubiquitous Spanish word that means both "deception" (something done to someone else) and "disappointment" (something you feel). He starts off with customarily deadpan, apparently innocent, observations before knifing the jugular:

I don't know what makes me naturally curious; I was born with a desire to know everything. I feel it bubbling through my veins compelling me to visit out of the way corners to eavesdrop upon the nonsense of others. This provides me with material for amusement during periods I spend in my room and sometimes in bed when I cannot sleep. In those moments I think over what I have heard, and laugh like crazy at the madmen I have listened to.

So this desire to know everything drew me the other day to a certain café of this court [i.e. Madrid] where two or three lawyers regularly meet to kill time and boredom, but who could not speak without putting on their spectacles. There are also a doctor who could not cure without his staff in his hand, and four walking chimneys who could not live if they had been born before the discovery of tobacco, so bound up with nicotine is their existence. Then there are also those who are vulgarly nicknamed dandies or blustering fools who would not venture into society if they were stripped of the boxfuls of jewels that adorn their chests like a jeweler's shop, and were ordered instead to think like rational beings and move like men, and above all if they threw a little more salt into their brains.

I, therefore, who belong to none of these groups, sat under the shadow of a hat made in the form of a roof that folded back upon itself... just another madman whose fancy was to pass as a foreigner in Madrid... I raised my cape up to my eyes, pulled down the brim of my hat and in this way prepared to catch whatever flights of foolishness that this bustling crowd was likely to produce.

Larra does not translate happily, but in any language he was a bitter man. It hardly needs adding that like most Madrileños, he was an astute watcher of people, if a misanthropic one. His mordant survey of café life turns up swindlers intent upon avoiding payment, pompous ignorant windbags sounding off about politics, affected would-be poets, vain, empty-headed pedants and scoundrels with nothing better to do than shroud themselves in smoke, impress their companions and idle away their time playing billiards. Reflecting at home on his impressions, Larra confesses that he does not feel like laughing on this occasion, and concludes that men live on their illusions.

Had his despair not overtaken him, Larra might have drawn comfort from the more intellectual, less gossipy milieu of the Ateneo, the establishment that eventually evolved from the efforts of his group of friends in the *tertulia* known as El Parnasillo who met at the Café Principe. The Artistic, Scientific and Literary Athenaeum had various homes in the center of town before moving in 1884 into the handsome building it still inhabits in the Calle del Prado, and where it boasts one of the finest libraries in Madrid.

The Ateneo, barely changed in more than 100 years, is today charmingly dilapidated, with fusty plush armchairs and dark wooden panels hung with lugubrious portraits of former members. Creaking corridors and crooked staircases lead you to blissfully silent and smoke-free reading rooms, the upper ones worn and shabby, their sagging ceilings supported with makeshift columns. Around examination time, the place is packed with students crouched over the ranks of desks, each space lit with its own lamp that you switch on by pulling a little chain. A notice reminds you to turn off the desk lamp when you leave. A shallow silvered dish is set into the wood separating each reading space. These dishes are not for cigarette ash—faded notices warn you not to smoke—but for pencil sharpening. The atmosphere is serene, conducive to study, tinged with melancholy. It goes with the bohemian, slightly anarchic reputation of the place, still trying to re-establish itself—with meetings, conferences and film seasons in the ornate concert hall — after suffering the cruel neglect of the Franco decades.

More than a century after Larra recorded his scorching vision of Madrid's flotsam and jetsam, the novelist Camilo José Cela casts a gentler but no less skeptical eye over similar social terrain. Despite the gap of 130 years that separates Larra's account from that of Cela's *Café de Artistas*, the panorama has scarcely changed. Cela's great novel *La Colmena* (The Hive) revolves around a café, which he portrays as a microcosm of Madrid society during the Franco years. The novel, written while the author made daily visits to the Café Gijón, includes, as in the novels of Pérez Galdós, personalities from every social stratum, each with their foibles and personal sufferings. He conveys, painstakingly, almost in real time, the banality and glacial slowness of social interaction among café regulars, until we gradually come to know them and care about their little doings, muted and constrained by their gray circumstances. Unlike Larra, who observes with a corrosive eye and mercilessly skewers his prey, Cela shows us how his characters feel from the inside. Even though they may be just as ridiculous as Larra's victims, we sympathize with them, grow fond of them, and find their predicaments heartbreakingly poignant. It is the perfect formula for a television soap opera—except that the social scene that Cela evokes had all but died before the genre was invented.

The Decline of Café Society

If it is possible to describe how café society arose, it is less easy to explain why it died. Were those who frequented cafés prosperous enough to have time on their hands but not wealthy enough to join exclusive clubs? Not hospitable enough to invite friends home but sociable enough to want frequent contact with them? Surely such people still exist. Did the café flourish in a period of political authoritarianism, providing a neutral ground for the exchange of dissident views? But Franco's regime appears to have killed off café society, in the sense of an informal forum for the discussion of ideas of all kinds, except in a very self-conscious way. Madrid's official historian Pedro Montoliú Camps, lamenting in his entertaining book on Madrid's traditions and fiestas the disappearance of most tertulias, notes that there was not much room for the open and uninhibited debate of the tertulia in the intimidated post-war society of the 1940s and 1950s. Then the advances, the period of economic development and a hastier pace of life conspired to bring the tradition to an end, he believes. The café atmosphere faded away, especially after the 1960s, when many cafés around the Puerta del Sol were closed to make way for banks. "The café-owners took the opportunity offered by prosperous new banks to make their sites more profitable, just when the cafés were anyway becoming obsolete in face of the proliferation of cafeterias, more in tune with the new times," Montoliu Camps writes. Before the Civil War, the journalist Corpus Barga wrote an article about a strike of café waiters that lasted two weeks, something that caused him serious alarm: "The epoch of the Madrileño café is obviously in decline. That's the only way to explain why Madrid's cafés have been closed for a fortnight without having any effect. In their heyday there would have been a revolution."

In *Strange Vignettes of Old Madrid*, an American reporter, Peter Besas, portrays the death agony of the one of the finest of the old cafés: the Levante on the Puerta del Sol, which closed in 1966:

I had the opportunity of sitting in its old tattered divans shortly before its knell was rung. To its dying day it continued to draw a smoky crowd of idlers during the afternoon hours. Dubious concessions to modernity were made with the installation of fluorescent lights in all parts of the cafe which gave a harsh, modern light that clashed with the old marble-topped tables, bentwood chairs and fluted pillars which burgeoned beside the spittoons. But the old men of the tertulias, most of whom must have remembered the Levante in the days of its prime, sat there like dazed penguins, knowing that their world had crumbled and left them behind. Some talked loudly in groups, gesticulating as thought the last thirty years hadn't occurred, while others scrutinized the newspapers through magnifying glasses. A few could be seen playing dominoes or dice; and occasionally you'd find one reading a book or bent over some papers, writing. Students sometimes wandered in as well. Smoke hung thick in the air and women were scarce. The room was broken into compartment-like sections, with panelled wooden screens, as in a maze, making it difficult to survey the whole room at a glance. In the rear, the café turned a corner, with tables lined up around the divans. A staircase led up to the first floor, which was mainly reserved for billiards. There were numerous billiard tables, all of them used in the afternoon, a remnant of the times when the game was still a pastime for the upper classes and had not yet sunk to the level of the now ubiquitous pinball machine. From the first floor of the Levante, you could peer down through an opening in the balcony into the downstairs part: a smoky vignette of the fossilized past.

But the Levante was obviously a losing affair. People would sit for hours over empty cups of coffee, and of course in this day of quick turnover such procrastination was economically ruinous.

Did the telephone kill off the need to physically meet your companion in order to have a conversation? Did television—what Spaniards call the "stupid box" (*la caja tonta*)—end the desire for conversation altogether? This does not seem convincing; many Spaniards seem to relish conducting their high-decibel conversations with the TV blaring companionably in the corner, especially at mealtimes. Did society become too broad and diffuse and lose the provincial sense of intimacy that guaranteed that one would probably bump into a few acquaintances in one café or another? But Madrid, more than most European capitals, retains that villagey, gossipy feel. At any rate, café society no longer exists in its original sense. Even the cafés themselves are fast disappearing. Of the traditional ones, the Gran Café de Gijón and the Comercial are the best-known survivors. The commentator Francisco Umbral, a habitué at the Gijón when he first arrived in Madrid in the 1950s as an ambitious young writer thirsty for recognition and material, says that for him in those days, Gijón meant "hunger and newspapers." Another remembers the time when the drink most frequently ordered by the motley assembly of clients in the post-war years was a glass of water with bicarbonate, because it was gratis and contained some minimal nourishment.

The Comercial and the Gijón keep up the old atmosphere, caught in amber as a palpable relic of a past age. Such cafés were the haunt of those, rich or poor, with time on their hands. Larra paints a hilarious portrait of a rich young man who has nothing to do all day but swan from salon to café, from dining room to gaming hall, before returning home to bed. Café society was for him a way of filling the empty hours. Similarly, many of Cela's characters are unemployed and impoverished, trapped in an enforced idleness where the café offers a welcome refuge from the cold of the street and the loneliness of their home. Such people have not died out. The Comercial may have introduced computer screens, but the Gijón has kept Alfonso, the gently cynical *cerillero* or match seller, who presides over his cigarette and newspaper stand just inside the door as he has for some 25 years. A wise old anarchist and friend, banker, messenger and confidant to generations of Gijón regulars, Alfonso greets newcomers with a smile and a word, and keeps alive the feeling that you are entering a world steeped in romance and sweet nostalgia.

There are indications of a revival of café society. There are often nights when you can hardly find a seat at the Gijón or the Comercial and you must struggle to make yourself heard. These traditional haunts seem to have embedded themselves into the city's social landscape, earning themselves a sort of spiritual heritage protection, as well as attracting new fans. They even serve as a model to new old-style cafés that have opened in recent years. The prosperity of the 1980s produced once again the atmosphere in which a group of people may wish to meet regularly to pursue no objective whatsoever except to show off and have conversation—Carandell's classic precondition for a *tertulia*. And lovely old shops or cafés—the Manuela, the Barbieri, the Central, the Latino, the Oriente, the Sastrería and many more—have been rehabilitated, with fake or genuine art-nouveau pillars, sewing machine tables, art-deco mirrors, baroque gilt and velvet benches, cut-glass windows, gentle lamps and all the trappings that encourage you to linger for hours doing not very much. The fiercely fashionable cafeterias with their bright, plastic-covered high stools and strip lighting, the places which killed off countless shabby cafés in the 1960s and 1970s, now look distinctly old hat and have acquired their own period charm.

Meanwhile, young *Madrileños* now value the older, softer, dimmer, more leisurely style of traditional café. The old/new cafés are further from the Puerta del Sol, more embedded in the bohemian haunts of Lavapiés, or Chueca or Huertas or Malasaña, cheek by jowl with the Irish pub or gay disco. There seems a desire to keep café society alive. What is less certain to survive, or revive, is the spark of debate, the productive uncertainty of an idea, the passionate desire to know and analyze what is going on, to discuss new theories of the future, or the past; where those steeped in cynicism and those burning with idealism harangue each other across a cup of coffee, a marble tabletop, an ideological chasm. But perhaps that is an unduly romanticized idea of what went on. From the quality of printed material that actually emerged from *tertulia* discussions in their glory days, I suspect much of it was hot air and gossip. The Paseo de Recoletos is not the Rive Gauche. Certainly, as Spanish political life has become more stable, predictable and indistinguishable from the rest of Europe, *Madrileños* seem less interested spending hours of their leisure time in talking about it. Films, love and future plans are likelier topics of café conversation these days. Until, that is, the owner sweeps away the sea of toothpicks and little screwed up paper napkins and cigarette ends that pile up on the floor of any Spanish café or bar, turns the chairs over the tables, and forces you to adopt one of the finest and most durable traditions of Madrid's café society, which is to continue your discussion in the street.

CHAPTER NINE

The "Resi": The Birth of Surrealism

Dominating Plaza de Cascorro, focus of the sprawling Rastro market area, is a high and handsome bronze statue of the patriot Eloy Gonzalo. The work commemorates a humble hero of Spain's doomed campaign against independence rebels in Cuba. The quixotic attempt to keep hold of one of the last of Spain's colonial possessions ended in a defeat so catastrophic that the event is known simply as "The Disaster." Gonzalo was a local boy, brought up in the Inclusa orphanage just around the corner, who, while on military service in Cuba, volunteered for a suicide mission to torch the enemy camp in the historic siege of Cascorro in 1898. He said he had nothing to lose, having no family back in Spain depending on him. So he set forth with a can of petrol, asking only that a rope be tied round his waist so that his body could be hauled free. He was shot in the attempt, but rescued by his comrades, survived for a few weeks during which word of his brave deed spread to Spain and he died a hero. The statue, unveiled in 1902, shows him carrying a can of petrol under his arm, and the rope for the other soldiers to pull him free.

The loss of Spain's last remaining colonies of Cuba, Puerto Rico, and the Philippines in a reckless war with the United States was a shattering blow to national pride. Within a few short weeks almost the entire Spanish navy was sunk. It was not so much the loss of the colonies that was so devastating—most of Spanish America had achieved independence earlier in the century—but that for the first time in the history of its empire, Spain had been humiliated by a foreign power. By the end of 1898, it dawned upon the torpid and shortsighted government in Madrid that Spain had been maneuvered into an unnecessary and suicidal conflict by a clutch of Spanish owners of Cuban sugar and tobacco estates. The US had actually offered to buy the island for $300 million, a deal that would have left the huge Spanish-owned estates virtually intact. But with their disproportionate influence in the Spanish parliament, this handful of "oligarchs," as they came to be known, persuaded the government to reject that offer and to rush to war with a vastly better armed opponent. Reluctant to cede an inch, they ended up losing everything and humiliating the nation.

The crushing defeat stunned the country into a political and cultural crisis that had long been brewing and took years to overcome. It revealed Spain's extreme international isolation; not one single ally could be called upon to defend it against US aggression, or to soften the humiliating peace treaty imposed upon Spain in the Paris peace talks. The country had become inward-looking, complacent, corrupt and passive. As the century dribbled away, Spain languished without strength or impulse; and those in a position to take action dithered, demoralized and bereft of ideas. This moment of despair prompted calls for reform and sparked a process of regeneration. An influential group of social critics and writers began to emerge, known as the "Generation of '98," who started to ask what Spain's problem was and how to solve it.

The Disaster revealed that Madrid had reached the lowest point of a decline that had lasted four centuries. As the court to a now ruined imperial monarchy, it had outlived its function without creating a new one. Madrid seemed incapable of transforming itself into the capital of a modern nation, and many must have pondered the wisdom of ever designating this unprepossessing spot as the hub of empire. On the brink of the twentieth century, the city confronted the same obstacles to development that had plagued it since its foundation in 1561.

Uniquely among comparable European capitals, Madrid remained marooned in its vast, virtually impenetrable tableland. Spain's most vibrant manufacturing and commercial centers were far from Madrid—in Barcelona, Valencia or Bilbao—and everything had to be hauled across harsh country to this booming metropolis that was at the same time bypassed by the currents of economic progress. Even at the end of the nineteenth century, Madrid continued to operate as the insatiable consumer of agricultural output generated throughout Spain. It consumed vastly more than it produced, bleeding dry the surrounding countryside without stimulating any productive activity in return. Over the centuries, Madrid had ruined the surrounding Castillian economy, precarious enough from the outset, stripping wealth and people from that parched land.

Madrid gave the impression in 1898, according to the charismatic republican leader Manuel Azaña, of an idle rural nobleman who lived off the produce of his—or others'—landed estates. Idleness was the overwhelming attribute of the main social classes in Madrid in the late 1800s: the nobles, the landowners, traders, bureaucrats, and the shifting mass of immigrants—which in Spain means incomers from the rest of the country. Those who consumed most and produced least were the nobles and beggars: both groups had literally nothing to do from the moment they got up late in the morning until they went to bed toward dawn. Traders and bureaucrats did not exactly sparkle with dynamism either, and a typical image of the time was that of a small trader who stood for hours behind the counter of his empty shop

The Disaster pointed up the city's political frustrations. Not only was it unable to control an empire that had abruptly fallen about its ears. It failed even to keep a grip on its Spanish subjects who were becoming increasingly alienated from the remote indifference of the government. The country's rulers barely set foot in the streets of their capital and made no attempt to replace the crumbling empire with a coherent and self-confident national project that would weld together the disparate peoples of Spain. Lacking economic strength and political conviction, Madrid was not much of an intellectual capital either, despite drawing intellectuals and artists from all over the country. Virtually all the intellectuals who emerged in these years came from outside Madrid, from Catalonia, Galicia, or the Basque Country. You were nothing until you had conquered the salons and cafés of Madrid. But the city itself transmitted no intellectual spirit or talent. Its home-grown culture reflected more the intellectual vulgarity and economic backwardness of the surrounding provinces whose impoverished migrants flocked to Madrid to find work as servants or builders.

Unable to impose itself as an economic, political or cultural capital, Madrid a hundred years ago was for the majority of its citizens a chaotic muddle, a nightmare of uncontrolled street life, dusty and frustrating. Since its foundation as the seat of the Habsburg court, Madrid had grown higgledy-piggledy without plan or consensus. A monarchy on whose far-flung dominions the sun never set laid out gorgeous rectilinear metropolises in the remotest corners of the new world, but treated its own capital with indifference and disdain. Royal favors and petty restrictions prevented aristocrats from building fine palaces or handsome boulevards with imposing panoramas. The streets remained—and largely still do—in the haphazard layout determined by the course of medieval rivulets or the plethora of churches and convents planted where the clergy fancied. Efforts to plan the city rationally had been endlessly shelved or forgotten, compounding the frustration and impotence of those who wanted to progress.

Comparable European capitals were bigger and finer. By 1910, London was a city of seven million, Paris had three million people, and even Berlin—a recently established capital of a new nation-state—housed two million inhabitants. Madrid, capital of a kingdom as ancient and glorious as Britain or France, had meanwhile barely half a million inhabitants, at least half of whom were migrants from elsewhere in Spain. Even Barcelona was bigger, handsomer and more prosperous. Those in positions of influence acknowledged that Madrid reflected a weak and inefficient state, constructed by small groups of friends upon a backward, rural society, introspective and marginalized from the political and economic mainstream of the modern world. The social shape of the city seemed hardly conducive to reform. Its nobility was withered and enfeebled, despite the brilliance that blazed from its salons. The pinnacle of ambition for the petty bourgeoisie—those getting rich through banking or the manufacture of soap or paper—

was to accumulate enough money to join the aristocracy. Some artisans ran shops or workshops, and a huge mass of poor, and beggars, struggled to survive. Late nineteenth-century observers recoiled at the filth, the noise, the laziness, and especially the provincial, rural feel of the capital. "For all its ridiculous vanity," wrote Benito Pérez Galdós in 1876, in his great novel *Fortunata y Jacinta,* "Madrid was a metropolis in name only. It was a bumpkin in a gentleman's coat buttoned over a torn, dirty shirt." After the turn of the century, the future President of the Republic Manuel Azaña wrote dismissively: "In Madrid nothing has happened because in two centuries almost nothing has happened in Spain, and the little that has occurred has done so elsewhere. Madrid is a town without history... the entire history of Madrid consists of hand-kissing and private or royal intrigues."

The events of 1898 cruelly exposed this sorry legacy and the ineptitude of those responsible for it. But it also marked a turning point. The Disaster sparked an intellectual awakening and the beginning of a process of self-criticism and a questioning of why Spain seemed unable to deal with the modern world. As the century turned, things started to move; the loss of the last colonies coincided with the moment that the trams of Madrid lost their mules in favor of electricity. Electrification and the final loss of empire marked the beginning of a new era that included the First World War, in which fortunes were made in neutral Madrid. Neutrality in this world conflict, although perhaps little more than another manifestation of the country's age-old isolationism, proved hugely profitable and a vital spur to the regeneration of the capital. Foreign investment flowed in during the 1920s, prompting rapid urbanization and the long-overdue modernization of Madrid's infrastructure. The atmosphere suddenly favored an unprecedented impetus for change and spiritual awakening. Madrid finally began to lose the somnolent apathy of a *manchego* township, and the 1920s must have been one of the most glamorous and exciting periods of twentieth-century Madrid's history.

The Generation of '98
The first couple of decades of the 1900s saw the flowering of the Generation of '98, the best poets and writers Spain had produced since

the sixteenth-century Golden Age. They included José Azorín, Pío Baroja, Ramón del Valle-Inclán, José Ortega y Gasset, Rubén Darío, Miguel de Unamuno, Antonio and Manuel Machado and the renowned *tertuliano* and leader of coffee house discussions, Ramón Gómez de la Serna. These writers are not well-known outside the Spanish-speaking world and, with few exceptions, their works do not translate happily into the English-speaking context. Painters like Joaquín Sorolla, Darío de Regoyos and Ignacio Zuloaga, scientists and historians like Santiago Ramón y Cajal and Gregorio Marañon contributed to an ambiance of feverish intellectual excitement. The first 36 years of twentieth-century Spain are sometimes called "a silver age" in conscious homage to the epoch of Cervantes and Velázquez. A generation of Spaniards like Pablo Picasso, Juan Gris, Salvador Dalí, the Machado brothers, Federico García Lorca, Manuel de Falla and Luis Buñuel lived or studied for a time in Madrid, even if they came from somewhere else. It was a short-lived moment of brilliance in Madrid's cultural life, culminating in the formation of the Republic in 1931. But was to end in the tragedy of civil war.

Prompted by the Disaster, polemic began to supersede gossip and to sharpen into political criticism, even to contain the seeds of programs for reform. Spain's best-known philosopher, José Ortega y Gasset, argued that human beings could not be separated from their historical circumstance; they were obliged to act upon it, joining together with a like-minded elite to lead the country to reform. He also, crucially, railed against Spain's isolation from the world and insisted that its future lay in closer contact with European neighbors. Unamuno, another influential thinker, argued for the freedom of conscience in Spain and condemned the climate of censorship and persecution organized by cliques of inept or frivolous rulers. His was a search for individualism and identity, the pursuit of an intellectual freedom that contained a strongly reformist impulse, although it had, for him, scarcely any practical political implications. These intellectuals and bohemians, for all their reforming liberalism and desire for national regeneration, did not seek contact with the ignorant, illiterate and disorganized popular masses. Their debates and demands for reform and renewal had no practical repercussions. They failed to connect with the anarchist and socialist movements gaining strength as the century turned, movements which, faced with the rotting structures of the old order, contributed to the process that drove the country to democracy. The Generation of '98 inspired future progressive thinkers, but their theories did not grip the imagination of those who might have been capable of carrying them into practice.

Spain's burgeoning anarchist movement became a mass phenomenon in Andalusia among impoverished day laborers and in Catalonia among the growing industrial working class toward the end of the nineteenth century. It was never to be as powerful in Madrid, but a nationwide anarchist workers' federation was formed in the capital in 1900, advocating as its main weapon the general strike. When a strike was called in Barcelona two years later, it was crushed, despite winning much support, and the federation collapsed. In Madrid the image of the anarchist as a crazed revolutionary was reinforced by a number of assassination attempts as the century drew to a close, especially when the Catalan Mateo Morral flung a bomb at King Alfonso XIII's wedding procession in the Calle Mayor in 1906, killing several people but making no perceptible impact on the decrepit monarchy.

The socialists, with their reformist methods and determination to win power through parliamentary means, were a more serious operation. The party was founded in the Labra tavern in Calle Tetuan just behind the Puerta del Sol in 1879 under the leadership of Pablo Iglesias. This atmospheric bar still exits and remains a hectic and popular haunt. Iglesias was a typesetter whose widowed mother was a *lavandera*—she washed the clothes of the rich in the Manzanares river. He was to suffer all his life from poor health as a result of early malnutrition, remaining a popular leader until his death in 1925. He led the 900-strong printers and typographers' union in a successful strike in 1881, although he was imprisoned for three months for his part in it. In 1888 the socialists formed a trade union federation, the Unión General de Trabajadores (UGT), the General Workers' Union that still exists today. It was moderate and disciplined, and sought reforms and improvements in workers' conditions through peaceful methods. The Socialist Party and its affiliated union urged parliamentary and municipal participation and eschewed anarchist tactics of violence or direct action. But national elections were corrupt and fraudulent, with results fixed in advance, so they were doomed to years of frustration. Iglesias fell back on a high-minded strategy of moral preparation, a position of almost Calvinist austerity that appealed only to small numbers of workers.

When the Disaster struck, everything changed: UGT membership shot up from 6,000 to 26,000 in a couple of years, with most party and union members based in Madrid. Compared with the shipyards and steel mills of Bilbao and the mines of Asturias and León, where socialists made rapid advances, the working-class base in Madrid remained overwhelmingly artisanal, with a corresponding lack of industrial muscle. The party set up workers' education centers with libraries, called Casas del Pueblo, and, often against Iglesias's advice, backed huge general strikes between 1910 and 1917 of Basque, Asturian, or Catalan workers that were savagely repressed. Each setback prompted a massive increase in members, as the socialists insisted they wanted only honest elections, moderate reforms, and a clean-up of political and administrative life. By the first decade of the twentieth century, the Spanish socialists were a serious political force, self-educated, disciplined and moderate, with whom many disaffected intellectuals of the time might have found common cause. But the artists and writers did not leap the gulf between words and actions.

The left-wing Azaña reproached the intellectuals for not grasping that Spain's real problem was not ethical, as they argued, but political: it was a problem of democracy. That much eventually became clear in the aftermath of the futile death of Eloy Gonzalo and hundreds of thousands like him, who perished in defense of a rotten, indifferent system.

One product of that intellectual blossoming did have a lasting international impact. The Students' Residence in Madrid—La Residencia de Estudiantes—has an uninspiring name but a sparkling reputation as the cradle of Spanish surrealism. It was the trench, as one young Madrid writer put it recently, from which a group of friends launched an assault upon the intellectual establishment. Situated in the northern reaches of the city's smart Salamanca quarter in a wooded hilly enclave, the "Resi" was an intoxicating cultural cauldron best known for the youthful friendship of Federico García Lorca, the painter Salvador Dalí, the filmmaker Luis Buñuel, and a host of poets and artists including Rafael Alberti.

When it was completed in 1915 on what was called the "hill of poplars," the site, slightly higher than its surroundings, was on the northern outskirts of the built-up part of town and backed directly on to the harsh Castillian plain. The spot offered stunning views of the sierra to the north but was only a twenty-minute tram ride to the heart of Madrid. Reached, as it still is, by a winding leafy road, it gives the impression of a tranquil refuge perfect for spinning iconoclastic theories of art and indulging exotic tastes. Huge efforts are being made to reclaim the Resi's original free-thinking mission after decades during which it was banished to oblivion and its revolutionary legacy all but expunged. The area still breathes the fresh breezes and birdsong that inspired prosperous young men (mostly men) who lodged there until the outbreak of civil war in 1936 brought its ambitions to an end. In a dazzling spell of less than twenty years, the Resi proved itself to be one of the most exciting educational experiments in modern Spain.

Full-scale restoration work is currently under way and the vast, fenced-off, clattering building site interrupts the tranquil, college-like, feel of the place. But this work nonetheless promises the revival of its original creative energy. One of the austere, but welcoming, red brick pavilions, with its green shutters and pretty wooden verandas, has already been fully restored and hosts a wide range of exhibitions and artistic events.

The Resi was inspired by the dynamic and enlightened educator, Alberto Jiménez Fraud under the guidance of the liberal-minded Free Education Institution. That mold-breaking body was set up in 1876 in revolt against state and Church interference, and particularly against a law that insisted teachers use only authorized textbooks. One of its founders, Francisco Gíner de los Ríos, once proclaimed that students should "work more, feel more, think more, want more, play more, sleep more, eat more, wash more and have more fun." Jiménez Fraud had been in England whose educational system he had studied with interest, particularly the colleges of the old universities. So when Gíner de los Ríos—who once declined an invitation by Britain to set up a university in Gibraltar—invited him to direct a little college, Jiménez Fraud, who was barely 27, accepted gladly. Originally based in a hotel in nearby Calle Fortuny, the first residence—with only fifteen rooms and seventeen students—was a huge success.

In 1913 enough support had been mobilized to move to Poplar Hill, and to create buildings whose architecture combines cool English taste with the more exotic Andalusian playfulness. The slim, brick-built three-story residence halls were well equipped with showers and baths, and the architect, Antonio Florez, carefully positioned the buildings so they would receive the maximum light. Austerity, cleanliness and good taste were the watchwords. Once all five buildings were completed, they housed some 150 students, a figure that remained roughly constant until 1936, enabling all the residents to get to know each other by name. The Resi offered something that Madrid had never previously known: a wide range of university studies, a tutorial system based on the Oxbridge model and a broad cultural perspective that sought to build bridges between sciences and humanities. It transformed the traditional image of the Madrid student. Until then, students from the provinces sent to study in the capital had little alternative but to live on their own in squalid digs, tempted to waste their parents' money on idle dissipation. The new hall of residence offered students comfortable, if simple, accommodation, unofficial tutorial supervision, and the opportunity to mix with students from other disciplines to broaden their horizons. The Resi also encouraged communal effort and personal responsibility, and the values of an austerity of style, evident in the way it was run and its décor.

"Oxford and Cambridge in Madrid!" enthused the English musicologist J.B. Trend: "The Residencia has begun from the point which English universities have already reached, and has gone indeed some way beyond it." The aim was to produce gentlemen—rather than the *señorito*, which has connotations of idleness and superficiality. The interior was simple, adorned only with reproduction works by Vermeer and Michelangelo, glazed tiles and traditional pottery from Talavera. The furniture was comprised of pine wood and plain cane chairs.

The bedrooms had a monastic air; everyone was encouraged to keep their voice down. "And of course, the place was kept spotless," writes the Irish hispanist Ian Gibson in his classic biography of Lorca. "In a country where floors have habitually been used as substitute dustbins, those of the Resi were sacrosanct, and Lorca was to recall the intense shame he felt when once Don Alberto [Jiménez Fraud] saw him drop a cigarette end in a passageway. The warden, without saying a word, bent down, picked up the butt and deposited it in an ashtray, while the poet looked on in agony." Fraud himself ran the place with consummate ease and tranquillity, "controlling everything as if he wasn't lifting a finger," one resident, Gabriel Celaya, admiringly recalled.

Students were encouraged by their tutors to delve into obscure points and to make up their own minds instead of accepting other people's judgments. These were, and remain, rare qualities in Spanish educational thinking. Jiménez Fraud had a vision of the university that demanded "a cultured style of life" and was "based on a solid intellectual and moral foundation necessary to form a solid public opinion that respects the values that the university represents." So the Resi, without having academic faculties of its own, sought to create a cultured minority that would lead the soul of the community that produced them. Its influence was indeed enormous, far greater than the small number of students who passed through, some 2,000 in all. It sought to create a ruling elite, like Oxford or Cambridge or Harvard or Princeton, steeped in the best traditions of the country. The spirit was forward-looking, based on a desire to modernize Spain through what Jiménez Fraud called "the liberal reformist ideal." He summed up his philosophy thus:

> Only a chosen few should work for the perfection of humanity, prevent-
> ing the multitude from disturbing with their passions the ordered move-
> ment of a wise progress. But it is wrong to think that minorities privileged
> by rank or intelligence should consider themselves isolated entities, and
> forget that they only exist and are justified as the expression of a superior
> unity, that they must share a faith with the multitude, and that the light
> of truth does not recognize privileges, but is shared equally among all
> God's children.

This was elitism, but not too much. Lead the people, for sure, but within limits.

The new Resi was generously supported by the most important intellectuals in Spain. In 1916 lovely gardens were laid out behind the two parallel pavilions, including the famous poplars as well as shrubs, roses, and a little stream, now alas covered over. The "college" started to attract the most select offspring of the liberal bourgeoisie and aroused fervent enthusiasm among some aristocrats. Jiménez Fraud was keen to persuade distinguished international men and women to lecture to his students and in 1923 set up an English-Hispanic committee to develop cultural links between the two countries. Visiting lecturers included John Maynard Keynes, H.G. Wells, G.K. Chesterton, Alexander Calder and Edwin Lutyens. In 1922 Einstein gave a lecture in the presence of King Alfonso XIII, while the philosopher Ortega y Gasset translated the German into Spanish. There were evening concerts with performances by Andrés Segovia, Manuel de Falla, Igor Stravinsky, and Maurice Ravel. The original Bechstein piano on which Lorca accompanied his singing on more informal musical evenings is still there. There were also visits from modern architects like Le Corbusier and Walter Gropius.

Dalí, Lorca and Buñuel

The Resi is best known as the place where Dalí, Lorca, and Buñuel became friends in the 1920s and where they developed their revolutionary ideas about art and poetry. Buñuel arrived in 1917 and stayed until 1925. Lorca, the young poet from Granada, arrived in 1919 and stayed, with a few intermissions, until 1928. Buñuel, along with his friends, appears to have subverted Jiménez Fraud's disciplined vision of the Resi. "You could study any subject that you wanted, stay as long as you liked and change your area of specialty in mid-stream," he recalled with relish in his memoirs, *My Last Breath*. He studied natural sciences at the Natural History Museum just down the road, went running every morning whatever the weather, in shorts and often barefoot, and one day even scaled the façade of the Resi. A contemporary, Moreno Villa, described him as "crazy":

> *Buñuel was athletic and well-built, the son of rich parents and so he always had money. He never stopped. On the coldest mornings of Madrid we used to see him go out with a pole vault to jump. Then he*

would rain punches upon a ball hung from a support. After that he would go out in his car to eat in some tavern outside Madrid, return and install himself in a café, attend a hypnotism session, hypnotize a young girl. He even tried to hypnotize the clerk of the Residencia, which frightened the poor man.

Dalí stayed there between 1922 and 1926, when he was expelled from the Fine Arts Academy of San Fernando for challenging the competence of his professors to assess his work. He had been expelled before, in 1923, but on that occasion allowed to return. A wide and influential artistic and literary circle of friends rapidly formed around this lively trio, although Buñuel remembers that Lorca was the center of attention:

Federico was brilliant and charming, with a visible desire for sartorial elegance—his ties were always in impeccable taste. With his dark shining eyes, he had a magnetism that few could resist... It wasn't long before he knew everyone that mattered, and his room at the Residencia was a popular meeting place for Madrid intellectuals... We used to sit on the grass in the evenings behind the Residencia (at that time there were open spaces reaching to the horizon), and he would read me his poems. He read slowly and beautifully, and through him I began to discover a whole new world.

Dalí was smitten by Lorca's extraordinary charisma. "The personality of Federico García Lorca produced an immense impression on me. The poetic phenomenon in its entirety and 'in the raw' presented itself before me suddenly in flesh and bone, confused, blood red, viscous and sublime, quivering with a thousand fires of darkness and of subterranean biology, like all matter endowed with the originality of its own form." Dalí then makes an extraordinary confession:

During this time I knew several elegant women on whom my hateful cynicism desperately grazed for moral and erotic fodder. I avoided Lorca and the group, which grew to be his group more and more. This was the culminating moment of his irresistible personal influence—and the only moment in my life when I thought I glimpsed the torture that envy can be. Sometimes we would be walking, the whole group of us, along El Paseo de la Castellana on our way to the café where we held our usual literary meetings, and where I knew Lorca would shine like a mad and

*fiery diamond. Suddenly I would set off at a run, and no one would see
me for three days.*

In each other's rooms, the young gentlemen took tea in the English
style—alcohol was forbidden on the premises; there was not even wine
at meals. They read and discussed Spanish poetry, and even mounted
some early surrealist experiments. Dalí and Lorca one day set up "the
cabin in the desert." Between them they created a desert in one
bedroom and set up a cabin and an angel made from a camera tripod,
topped with an angel's head and wings made from starched collars.
"Let's open the window, and call for help," said Lorca. "Half Madrid
came trooping through our cabin," the poet recalled.

Buñuel relates in *My Last Breath* the lively antics he got up to with
his friends Lorca and Dalí, including his entertaining encounter with
King Alfonso XIII:

*I was standing at my window at the Residencia, my hair slicked back
fashionably with brilliantine under my boater. Suddenly the royal
carriage, complete with two drivers and someone young and female,
pulled up to the curb directly below me; the king himself got out of the car
to ask directions. Speechless at first (I was theoretically an anarchist at the
moment) I somehow replied with perfectly shameful politeness, addressing
him correctly as "Majestad." Only when the carriage pulled away did I
realise that I hadn't removed my hat. The relief was overwhelming: my
honour was still intact. When I told the story to the director of the Residencia, my reputation as a teller of tall tales was already so great that he
called up a secretary in the Royal Palace for verification.*

It was hardly surprising that the young men frequently headed off
downtown to the center of Madrid, to the Ritz and Palace hotels. Dalí
adored the double vodkas and olives and the hot rhythms of the black
jazz band, the Jackson Brothers from New York, who played in the
fashionable Rector's Club on the ground floor at the Ritz. It was the
roaring twenties and the young men enjoyed it to the full. Dalí became
a Charleston fanatic, and the friends became so passionate about jazz
that Buñuel tried to persuade Don Alberto to allow the Jacksons to give
a concert in the Resi. But Jiménez Fraud refused; such music was
incompatible with the spirit of a house where even dogs were banned
lest they barked at night and disturbed the scholars at their books.

"For us money did not count," Dalí wrote. "We were really of a limitless magnificence and generosity with the money earned by our parents' labors." Much of their money went in cafés, theaters, and night-time strolls around Madrid that Dalí illustrated in 1922 with a cubist-inspired monochrome watercolor entitled *Night-Walking Dreams*. Buñuel recalled: "In Madrid I often dressed up as a priest and strolled through the streets, a crime punishable by five years in jail." He remembers nocturnal visits to brothels. And Dalí recounts in self-indulgent detail a deliciously surrealist action he perpetrated when he visited the Ritz for a haircut one day in 1926, but decided instead to head for the bar where he asked for a cocktail. The tale involves a cocktail in which he dripped his own blood after inadvertently cutting his finger, and which he decorated with a false cherry that he twisted from the hat of a lady who entered the bar. Exalted by his surrealist act, he scampered off, convinced that everyone would think him "as crazy as a goat."

Buñuel's account of those wild, but mostly innocent, years at the Resi strike a chord with any former student:

> *It's impossible to describe the daily circumstances of our student years—the meetings, the conversations, the work and the walks, the drinking bouts, the brothels, the long evenings at the Residencia. Totally enamoured of jazz, I took up the banjo, bought a record player, and laid in a stock of American records. We all spent hours listening to them and drinking homemade rum. (Alcohol was strictly taboo on the premises. Even wine was forbidden, under the pretext that it might stain the white tablecloths.)*

He also describes how, during the summer holiday, he took a crowd of innocent Americans on a guided tour of the Prado, telling them with a straight face that Goya was a toreador who engaged in a secret and fatal liaison with the Duchess of Alba, and that Berruguete's *Auto-da-fé*, showing a mass execution by the Inquisition was a very valuable painting on account of the large number of people in it. They all listened attentively and some, to his delight, even took notes. The students also adopted the habit of not wearing hats—a daringly provocative gesture in Madrid where absolutely everyone wore a hat. The fashion, which the friends called *sinsombrerismo* ("nohattism"), caught on, but, a woman friend remembered: "People thought we were positively immoral, as if we had not clothes on, and almost attacked us in the street." Despite these excesses, Lorca wrote: "It seemed to me that everyone at the Residencia was very respectful. I don't think anyone dressed outrageously, except when we went out in fancy dress. We used to go to those chaps in the Cava Baja (the old heart of the city) who sell costumes for the theater. And we would parade around the streets and even home to the Residencia. But we never wore them in the salon."

Prompted by Dalí, the group of friends dismissed anyone they considered philistine or stuffy as *putrefacto*—spiritually dead and rotten. They developed an elaborate vision of what these living *putrefactos* looked like and how they behaved. Dalí made many drawings of a wide range of *putrefactos*, of which the poet Rafael Alberti remarked: "Some wore scarves, coughed a lot and sat alone on street benches. Others were elegant, with a flower in their buttonholes, carried a stick and were accompanied by a little beasty. They came in all genders—masculine, feminine and neuter and were of all ages." Dalí regarded his teachers at the Academy of San Fernando as almost all *putrefactos*.

He and Lorca planned a book of that title that marked the beginnings of Spanish surrealism. The work was never published, although the Resi recently assembled all the drawings and poems in a remarkable exhibition and catalogue. The work reveals the preoccupation of both young men with death.

George Orwell was to condemn Dalí for "necrophilia" in *Some Notes on Salvador Dali*, written in 1944, where the Englishman described with disgust Dalí's liking for putrefied donkeys and a mannequin rotting in a taxicab. His work stank, Orwell thought, constituting an assault on sanity and decency. But Dalí was nonetheless "a draughtsman of very exceptional gifts," he wrote. Which prompted him to reflect on the contradiction that few of Orwell's contemporaries wanted to accept. They said either that Dalí was morally repugnant and therefore his art had no merit, or an artistic genius who was exempt from the moral laws binding on ordinary people. "One ought to be able to hold in one's head simultaneously the two facts that Dalí is a good draughtsman and a disgusting human being... The two qualities that Dalí unquestionably possesses are a gift for drawing and an atrocious egoism." The important thing was to explain his success. Orwell sniffs:

> It is clear that Dali has not had to suffer for his eccentricities as he would have done in an earlier age. He grew up in the corrupt world of the nineteen-twenties, when sophistication was immensely widespread and every European capital swarmed with aristocrats and rentiers who had given up sport and politics and taken to patronising the arts. If you threw dead donkeys at people, they threw money back...

Such was Orwell's disapproving view of those crucial, self-indulgent, years in Madrid. Dalí's phobias and his artworks were, Orwell concluded, diseased and disgusting. The poet José Moreno Villa, who was a tutor at the Residencia, has an altogether kindlier interpretation. He recalls his experiences there in a nostalgic memoir written after he had fled into exile in Mexico following the outbreak of the Civil War:

> I think of my room, full of the morning sun on a Sunday. I would put on my fox-trot records or old zarzuelas while I painted. "Eternal youth"—the students—ran about on the games fields, sang in the showers, sunbathed on the terraces or held discussions in their rooms... Madrid was heaving, my friends wanted to surpass themselves. It was a hive of activity... How marvelous! For twenty years I felt this repeated rhythm and I said: this is what makes life worth living. A hundred or so first-class people working with maximum enthusiasm, at full steam. What more could a country want?

Dalí never returned to Madrid after he left in 1926, but decades later, in his old age, he confessed that Madrid was the European city that meant the most to him: "The places that Velázquez painted and the most important memories of my life—the years with Lorca, Buñuel... For me that's Madrid."

If you ask today at the Resi to see the room where Dalí, or Lorca, or Buñuel lodged, the open-faced young information officers tell you they do not know. Most of the institution's records were lost in the Civil War, making it almost impossible to fill in details of the passionate high-octane friendship forged between three of Spain's most gifted and original twentieth-century artists. The conferences and the most famous visiting personalities were apparently filmed, but Jiménez Fraud burned the films on the outbreak of the Civil War for fear that the material might provide evidence for persecutions and denunciations. The Resi's golden age, which flourished between 1931 and 1936 during the Republic, was cut short. Its theater was transformed into a church, and the laboratory building—dubbed the *Transatlántico* for its long balcony that recalled the elegant lines of a passenger cruiser— became the home of an Egyptian sultan. It later housed a science research institute, before reverting to its original use as a student hall of residence. For more than forty years its creative flame was snuffed out.

But in recent years, the Resi has blossomed anew. It is the seat of the Lorca Foundation, which preserves all the poet's manuscripts under the loving direction of Lorca's nephew, Manuel Fernández-Montesinos García. And every few months, the Resi mounts exhibitions and organizes conference seasons about the artists and poets who stayed and first developed their ideas there. The future destinies of the three friends could not have diverged more: the brilliant Lorca was shot dead in his native Granada by Franco's firing squad in 1936; Dalí became the international symbol of Spanish surrealism and the darling of America, to die old and batty in his Catalan home in Figueres in 1989. Buñuel, who with Dalí created the first surrealist film, *Un Chien Andalou*, developed his skills in Mexico and Paris and became Spain's best-known filmmaker until his death in 1983. In the latest of its increasingly ambitious exhibitions, the Resi became the focus of activities in spring 2000 to mark the centenary of Luis Buñuel's birth. As the mists are rolled away from the Resi's glory years of youth and optimism, more and more of its treasures reveal a brief, unique and brilliant moment in Madrid's cultural history, before the moment was expunged for ever.

CHAPTER TEN

Gran Vía: Bright Lights and Cannon Fire

The Gran Vía is the pulsing aorta of Madrid, a swaggering art-deco, jazz-age boulevard lined with some of Europe's finest baroque follies, earliest skyscrapers and glitziest movie palaces. Fourteen streets were scythed away in 1910 to make way for this roaring thoroughfare, designed to allow the smooth access for the newfangled motor car from Calle de la Princesa to the hub of important highways around the elegant Cibeles fountain. You can still glimpse dozens of little streets to each side of the avenue, and a few steps will bring you swiftly into the humble, often rundown, neighborhoods through which the Gran Vía sweeps.

In its heyday in the 1930s and 1940s it was handsome and imposing without being pompous, glamorous but not snooty. It was modern, swanky and bohemian, or, as Gerald Brenan, the distinguished English writer on Spain called it, "vulgar and blatant." That raffish spirit persists, amid the garish strip lighting and the endless stream of impatient honking traffic, the churning torrent of people bent on having a good time, piling into the cinemas, cafés and fast-food restaurants. Clashing with the neon are the hand-painted cinema posters up to thirty feet high, perhaps the last redoubt in the western world of this engaging, in-your-face art form.

It was a more somber scene one cold November morning in 1936, when troops formed up along a Gran Vía that monochrome photographs taken at the time by Robert Capa and others show was all but deserted of vehicles. The soldiers marched in battalions with exotic names drawn from around the world: Mickiewicz, Dombrowski, Garibaldi, Mackenzie-Papineau, Lincoln. It was a fine avenue for an irregular, albeit disciplined and committed, army to march down, composed of young men of all nationalities, races, and walks of life. Many were fleeing Mussolini's Fascism or Hitler's Nazism. Others—British or Americans—were idealists who wanted to stop Fascism before it conquered Europe. They were not well armed or equipped. They were not even very many—fewer than 2,000 men marched down the Gran Vía on November 8 on their way to the front. Two days later, another 2,000 arrived. Their contribution to the defense of Madrid in the three years of war that followed, historians now say, was not decisive. But their contribution to the morale of the capital of a country in combat with its own insurgent army was immeasurable. Their battle cry *No pasarán* ("They shall not pass") has been immortalized by history. One Madrid resident recalled the impact: "'No pasarán! No pasarán!' That's what you heard and saw everywhere all of a sudden. It was like an ad which says 'use instant shaving cream' and you do. Everyone believed it."

The Spanish Civil War began in July 1936 after General Francisco Franco led a military uprising against a pro-working-class Popular Front government of the Republic. The immediate trigger of war was, in other words, a military coup that failed. Franco's forces never expected those loyal to the Republic to defend it so fiercely for three terrible years. But the underlying social inequalities that divided the country were deep-seated and went back decades, if not centuries. The "siege of Madrid" between November 1936 and March 1937 was a prolonged battle within the Civil War: during those months, Franco concentrated his firepower upon the capital, subjecting it to daily bombardments. Only when Madrid failed to fall did Franco focus on targets elsewhere in Spain, especially the Basque Country and Aragón. But pressure on Madrid remained intense throughout the war.

Unlike the militiamen who wore workers' overalls and rope-soled sandals, the International Brigade wore boots and leather jackets, had steel helmets attached to their belts and rifles slung over their shoulders. They were singing the *Internationale*, but with unfamiliar French or German words. The brigaders were applauded as they marched down the Gran Vía that day and subsequent days, a motley troop whose assortment of flags and ranks of bayonets offered the people of Madrid the conviction that their Republic was not alone against Franco's rebel forces pressing on the western and southern flanks of the city. These romantic warriors had enlisted to defend the cause of liberty in a foreign land. Decisive or not, the heroism—some say romantic idealism—of the International Brigades, was born that cold morning early in November 1936. The Chilean poet Pablo Neruda later dedicated a poem to them, which begins "One morning in a cold month."

The filmmaker Luis Buñuel had been in Madrid as the first moment of combat occurred in July that year, when a disorganized group of Republicans assaulted the Montana barracks, south of the Plaza de España at the western end of the Gran Vía. He wrote in his memoirs: "Early one morning, I was jolted awake by a series of explosions and cannon fire; a Republican plane was bombing the Montana army barracks." The barracks is no more and the spot is part of a pleasant park that slopes down to the river. It was a fairly shambolic little skirmish. Some of the wounded soldiers were treated in a makeshift hospital set up in the Velussia cinema, now the Azul in the Gran Vía. Perhaps 150 died in the attack.

"Two weeks later," Buñuel remembers:

Élie Faure, the famous art historian and an ardent supporter of the Republican cause, came to Madrid for a few days. I went to visit him one morning at his hotel and can still see him standing at his window in his long underwear, watching the demonstrations in the street below and weeping at the sight of the people in arms. One day, we watched a hundred peasants marching by, four abreast, some armed with hunting rifles and revolvers, some with sickles and pitchforks. In an obvious effort at discipline, they were trying very hard to march in step. Faure and I both wept.

Most cars carried a couple of mattresses tied to the roof as protection against snipers, Buñuel says, adding that it was dangerous even to hold out your hand to signal a turn, as the gesture might be interpreted as a Fascist salute and provoke a fusillade of gunfire.

"Howitzer Alley"

Throughout the three years of the Civil War, the Gran Vía was the part of the city center most directly targeted by Franco's troops. From their trenches and their wooded knolls in the parkland of the Casa de Campo west of the capital, they trained their sights on the soaring angular mass of the Telefónica building. Spain's first skyscraper, built in 1929 and the tallest building on the Gran Vía's highest point, Telefónica was Madrid's most heavily bombarded target in the whole war. Franco's nationalist artillery used it as a point of reference from which they then aimed their guns at the zone that they decided each day had to be attacked. In consequence, the ornate entrance and the windows had to be protected by sandbags. But from its upper floors, the Republicans who had taken over the building had an excellent view of the nationalist front line to the south. Journalists reporting the war, like Ernest Hemingway and the photographer Robert Capa, would dodge shells and snipers' bullets fired from terrace rooftops as they scuttled from the Hotel Florida in the Gran Vía's Plaza del Callao or the art-deco cocktail bar Chicote further down the avenue to file their stories in the Telefónica building, where they first had to subject their copy to the Republic's censors.

"The hotel window is open, and as you're lying in bed you can hear the shooting on the front, 17 streets away," Hemingway wrote:

The shots go on all night. The rifles go tac crac pac tac; and then a machine gun opens fire. It's a bigger caliber and much noisier: ran cararan ran ran. Then comes the sound of a mortar or trench howitzer, and a machine gun rattle. You stay lying down; and it's marvelous to be in bed, with your feet stretched out, warming little by little the cold at the end of the bed, and not [at the front] in the University City or in Carabanchel. A man sings with a hoarse voice down below, in the street, and three drunks argue while one dozes off.

In the morning, before they call you from reception, the deafening explosion of a mortar bomb awakens you and you go to the window to look into the street, and you see a man running, with his head bent and the collar of his jacket raised, at full speed over the paving stones. You note the acrid stench of the chemical explosions, which you never wanted to experience ever again, and in your dressing gown and slippers, you go quickly down the marble staircase and are on the point of tripping over an elderly woman, wounded in the abdomen, while two men in blue overalls help her into the hotel lobby. She has both hands crossed over her large breast in the old Spanish style, and from between her fingers runs a trickle of blood. On the corner, 30 metres further on, there is a heap of rubble, asphalt broken in pieces, churned-up earth: and a dead man, with his clothes ripped to pieces and covered in dust; there is a big hole in the

ground, from which escapes gas from a broken pipe like a hot miracle in the cold morning air.

"How many dead?" you ask a guard.

"Only one" he replies. "The mortar buried itself into the asphalt and exploded underneath; if it had gone off on the pavement there could have been 50 deaths."

A guard uncovers the upper part of the body: the head is missing. They call for the gas pipes to be repaired; and you return to the hotel to have breakfast. A waitress with reddened eyes wipes blood from the marble. The dead man was not you or a friend; and everyone is hungry in the morning after a cold night and the long day before in Guadalajara… We go that way dozens of times a day. Precisely that corner… Everyone has that feeling that characterizes war. "It wasn't me. You see? It wasn't me."

…A mortar has just fallen on a house a little way away from the hotel in which I am writing. A child cries. A militiaman takes him in his arms and comforts him. There were no deaths in our street, and people who started to run slow down and smile nervously. One who didn't run at all looks at the others with a very superior air, and the city in which we are living is called Madrid.

So frequent were the attacks that the Gran Vía came to be known as "Howitzer Alley," or "Fifteen and a Half Avenue" in homage to the caliber of the shells that fell upon it. A joke ran thus: "has the 17 tram arrived?" "No," comes the reply. "The only thing that comes down here is the fifteen and a half." For fun children used to collect the red-hot shrapnel. One veteran recalled how as a 15-year-old he would wait with his friends in the side streets off the Gran Vía until they heard the cannon open fire in the evening attack, the whine of the shell through the air and the boom as it exploded against the Telefónica building. Then they rushed into the avenue to pick up the hot metal. "It seemed a very precious thing for us kids to collect. One evening when things got a bit hotter than usual, I took shelter in a shoemaker's shop; when the smoke cleared I saw a man in the street whose head had been blown off."

Capa's photos show the wide handsome boulevard empty but for a few frightened people darting for cover in the subway station, and the whole scene, including the elegant wrought-iron street lamps, shrouded with thick smoke from the explosions. In his memoir of the Civil War years the veteran journalist Eduardo Haro Tecglen remembers the curfew imposed by the aerial bombardments, the sticky tape that was stuck across windows to protect them from blasting into the rooms, and the constant exhortations to turn off the lights.

The battle for Madrid lasted from that chilly November morning throughout the winter of 1936 until the following March, when Franco realized that he was able neither to seize the city as he had hoped, nor to break the morale of the people and bombard them into surrender. He therefore turned his attention to other fronts elsewhere in Spain and prepared for a long war. But while the Spanish capital was besieged by Franco's rebel forces, its daily life was disrupted with constant bombardments from Italian and German aircraft, shortages of food, fuel and other essentials. And the stream of refugees fleeing either away from the city to avoid the bombs and the privations, or into it to escape the advancing troops, provided images of the worst horrors of modern war.

Rationing, controls, the black market, queues, fear of fifth columnists and cowering from air attacks in the subway stations, like Callao in the Gran Vía, became second nature to *Madrileños*. But amid the fear and chaos, the normal bustle and daily routine of the irrepressible residents of the capital held up. Children played in the streets; the cinemas, theaters and cafés all along the Gran Vía remained open and full of people, including members of the pro-Republican militia. Despite the progressive encirclement of the city, communications remained open to the southeast, enabling supplies to be brought in from Valencia, albeit painfully slowly and erratically, and never in sufficient quantity. Public transport continued to operate, allowing locals to take the tram to and from the front. It must have been the only city where you could take a tram to the front. "To the front, five *centimos*," tram-drivers would call, and young women, knowing that their boyfriends had an hour or two off duty at the front, would hop on the tram to see them. "And there, behind the barricades and the parapets, you could see them making love with firing going on all round them. Now and then a couple would be killed and their bodies found still clasping each other in a last embrace," one veteran remembered in Ronald Fraser's *Blood of Spain*.

Haro Tecglen relates how his family's young housemaid Victoria announced one morning to his mother:

"Señora with your permission I'm going to the front. I'll make every effort to be home in time to serve dinner." She returned that night, in her blue overall with a pistol at her waist and her soldier's beret. She had left her rifle with the comrade who was serving the nightshift at the front. Many did the same; those who spent the night at war returned to work during the day, so as not to lose the day's pay. Victoria spent the day fighting, but returned at dusk. Sometimes she picked me up from school; she'd stand on the pavement and stop a car with her pistol in hand. "Comrades, do me the favor of giving me and this comrade (that was me!) a lift because it's very cold." My mother forbade this: "Don't do that ever again: think of those in the car. If they see you with a pistol they might open fire." "Just as you say, señora."

The city bubbled with pride, even euphoria, throughout those dark months, despite the bombing and the lack of proper food. Combatants remember taking the tram from the front to the Gran Vía in the evenings—to go to the cinema. Everything somehow kept working amid the random disorder of war, writes Haro Tecglen: the gas, the water, electricity, the metro, the trams all operated normally as if indifferent to the siege they were under and the prospect of instant death at any moment. "In the Molinero tea shop on the Gran Vía they had neither tea nor coffee, perhaps chicory, some doubtful infusions; there was no butter, but a peanut paste and strange currant marmalade. But the waiters in their white tie and tails continued to serve the ladies who came in the late afternoon. People went to school, to concerts and exhibitions, and to the theater."

Life Under Fire

Surviving the Civil War and the years of dictatorship, is the Gran Peña, a club for retired military officers and their friends, just a few yards from Chicote at Gran Vía 2. This is arguably the most reactionary corner of the city, where a statue to Franco in the main lounge not only still existed as late as 1999, but was not erected until the 1970s, well after the dictator's death. It remains perhaps Madrid's most exclusive gentlemen's club, where women are permitted only as guests, but whose opulent basement bar is dominated by the portrait of a gorgeous femme fatale, said to be a distinguished member's mistress, who broke his heart and ruined him. The clientele of this venerable institution was transformed in the early days of the war, when, in the autumn of 1936, well-born gentlemen were pushed aside in favor of militiamen who casually put their rifles on the tables. This, despite critical press reports complaining that true fighters for freedom and democracy would not take their coffee clutching machine guns. The number of armed militiamen who strolled around Madrid grew to such an extent that some restaurants in the Gran Vía posted notices requesting clients not to deposit their weapons in the cloakrooms, since this gave rise to confusions and unseemly confrontations. The newspapers reported in August 1936 that a *novillo*, a young bull, had succeeded in jumping the barrier in the bullring and caused havoc, not by goring anyone in the audience, but because several militiamen present had fired their rifles at the beast, and a spectator had died in the mêlée.

Other customs changed rapidly in those early days of war. It became fashionable to stride about wearing blue or gray or green workmen's overalls, and sandals. Suits, ties and hats began to vanish from the streets of Madrid, and everyone addressed each other with the informal *tu*. The well-to-do dressed down to pass unnoticed, to the point that in August 1936, the association of ladies' hairdressers announced that the sector was in crisis. The clenched fist salute became a common greeting, and even matadors saluting the presidential balcony at the start of Madrid's bullfights did so with a raised fist.

The war period saw a surge in the numbers of people going to the cinema and the theater, perhaps as a way of forgetting for a brief while the horrors that surrounded them. Those who remember those days recall the astonishing variety of films shown in the cinemas of the Gran Vía throughout the entire war, by far the majority of which were American. The Spanish Civil War saw the supremacy of American film stars, seen in all their big screen glory in the Gran Vía's vast glittering movie palaces. They included films starring Laurel and Hardy, Betty Boop cartoons, Mae West and Cary Grant in *I'm No Angel,* Boris Karloff in *Satan,* Greta Garbo in *Queen Christina,* Claudette Colbert and Shirley Temple, Clark Gable and Jean Harlow, Myrna Loy, Charlie

Chaplin, James Cagney, and Edward G. Robinson. Soviet films were also shown, including Sergei Eisenstein's classic *Kronstadt* at the fine Capitol cinema on October 19, 1936. This was a screening of such importance that arrows were pasted on lampposts all along the Gran Vía leading to the cinema, whose façade was covered by an enormous poster. The foyer was draped with banners of the Republican Fifth Regiment, and the Symphony Orchestra played Catalan, Basque and Castillian anthems of freedom and independence. The screening was attended by the President of the Republic, Manuel Azaña, together with his ministers and military chiefs, but was overshadowed by news that Franco's troops had taken the town of Illescas, just 25 miles south of Madrid, the day before.

So popular were films or plays that nationalist bombardments were timed for when the spectacle was ending and crowds surged into the streets. Eduardo Haro Tecglen recalls: "One day a bomb fell near the Fuencarral theater [behind the Gran Vía]. One of the actors fled down the street dressed as a prior, in the middle of the civil war. He was saved by a CNT [anarchist union] car. It was usual to interrupt the performance during a bombardment, wait in a nearby shelter, then return to the theater to continue the play." Some were not so lucky: soldiers who had gone through the worst of the fighting at the front were killed leaving a cinema in the Gran Vía at night. For young Alvaro Delgado who had collected red-hot shrapnel, half the excitement was the fear of whether you would get home safely from the cinema. "If you could reach the Plaza del Callao and the corner of Calle Preciados then you knew you were OK." One evening he was watching an American film, something to do with Mexico, when the noise of the shooting on the screen seemed to get much closer and, suddenly, the lights went out, as a shell hit the cinema. Haro Tecglen relates that the spectacles offered were overwhelmingly comic farces and vulgar variety shows, and that the favorite films were melodramas with plenty of violent shoot-outs. Admittedly, alternative forms of entertainment were scarce; bullfights were suppressed as cattle were slaughtered to provide meat, and football was confined to Catalonia and Valencia.

The eminent historian Pedro Montoliú describes wartime Madrid and its strange atmosphere in his *Madrid en la Guerra Civil*:

The cafés, cinemas, theaters and brothels were full of people who, despite the unpromising progress of the war, were curiously optimistic. In the streets, in a street market, or crossing in front of a passing photographer or shoeshine boy you could see personalities like the surrealist artist Tristan Tzara, [the French writer] Antoine de Saint-Exupéry or Ernest Hemingway who had traveled to Madrid to be near the people who had succeeded in holding back Franco's troops. They all stayed at the Florida hotel at the Gran Vía's Plaza Callao. [The poet] Antonio Machado wrote in the newspaper El Sol on 7 February 1937: "Madrid has resisted three months under siege, subjected to iron and fire, and it still has, as they tell me, a smile on its lips." Machado adds: "the fact that Madrid approaches complete tragedy and heroic sacrifice without losing its smile is worthy of admiration but comes as no surprise."

Certainly, the patrols of the International Brigades throughout the streets of the capital, as they marched to confront the enemy in the Casa de Campo, lifted people's spirits. *Madrileños'* determined defense of their city had been the first serious check to the advance of Franco's troops across Spain since his rebels had set out from North Africa in the summer of 1936. But it was a period of severe shortages, queues, hunger, fear, and the to-ing and fro-ing of hundreds of thousands of refugees. "Today you can say with certainty that the people of Madrid practically don't eat," wrote a public order official for the local authorities in January 1937, as the winter entered its bitterest moments, adding: "There is no point in having war supplies if Madrid is going to die of hunger." Queues for bread and milk had started early in the war. You had to join the queue at 7AM to stand any chance of getting something later in the day; family members took turns spending a couple of hours each in the queue. It was where people talked, exchanged gossip about the front, kept up morale. But as the war progressed and food shortages worsened, people suffered vitamin deficiencies. Alvaro Delgado remembers that great boils broke out on his neck and under his arms. His hands were broken with chilblains. A bowl of lentils, some rice, was what he mostly ate. He never saw meat, never tasted coffee.

As food became scarce in the besieged city, a grotesque "war cuisine" emerged, including recipes such as egg-free mayonnaise and egg-free tortillas. Some cafés sold cups of anonymous soup for a peseta—one peseta 10 cents with added red pepper—and coffee-free "coffee" made with malt without milk or sugar. They also served drinks with a strong taste of chemicals, prompting some typically *Madrileño* black humor: a customer takes a sip of one of these dubious drinks and tells the waiter, "Hey, this anis tastes of bleach," and the waiter replies "Oh, I'm sorry, I gave you brandy by mistake. Today the anis tastes of petroleum." Hemingway, a committed drinker, lamented the shortage of supplies: "Beer is scarce and whisky practically unobtainable. Shop windows are full of Spanish imitations of all the drinks, whiskies and vermouths. They are not to be recommended for internal use, but I sometimes use something called 'Milord Escosses Whisky' for my face, after shaving. It stings a bit, but makes me feel clean…" The authorities were incapable of controlling the flourishing black market which, for a price, could provide delicacies like suckling lamb and chocolate.

While many had to go to extreme lengths to procure food, others took every opportunity to profit from the shortages. This was a painful echo of the experience of the First World War when Madrid had been a hotbed of black market profiteering. Spain's neutrality between 1914 and 1918 made the capital a haven for spies, dealers, entrepreneurs and smugglers who took up residence in new luxury hotels and hung out in the smart cafés and bars on the glamorously louche Gran Vía. The situation created a lively atmosphere, thick with gossip and intrigue, but it swiftly collapsed when the persistence of the conflict caused the destruction of the export market. But the similar social conditions resurfaced, with a darker undertow, during the Civil War.

Alvaro Delgado tells how his family was divided: his mother's side "exceedingly right-wing," his father's communists. During the war his mother's side became much better off than the rest of the family. They moved to a large apartment away from the shelling, which they shared with two other families; the husband of one of them seemed able to procure all the meat he wanted. "One of my cousins was a draft-dodger who got himself a job as a clerk in the SIM, the counterespionage service; he belonged to the clandestine [far-right] Falange. We, who were on the left, had virtually to beg food from my right-wing family who always seemed to have enough bread, soap, milk. In fact I used to go to the SIM headquarters where my cousin would give me green soap for washing clothes, and condensed milk."

As the war drew to an end early in 1939, an international charity commission estimated that existing levels of food supplies could not support life for more than another three months. The basic problem was that the peasantry in the countryside around Madrid would not hand over their wheat. Despite rationing there was plenty of bread in the villages. And at that point the nationalists bombed the capital with bread. According to Delgado: "It came down in sacks with propaganda wrapped round it saying: 'This bread is being sent to you by your nationalist brothers'... Some came through a broken skylight at the Fine Arts School [where Delgado started studying during the war] and when no one was around I and other students ate so much we felt sick." But in the streets, people trampled the bread with rage. "I did so myself; we were almost dying of hunger and yet people were shouting at each other 'Don't pick it up,'" another eyewitness recalls.

Demoralization, Resistance and Defeat

The rapid initial success against the subversive nationalists in the capital had given *Madrileños* perhaps an overoptimistic vision of imminent victory. Newspapers in Republican hands brushed over defeats and presented small advances as great triumphs. Fighting in the sierra, once the front was established, became virtual weekend spectacles for politicians and the curious. Montoliú writes: "Newspapers scarcely spoke of those killed or wounded in combat, unless it was to announce the burial of a combatant who died gloriously defending the Republic, or a famous militia leader, in which case people filled the streets to accompany the funeral cortege that filed through the city. These showpiece burials began to tail off after September 1936 because their announcement in the press served only to prompt the nationalist airforce to conduct bombing raids."

Without military victories to offset cold, hunger and air raids, the mobilization of the rearguard became increasingly difficult. While morale at the front remained high, the rear began slowly to crumble. The fact that it survived for so long was due to the decisive role of the Republican women, according to a recent scholarly study that has become a best seller, by Mary Nash, an American historian based in Barcelona. In her readable and passionate account of the experience of Republican women during the Civil War, Nash argues that the women were neither "heroines" nor "victims" of the war, but in their desperate struggle against the privations and hunger of war, broke down their existing stereotypes as "the angel of the home" or "the perfect wife" that had defined their roles until then. So determined and resourceful were they that their collective experiences contributed decisively to the survival of the rearguard in the war. But they remained constrained by the force of traditional values. The image of the woman in arms, the militiawoman fighting at the front alongside the men, was never accepted, except by a tiny minority. Most women accepted the limitations of their new more liberated role, and concentrated on tackling problems of health, education and child-care, albeit in new ways that broke traditional molds and crucially maintained the rearguard. "They were a decisive force in the resistance of the Republic for three years. If it had not been for the women of Madrid and other cities and towns, the Republic would not have survived as long as it did. The quiet, almost invisible collective experience of women and their ability to bring in the bread was decisive to the resistance of the Republic," Nash said when she presented her book in Madrid in September 1999. This fledgling process of emancipation was broken with Franco's victory in 1939, which prompted a brutal return to traditional conservative definitions of a woman's role: that of wife, or mother, plaything, or child. But beneath the suffocating blanket of the new orthodoxy, a learning process had occurred, a transmission of values of self-esteem and women's self-belief survived even the years of dictatorship that followed.

By the end of March 1939 it was all over. Suddenly everybody started handing out cigarettes. Someone who had been hiding in an embassy for two years said: "I don't know where they had kept them hidden for so long. We threw open the shutters. It was the first time I had seen the street for two years and nine days. I leapt out. It was true, there were people shouting 'Viva España.'" At the western end of the Gran Vía, the Plaza de España was crammed with demonstrators.

Right-wingers in a lorry stopped and forced Encarnación Plaza's cousin in his Republican uniform to give the Fascist salute. All around her people were raising their outstretched arms. Her girlfriend and her girlfriend's mother were doing the same. Encarnación was frightened they would notice that she did not follow suit. But she was only a child and no one paid any attention. The daughter of a life-long Republican, she could not bring herself to give the salute. Everywhere there were blue shirts. The women impressed her most; the *señoritas* of good families from the Salamanca neighborhood shouting "At last, at last, and singing *Cara al Sol.*" She says: "On all their faces I saw not joy but hatred and rage. Hatred for the population amongst whom they had been living, the ordinary working people of Madrid."

Haro Tecglen remembers the day after three years of fear and fighting when the nationalists finally entered Madrid:

> *"They're here," my mother said. The hand that had gently aroused me from sleep throughout my tiny life now shook me hastily, as when a bombardment started in the middle of the night. There were shouts, trumpets, hymns, loudhailers. It was March 28, 1939. Madrid had fallen. They had passed through. My father was sleeping. He had worked all night on what would be the last edition of the newspaper he ran: the copy that he had brought home was still fresh. It went on sale for barely a moment: he never returned to his office. It was already taken over—while he slept, waiting for them to come for him—by those who would put out on the same day another newspaper, that of the victors.*

He saw pale priests stumble into the streets clutching enormous crucifixes and blessing the incoming nationalist troops. "People knelt before them, and some fainted at the sight of the first scarlet and gold nationalist flags. Moors shrieked, legionaries sang and nuns prayed. They handed out food parcels from the back of lorries. Loudspeakers played hymns and pronouncements and the voice of Franco. Some people were running from pursuers, and the Civil Guard already had handcuffs on others. Some could not contain their grief and their weeping. At home many burned books, flags, party cards; others hid them, hoping for better days. They buried my [anarchist] CNT card forever. The Republic died that day and it will never come back."

Chicote

Chicote, at 12 Gran Vía remains relatively unchanged, despite renovation, since its heyday in the 1930s and 1940s, although its glory days as the focus of high society and cosmopolitan, sometimes sleazy, glamour are long past. This elegant, raffish bar prided itself on never closing even during the fiercest fighting and worst shortages of the Civil War. The establishment was founded in 1931 by Perico Chicote, who became known as "the king of the cocktails" when these stylish aperitifs were the height of fashion. Chicote's curved leather seats and chrome and mirrored décor still project a timeless, if faded, elegance. The bar is actually called "Museo Chicote" in reference to the founder's collection of 25,000 drinks from all over the world that he kept in the cellar. The bottles ranged from the smallest, which contained eight drops of peppermint, to one that held 82 liters, but I don't know what the giant bottle contained. Some were more than 100 years old. Chicote was prompted to form his curious museum when the commercial attaché from the Brazilian embassy presented him with a bottle of Brazilian Paraty rum while he was working as a barman at The Ritz in 1916. His frequent travels abroad served an additional purpose: to obtain bottles for his collection. They were arranged geographically in the vaults of his bar, and access was by a tiny staircase. There was a time when it was joked that his was the most visited museum in Madrid after the Prado, but alas the collection was recently sold, reputedly to the Walt Disney Corporation, but no one at the bar today really knows, or if they do, they're not saying.

The rich, glamorous and famous hung out there, including Hemingway, Ava Gardner, Frank Sinatra, Orson Welles, European princelings, scientists, artists and intellectuals, whose photos adorn the walls. Hemingway said of Chicote: "The most attractive girls in the city went to Chicote and it was the place from which you could begin a good night out; well, everyone has begun some good nights from there. It was like a club, with the difference that you didn't have to pay subs and you could pick up girls there. It was without doubt the best bar in Spain, and I think one of the best in the world… Another reason is that the drinks are marvelous." The clientele during the war was comprised of the international brigaders, the foreign correspondents, and a regular clutch of young women who engaged in a covert prostitution.

Chicote became renowned in the post-war years for its beautiful women of a certain kind known as *señoritas putas de derecha*—sluttish right-wing young ladies. The satirist Miguel Mihura says with typical *Madrileño* deadpan humor that Chicote was the best reason he could find for having been born in Madrid. "I decided to be born in Madrid because I thought it was the place that would put me nearest to the Chicote. I could have been born in Burgos or Seville without any problem, because both cities were already complete; but this would have meant a very long journey to have an aperitif." Throughout the post-war period of hunger and deprivation, the elegant of the city rendezvoused in Chicote in pursuit of the latest imported sensation, the latest *estraperlo*— black market—offers in apartments, cars, overcoats, or penicillin. Here you would also hear the latest joke against the *Generalísimo* or the latest piece of gossip about improvised fortunes or well orchestrated adulteries. As prosperity pricked up in the 1960s, Chicote reflected Madrid's fascination with Americanized consumer society, fast living, high-class affairs, and property speculation. One long-standing expatriate English woman living in Madrid today still remembers Chicote as a renowned pick-up joint, and recalls that up until only a few years ago respectable ladies did not frequent the bar unaccompanied, and decamped altogether after 8PM in favor of looser women.

Frontier Zone

A few years ago, the local authorities described the area around the Gran Vía as "the most derelict and socially marginal in the city." The district abounded with prostitutes, drug dealers and "urban tribes," they said, and they pledged an extensive and expensive cleanup package. The success of these efforts is still to be proved. Former no-go areas have been rehabilitated with traffic-free walkways and proper lighting. But you can still see prostitutes peeing in doorways after dark, a down-and-out settling himself down for the night in a bank entrance that he has frequented for more than twenty years. It is wise to move on when someone approaches you with a publication or a petition to sign, for it is one of the spots of the city where the traveler is likely to be deftly—sometimes roughly—relieved of wallet or handbag.

The Gran Vía remains what it was from the start, an ambiguous frontier zone where smart and louche, high and low, rub along side by side, constantly eyeing each other and acknowledging the presence of the other. One particular proposal by the authorities provoked a huge polemic: someone in the town hall called for the vast hand-painted posters that announce forthcoming films to be removed from the cinemas, to reveal the fine facades of the handsome buildings they cover. They suggested replacing the posters that have adorned the Gran Vía since the cinemas were built with luminous projections that would be shone upon the facades at night. But *Madrileños*, especially the cinema owners, consider the posters to be of greater social and historic importance than the buildings they adorn. They raised howls of outrage at an idea they thought would cause a drop in audience figures. The much-loved hand-painted posters, said critics, were part of the landscape of the city, contributing beauty and cheeriness to the area.

What is more, they have sustained a historic artisan industry unique to the capital. On the Monday of the week when the film is changed, a little workshop in a rundown part of the city receives notification from the Gran Vía cinemas of the new screening, with publicity photos on which to base the new posters. "That's the day they decide to change the program if the weekend box office takings have been poor. We have to work quickly because the posters must be ready by Thursday. We put them up on Thursday night ready for the first showing on Friday," says Inés Sánchez, who runs one of the last cinema poster painting workshops in Madrid. The vast canvases—some of them the area of a good-sized apartment—are recycled, washed, primed and repainted, "although it's a shame they can't be preserved in some museum." She adds sadly: "Without the posters, the Gran Vía would be nothing, just a barely camouflaged strip joint. The beauty of the avenue is in the facades and the cinema posters. We decorate the street at no cost to the authorities." During the Civil War, the technique was used to paint gigantic posters of revolutionary heroes—of La Pasionaria, Lenin, Marx, the poet Federico García Lorca—which were then slung from the protective structures built over national monuments like the Puerta de Alcalá. Some criticize today's huge posters, saying they are kitsch, garish and of poor taste. But for those who love the Gran Vía and its rollicking past, that is all part of its appeal.

CHAPTER ELEVEN

The Valley of the Fallen: The Franco Years

Every November 20, on the anniversary of the death of Franco, a diminishing number of the former dictator's supporters—dubbed *nostálgicos* by opponents—gather to render homage to their hero. They assemble in the only square in Madrid where a statue of Franco remains, the *caudillo* astride a horse with his hand imperiously outstretched. It is the Plaza San Juan de la Cruz, to the north of the city near the vast concrete stretch of official buildings planned during the brief Republic of the early 1930s but erected and inflated to their full grandeur during the dictatorship. These buildings are known as "Nuevos Ministerios." Here the *nostálgicos* listen to an ear-shattering rant full of imprecations against "traitors" and "separatists," by which the orators usually mean conservative Popular Party politicians or extreme right-wing splinter groups who congregate in another part of town.

And from here they make a pilgrimage to the mausoleum that Franco built in the Valle de los Caídos, the Valley of the Fallen some thirty miles north of the capital, and where he is buried. More than 25 years after Franco's death it is still quite easy to find *Madrileños* who confess their belief that things were better during his rule. They do not make themselves conspicuous and they keep to their favorite parts of town, the smart Salamanca area (known as the *zona nacionalista*) and adjoining neighborhoods, including the areas around Nuevos Ministerios that were built during the 1950s, 1960s, and 1970s, as the Franco era gradually emerged from the shocking poverty of the post-war years into a period of relative prosperity. These are the areas colonized by those who backed the winning side in the Civil War, drawn from all parts of Spain to share in the economic benefits of the new order. Initially, their migration to the capital may have been driven by the terrible rural hunger and starvation of the 1940s and 1950s. Those who benefited from Madrid's gradual economic development and stability attribute their improved conditions to Franco, and turned a deaf ear and blind eye to the repression, censorship and intellectual stultification that accompanied the process.

Una España Grande y Libre—"One Spain, Great and Free"—say the banners sold around the Plaza San Juan de la Cruz every November 20, slung from stalls similar to those outside a football match, with their stickers, scarlet-and-gold flags and scarves. Indeed, those crowding around to buy their souvenirs resemble football fans. They are overwhelmingly young men, with bomber jackets and close-cropped hair. You will see the occasional grizzled old-timer or mink-clad lady with carmine lips, right forearm held firmly aloft while the Fascist anthem *Cara al Sol* blares from loudspeakers at a volume totally disproportionate to the aural needs of the few hundred in attendance. But the relentless earbashing conveys the sense of excitement and intimidation that the reduced numbers fail to provide. Some even assemble together for a group photo like a football team, arms outstretched, a swastika raised, and a fierce look on their faces. When one of their number asks for a smile for the camera, they snarl.

You have to take a bus or train to El Escorial, Felipe II's imperial folly, then buy a ticket at the Casino bar around the corner for the special bus to the Valley of the Fallen, laid on every afternoon. The bus does brisk business most weekends, but especially around November 20, when enthusiasts sing *Arriba España* with gusto, prompting even the impassive bus driver to ask them to calm down. At the mausoleum, which is at once absurdly kitsch and cruelly frightening, delegations from the French Marshal Pétain association and similar international like-minded bodies lay wreaths at the dictator's grave. However many visitors are there, mere mortals still tend to be swallowed up in the numbingly vast granite and marble acreage of this ugly spot.

The 850-foot underground basilica hewn into the side of the mountain claims to honor "the civil war dead of both sides," but you can see at a glance that this is a memorial to the victors of Franco's Spain. "Fallen for God and Spain" the inscriptions repeat throughout the cavernous mausoleum; they should more accurately read "Fallen for Franco's Spain." A gigantic cross towers 500 feet above the rocky

hill and dominates the scene for miles around. Only two men lie buried at the high altar: the *generalísimo* and his right-hand man, the well-born Falangist José Antonio Primo de Rivera who was shot dead by Republicans at the beginning of the war. In a bizarre episode in the early days of Franco's rule, José Antonio's cadaver was exhumed from its burial spot at the bottom of a ditch in the southeastern city of Alicante, to be placed in a cemetery nearby. The fallen *caudillo* was then borne on the shoulders of Falangists who carried the coffin in a macabre pilgrimage to lay their hero to rest in the Valley of the Fallen. There are those who say the Falangist leader's death was convenient for Franco, because it removed a possible challenger to his power. This, they insinuate, is the reason for the elaborate homage laid on for him after his martyrdom.

Some *nostálgicos* still pointedly devote their loyalties to either Franco or José Antonio. One young passenger on the special bus wore a beautifully pressed blue shirt with the crimson yoked-arrows insignia and two metal stars on the breast pocket, a neat silken lanyard looped over his shoulder. He was accompanied by a broad, sweet-faced girl, who towered above him, wearing a black shiny tracksuit trimmed in scarlet and gold. The pair joined the group entering the crepuscular gloom of the granite vault, barely illuminated by wrought-iron lanterns attached to the walls. The customary metallic shriek habitual to an assembled group of Spaniards dropped to a murmur, out of respect, or perhaps muffled by the portentous enormity of an architectural style that many consider impressive because of its power to extinguish the human spirit. The young man headed for the tombstone of José Antonio, a flat granite slab laid into the floor beneath the huge mosaic-decorated and gilded cupola. It was adorned by a couple of bunches of scarlet roses. He stood there for a moment, suddenly bent down and kissed the granite, then in a single fluid movement clicked his heels and swung his right arm aloft before turning and striding swiftly down the nave, his girlfriend loping behind him, her little camera swinging from her wrist. Outside they asked an elderly lady to take a snap of them, "and please make sure you get all the cross in." Another smooth heel-click and arm-swing, and they headed for the bar.

Monumental Obsession

Franco announced his megalomaniac project on April 1, 1940, on the day of a victory parade celebrating the first anniversary of his triumph. With the country on the point of economic collapse, thousands dying of starvation and Europe consumed in war, Franco found time to conduct several exploratory trips into the barren countryside around Madrid in pursuit of a suitably impressive natural spot for his monument. Once he had settled on the grimly imposing valley of Cuelgamuros in the Sierra de Guadarrama, he swept his top brass to the site (after a good lunch) in a cavalcade of cars, detonated the first charge of dynamite, then addressed the company on his vision:

> *The dimensions of our Crusade, the heroic sacrifices involved in the victory and the far-reaching significance which this epic has had for the future of Spain cannot be commemorated by the simple monuments by which the outstanding events of our history and the glorious deeds of Spain's sons are normally remembered... The stones to be erected must have the grandeur of the monuments of old which defy time and forgetfulness.*

Franco kept a close and active eye on development of the design and during construction sketched his own plans for the architect Pedro Muguruza. The monument's purpose was explicitly to link Franco's era with that of the imperial monarchs Carlos V and Felipe II. Originally planned to take twelve months, the project took twenty years to complete. It became, as the British historian Paul Preston puts it, Franco's obsession, one as passionately consuming as if it had been "the other woman."

The labor was carried out by Republican prisoners who had escaped execution. These survivors of the army that remained loyal to the government elected in 1936 worked in "penal detachments" and "labor battalions" used as a coerced workforce to build dams, bridges and irrigation canals. Twenty thousand worked on "quarrying duty" at the Valley of the Fallen: fourteen died and were reputedly buried where they fell, entombed beneath the Guadarrama granite on which they toiled. Their deaths are unrecorded and remain a lingering source of bitterness to their families. Countless more lost limbs in accidents or were stricken with silicosis. The crypt—doubled in size from the original conception—was finished in August 1954, hewn from solid granite, over 850 feet long and 125 high. The cross, nearly 200,000 tons of it, took another two years to complete. The monument was finally inaugurated on April 1, 1959, on the twentieth anniversary of the end of the Civil War. This was the high point of the dictator's rule. Franco in his Captain General's uniform, accompanied by his wife Doña Carmen, dressed in black with a mantilla and high comb, walked up the central aisle under a canopy to special thrones near the high altar. Thousands of workers were given a day off with pay plus a packed lunch, and bussed in for the occasion. The whole enterprise had cost the equivalent of $300 million. Franco saw his Valley of the Fallen as his El Escorial, the two monuments each symbolizing the greatness of their era. His speech about the heroism of "our fallen" in defense of "our lines" was, reports Paul Preston in his biography of the dictator, "triumphant and vengeful. He gloated over the enemy that had been obliged to 'bite the dust of defeat' and showed not the slightest trace of desire to see reconciliation between Spaniards."

Democratic Spain has taken the pragmatic but understandable position of scooping up the Valley of the Fallen as a sort of offshoot of the El Escorial complex, a further example of how a Spanish ruler created a monument to his own glory. The lavishly illustrated visitor's guide to the Valley is produced by the organization responsible for royal monuments and describes the site, the statues and the tapestries depicting scenes from the Apocalypse with the same effusive pedantry as it describes El Escorial or the Royal Palace. "The Cross, together with the Royal Seats, has become one of the greatest and most popular tourist attractions in the area around Madrid," the guide says, making a glancing reference to the employment of prisoners of war, "who opted for the 'remission through work' system according to which they could work off up to six days of their sentence for one of toil." The divisive and vengeful spirit of the place is played down in favor of a studied, apologetic neutrality. This may be distasteful for those visitors who do not share the views of the young man with the blue shirt, but at least it has the merit of keeping the tourist propaganda from the influence of the *nostálgicos*. This approach is in keeping with the way Madrid has dealt with its dictatorial past.

Unable to denounce it, unable to celebrate it, unable to forget it, the solution is to de-politicize it, neutralize it in the blanket of deadpan bureaucracy, squeezing from it any potentially dangerous signs of political life that might stir within. Hence, in the gloomy echoing entrance hall, the stall of tourist kitsch offers Valley of the Fallen candlesticks, Toledo steel swords, key-rings, gilded plates, coasters, lighters and ashtrays. Supplies are bulked out with generic "royal" souvenirs of fleur-de-lis soap, Velázquez cologne, cherubs, T-shirts, silver spoons, thyme vinegar... But the only portraits available, the only figures honored on a key-ring are those of King Juan Carlos and Queen Sofia. Of the two men entombed in the granite vastness, one of whom ruled for forty years within recent living memory, there is not a trace.

Divided City

Those cold November days when Franco's supporters are most fervent in their demonstrations of loyalty are the most miserable and monochrome in this vibrantly technicolor city. The Valley of the Fallen is monochrome, the Monastery-Palace of El Escorial is granite-gray. The tones reflect the Franco years, which most who remember them recall as being uniformly bleak, dull and boring. The writer Antonio Gómez Rufo evokes the spiritual grimness of those times in his novel *El Desfile de la victoria* (The Victory Parade). The action takes place in mid-May 1953, just as the worst of the post-war austerity was about to lift. That year the Eisenhower administration in the US finally decided to recognize Franco's regime, breaking Spain's international isolation. It was the beginning of a slow thaw. But Rufo's opening description of a divided Madrid is steeped in a dreary chill:

> *It was a city inhabited by new soldiers and young functionaries drawn from the countryside, their stomachs satisfied, gold diggers, war victors; but the other city, the defeated city, continued crouched on its knees surrendered to sadness, a people with lowered glances who in moments of greater lucidity were gradually casting off the bonds of the recently suppressed ration book in a black and white landscape that did not diminish with the exalted fervor of coming days.*

Rufo's entertaining and atmospheric tale is of an anarchist conspiracy to kill Franco that is thwarted in the days leading up to one of the annual victory parades laid on by the regime to convince its citizens and the world that peace and order reigned in Spain. "It was Monday, it was May, but Madrid smelt like a January dawn... Madrid's black and white life was about to change fractionally, perhaps only by a detail, but the reality was that up till then the most fortunate children had to content themselves with balloons of gray rubber, as sad as their ample overcoats, handed down and not always altered to fit."

The author evokes a city divided between victors and vanquished, and describes the pain and anguish of those who had resisted for three years of war only to suffer the bitterness and humiliation of losing. The silent daily confrontation between Republicans and nationalists, and between rich and poor, was clearly demarcated geographically within the capital. The feeling among *Madrileños* as the day of Franco's victory parade approached varied starkly according to which part of town you observed. On the eve of the parade, smart women with bright lipstick and a permanent smile and men in check suits and good hats were cheerfully taking glasses of vermouth in smart bars in Calle Goya or Calle Serrano in the prosperous Salamanca district. Meanwhile, in the working-class suburbs further from the center, in Ciudad Lineal, Atocha, Tetuan, or Vallecas, police patrols harried people for their papers, took them in for questioning and made every effort to prevent a hint of rebellion, protest, or civil disobedience from marring a perfectly orchestrated occasion to honor the *generalísimo*. The transition from one sector to the other could be brusque: "The main thoroughfares were garlanded with decorations, but the nearby side streets stank of oilcloth and stew, of onion and bread, fried fish and fear." Gómez Rufo's story is fiction, but based on the memories of those living in Madrid in 1953 and records of the time. The dismal, fearful and suspicious spirit is confirmed by emerging historical studies of a period that has for more than two decades been airbrushed by what became known as the "pact of forgetting." When the dictatorship fell in 1975, opposing political factions made a mutual agreement to let sleeping dogs lie, the better to overcome fears and resentments that could have sabotaged a peaceful transition to democracy. Such tactical amnesia helped secure the transition, but left many scars unhealed.

Adding to what the historian Santos Julía calls the overwhelming sense of "hunger and silence" was the crepuscular gloom, a feeble half light not only in the streets that were dark and empty of people, but in the home, where a dismal illumination was provided by the ubiquitous 25-watt light bulb. Still today in Madrid, when you take possession of an unmodernized rented flat, your first instinct is to rush to replace those palely glimmering bulbs. In theory, the nightwatchman, the *sereno*, who patrolled his designated patch all night long, protected you on the street at night. And among the things most missed by the *nostálgicos* is the sense of safety on the streets. Apologists for dictatorship around the world always seem to complain that in those days you could walk around in safety. I remember as a young student rolling home late after the big doors to the hostel in central Madrid where I was lodging had been locked, and the *portero* had gone to bed. You clapped your hands in an imperious summons. The sound echoed against the walls in the deserted dark street and the *sereno* would appear, select the right key from a vast bunch strung on a large ring hung at his belt, and ceremoniously let you in, perhaps with a dark and suspicious look suggesting that he knew you had been up to dangerous practices or at least harbored dangerous thoughts. *Serenos* were invented in 1765 by King Carlos III in an effort to control the disorder that reigned on the streets of Madrid after dark. For centuries they patrolled the night streets with their tall pike and their ring of keys, discouraging criminals, calling out the hour and *todo sereno*—"all quiet." They died with the dictatorship, in the mid-1970s, to the regret of many. Madrid's socialist mayor Enrique Tierno Galván tried in the 1980s to bring them back. But, in the era of electronic locks, the attempt was a failure.

More durable, and even more redolent of the Franco years, the *portero* or doorman continues to thrive as a Madrid institution. The *portero*, who watches everyone who enters and leaves his building, takes out the rubbish and takes in the post and generally makes himself indispensable to the residents, was in the Franco years often considered a police informer: a *soplón*, the expression goes, with its suggestion of a puff of air from lips held to the ear of the authorities. In Rufo's novel, the *portero* Zacarias is eaten up with frustration and curiosity at the comings and goings at his house that are closely scrutinized from police cars parked nearby, but no one will tell him what is going on. It is intolerable that he, the one supposed to impart information to everyone else, is being kept in the dark. Rufo describes this mentality, which he said was fostered by Madrid in the Franco years: "A refuge for traffic wardens, debt-collectors, bank clerks. A setting for functionaries, janitors and ushers proud of the minuscule power conferred by the borrowed uniform they put on every morning so that, within its sheltering protection, they might order, permit or prohibit, behind a desk to which they clung as if it belonged to a general or a minister." The *portero* in his little cubbyhole at the foot of the stairs or by the lift, from which he could monitor every movement in and out of his domain, reflected the lowest rung of a structure of power in which, as many survivors bitterly recall, "whatever was not forbidden was compulsory." Today's *porteros*, particularly the younger generation, are free of this lugubrious legacy, but residents nonetheless usually feel it is worth paying the customary monthly tip, not just for favors like taking in parcels or letting in the plumber to repair a dripping tap when they are at work, but simply to keep him "on-side."

"A Long Winter"

Franco's dictatorship exercised control not only through its omnipresent security forces but also, crucially, through censorship and what one recent study of the early Franco years calls "the dictatorship's enormous avalanche of propaganda." According to the authors, Nicolas Sartorius and Javier Alfaya, each of whom served prison terms for opposing the dictatorship, Franco's ideological strategy was to present Spain as a prosperous, peaceful country besieged from abroad by a vast communist conspiracy, and from within by extravagantly rewarded secret agents who exploited the innocence and good faith of honorable Spanish workers. Those most under suspicion were the intellectuals or, as the publications of the regime called them, "pseudo-intellectuals." Among them were the distinguished authors, the brothers Juan, Luís and José Augustín Goytisolo, who had lost their mother in Franco's bombardment of Barcelona and who fiercely criticized the regime. A Francoist newspaper commented brutally that their works were better known in the country's police stations than in its bookstores. In the 1960s and 1970s, the professional middle classes came under scrutiny, as increasing numbers of architects, doctors, economists, lawyers and journalists began to express their opposition to Franco's rule. As their numbers grew, Franco's methods of propaganda backed by terror began to lose their effectiveness. The misery of the 1940s and 1950s gave way to economic development of the 1960s and 1970s, creating a climate of conformity that helped mute the desire for liberty. But Sartorius and Alfaya emphasize the massively extensive network of *soplones*, paid informers, who permeated the length and breadth of Spain, especially in Madrid which had stood defiant for so long. It is impossible to say how important this network was, they say, because crucial police and security services archives remain closed, or in many cases have been destroyed. At any rate, the sums spent on this endeavor by Franco's government must have been huge, "given that the Francoist Ministry of Government had a vast budget, greater than the Ministry of Education." The authors conclude: "Unfortunately, the active or passive participation of sectors of Spanish society in the repression was more important than we care to remember."

The commentator Francisco Umbral described those years as "a long winter" for the less well-off: a Spain of queues, hand-me-down clothes, repulsive food, collective misery with no escape-valve except that of the cinema. There are still Spaniards who remember never having eaten a proper meal for ten years after the Civil War ended in 1939. Rationing was in force until 1952, which produced a flourishing black market. Black market dealing, known as *estraperlo* after a roulette fraud in the 1930s, became "a national sport," Francisco Umbral remembers, in which packets of food were thrown from the windows of an approaching train before it entered the station, in order to elude the watchful eye of the police.

One survivor of those years of hunger, Remedios, worked as a maid in a prosperous household in Madrid. She confessed years later to an American journalist how she swallowed her scruples to survive and prosper in a society built on deception and profiteering:

The Suarezes were highly placed; although he was a civilian, his position in the [pro-Franco] Falange had gotten him the job of managing an Army warehouse which also carried supplies for other government ministries. All receipts and disbursements were signed by him, and his signature on a chit for any goods in the warehouse was unquestioned. "They stole, not just for themselves but for their rich friends as well. The manservant and the maid with whom I was first sent to the warehouse were so well known there that they scarcely looked at the chits that we brought signed by Don Joaquín. They gave us whatever the manservant asked for!" Remedios laughs nervously at the recollection. "I believe the men working there added things to those orders and kept them for themselves. The manservant himself said to me the first day, ' Here, this is for you—a can of sardines!' And when don Joaquín's wife discovered that I was a good cook and turned over the kitchen to me, I often went to the warehouse alone to get things for the table. I believe that nothing which came into that house was paid for.

"After a while, I did not even need to bring a chit or a list of things they were to give me. But I only stole food. I made them into small packages with cloth wrappings and closed them tight with needle and thread and I ran down to Atocha Station and put them on a train that each day stopped at Cavares. I did not have a package for each train, only for two or three a week, but I alerted my family and to be sure, one of them met the Madrid train every day... Those were years of hunger. Not only because the people had no money and no jobs, but because there was also a scarcity of food that even money could not always buy. A gallon of olive oil on the black market cost my month's salary!"

Children in the Franco years had their heads shaved to protect them from lice and the boys were clapped into uniforms and treated as little warriors. Coeducation, which had briefly flourished under the Republic, was stamped out, and boys and girls were segregated to the maximum degree possible. Coeducation, according to the ministerial decree of May 1, 1939, "was entirely contrary to the religious principles of the glorious National Movement, and necessarily suppressed as anti-educative." The fate of women was particularly grim after the brief flowering of autonomy during the Republic. The regime tried to create within the family a little authoritarian state in miniature.

A woman was defined primarily as a wife who was encouraged to stay at home and produce babies. If she had to work, the professions deemed suitable included teacher, telephonist, seamstress, or beautician, and these were only thought appropriate for single women. A grueling regime of toil in the home was recommended, occupying every waking moment of a woman's life. Going to university was discouraged. She was expected to organize every aspect of the domestic economy of her family, without having any control over the money—a miserable challenge during the period of shortages and rationing between 1939 and 1952. In law, a woman was the property of her husband or father, without whose permission she could not open a bank account, obtain a passport or a job. Adultery was punishable by prison for a woman, but it was not a crime for men unless they were blatant about it to the point of causing a social scandal. Divorce was abolished in 1939, but desertion was common, and women endured the painful experience of being abandoned with small children and being unable to remarry, although their husbands never reappeared. The traditional option of a single woman without education or economic resources was either prostitution, which flourished covertly with the tolerance of brothels, or to open an *estanco* or cigarette kiosk, those lugubrious brown corner shops whose proprietors still often seem as miserable as their surroundings.

Under the new order, men and women were subjected to a fierce dress code: underwear had to be white or flesh-colored; men wore hats. Ecclesiastical censorship expunged any trace of political criticism and of eroticism too: under the influence of the Catholic hierarchy, puritanical aversion to the depiction or mention of bare flesh reached what Juan Pablo Fusi and Raymond Carr called, in their study of culture under Franco, "levels of comic absurdity." Boxers' torsos were concealed in painted vests and film stars' busts reduced; the word "thigh" was struck out from a play. The imported melodramas that filled the cinemas were rigorously dubbed, and voice-overs ludicrously distorted to preserve moral propriety. Lovers were rendered as siblings to prevent the suspicion of adultery. When, in one example of crass censorship, a woman is asked if the man is her lover, her dubbed voice says no, while on the screen she nods her head in assent.

"The cinema," wrote Francisco Umbral, "gave us the measure of our misery." Despite their best efforts, censors could not tame exuberant femmes fatales like Rita Hayworth or Betty Grable to the chilly sexual desert imposed by the regime. Over-excited Falangists flung bottles of ink at the screening of *Gilda*, which bishops denounced as anathema and "the collective heresy of the West." Spanish films, whose scripts were censored until 1976, were mainly vulgar folkloric comedies and spaghetti westerns. Theatrical offerings were confined to light musical comedy. The press was "inconceivably boring," say Fusi and Carr, offering little more than flat accounts of official functions. In this climate *Hola!* magazine emerged with a winning formula: a picture weekly devoted to the glamour and domestic detail of the rich and famous of Madrid society and European royals. Everything in *Hola!* was rendered without comment, certainly without criticism and nothing political ever appeared. Radio offered perhaps the greatest escape of all, especially for women confined to the home, broadcasting sentimental, "typically Spanish" songs sung by a clutch of wholesomely glamorous stars like Carmen Sevilla and Lola Flores, who were ironically dubbed "missionaries of optimism" by a later critic. Melodramatic radio soap operas held half the nation in thrall, rather as Latin American *telenovelas* do today. Throughout the 1950s, radio shows, songs, quizz shows and football commentaries formed the falsely cheerful soundtrack of a generation. They cast, wrote the gifted and acerbic author Carmen Martín Gaite "an artificial silence" over the real problems of the country by avoiding any reference to the present or the immediate past. Then, in the 1960s, came television, whose achievements Fusi and Carr summed up in 1978 thus: "Theatrical productions were rare and poor; serials based on novels were deplorable; cultural programmes irrelevant; political information grotesque; political interviews non-existent until Franco's death. Spanish television remains rooted in mediocrity."

El Escorial
Felipe II built his great palace monastery of El Escorial del San Lorenzo thirty miles north of Madrid nearly four centuries before Franco came to power. But its oppressive style and megalomaniac scale imposes a

sense of impotence and despair comparable to that experienced by a generation of Spaniards between 1939 and 1975. The pompously overbearing architecture was the inspiration for Franco's similarly obsessive Valley of the Fallen monument just five miles up the road. The creations share a spiritual as well as a geographical proximity. But while Franco's folly has only one altar, Felipe's basilica contains more than forty, enabling scores of masses to be celebrated at once.

Felipe II, who invented Madrid as the Spanish capital, conceived of a building that was at once a royal palace, church, monastery, college, seminary and library, a total vision that has been described as the spirit of the Inquisition raised in granite. He pronounced the inhospitable site at the foot of the Guadarrama mountains an ideal spot for his project, which he called San Lorenzo in honor of the saint on whose day—August 10, 1557—the king won an important battle against the French. The fiercely geometrical gridiron plan on which the palace was designed is said to represent the grill on which the saint was burned to death. The king's instructions to the architects, Juan Bautista de Toledo who had trained in Naples and worked on St. Peter's in Rome, and later Juan de Herrera, fit his austere personality: "Above all, do not

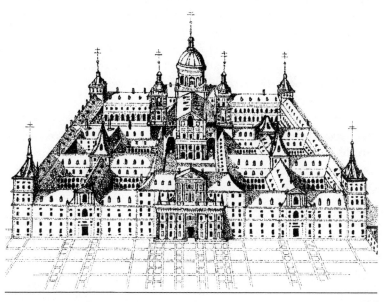

forget what I have told you: simplicity in the construction, severity in the whole; nobility without arrogance, majesty without ostentation."

Felipe II's building, like Franco's, conjures up unhappy associations of cruelty, repression, war and death, and the effect of the grandiose architecture of El Escorial is to intimidate and cow the spirit of any visitor. It also conveys what visitors to Madrid constantly remark upon: the Spanish obsession with death. The nineteenth-century French writer Théophile Gautier found even getting to El Escorial a lowering experience: "You cannot imagine anything more arid or more desolate than the countryside you have to cross to get there: not a single tree, not a single house; great slopes of rock folding in upon themselves... But such a landscape does not, however, lack grandeur. The very absence of vegetation gives the contours of the terrain an extraordinary severity and nobility." The place itself first impresses by its size: "the biggest accumulation of granite after the pyramids of Egypt," Gautier writes before launching into one of the most extraordinarily bitter invectives that can ever have been written about a Spanish building and the monarch who inspired it. El Escorial was, he concludes: "the most boring and disagreeable monument that a taciturn monk and a suspicious tyrant could dream up for the mortification of his fellow creatures." Visiting it, he felt the marrow freeze in his bones and his blood "ran colder than that of a viper." The building, he said, was inspired by the ideal of a barracks or a hospital, and was monotonous, cold, overpowering, sinister and sad. "I left this granite desert, this monkish necropolis, this architectural nightmare, with an extraordinary feeling of satisfaction and relief." And just to drive the message home, the French visitor offers the following advice to those who boast that they never suffer from boredom: spend three or four days in El Escorial. "You will learn what real boredom is, and you can amuse yourself for the rest of your life by thinking that you could be in El Escorial but are not."

Gautier's loathing was almost matched by that of the distinguished English traveler Richard Ford, who uttered similarly patriotic denunciations of Felipe II, with his "bigot grey eyes cold as frozen drops of morning dew... which even the pencil of Titian could not warm." And the German traveler Wilhelm von Humboldt, more moderate in his criticism, nevertheless shared the sense of gloom that engulfed him when he entered the church: "Every hour bells sound lugubriously in memory of the death of this or that prince, and the building itself lacks light and breadth." Humboldt describes how he spent some hours in the chamber of the Prince of Asturias and looked through the window at the mountains that, neither beautiful nor varied, offered at least a broad and impressive outlook. He goes on: "I was invaded by a peculiar sense of monkish emptiness as I looked through those narrow windows, that I will always remember. It was a melancholy but sweet sensation, and for a moment at least I could have lived in that place." The place had housed a strange and peculiar community of monks and monarchs, and "from here Felipe II ruled half the world."

One of the worst legacies of Franco, recalled the Basque philosopher Fernando Savater recently, "was the antipathy felt by Spaniards for our own country and the symbols of our own country. Even the use of conventional national symbols—even the national flag—to legitimize the regime. It all smells of fascism to us, as though Francoism had contaminated all the symbols of national life. We all felt in some ill-defined way ashamed, as if our socks smelt." And apart from shame, fear was the dominant feeling, a dull nameless fear caught in the influential journalist Juan Luis Cebrian's novel *La Agonía del dragón* (The Dragon's Agony). The novel covers the period from 1968 to the moment in 1973 when Franco's designated successor, Carrero Blanco, was blown to smithereens in an ETA car bomb. Savater recalls "an absurd, vulgar life of Francoism: totalitarianism cemented by a failure to implement the laws." Francoism maintained up until the last minute all the apparatus of repression, firing squads and all, but was corrupted from within and only awaited a puff of air to blow it all away. Like a mummy that maintained its appearance unchanged for eons, it collapsed to dust at the slightest movement. Built to survive for generations, the regimes of both Felipe II and Franco fell when no one cared to prop them up. Their granite monuments remain a source of wonder to skeptics and supporters alike.

CHAPTER TWELVE

Bernabéu and Calderón: Passion for Football

When you gaze up at the Santiago Bernabéu stadium, temple of Real Madrid Football Club, it is worth reflecting that this soaring concrete pile with its swirling stairwells at each corner was built during Spain's most pauperized post-war years when thousands of Spaniards were starving. Madrid's biggest and most splendid stadium, situated just north of the elegant plazas and palaces of the city's smartest Salamanca quarter, is in the street that was called at the time Avenida Generalísimo Franco, now the Paseo de la Castellana.

Franco's decision at that moment to pour enormous sums into building a shrine to football accommodating more than 100,000 spectators illustrates what historians have called "the culture of evasion" in which most Spaniards immersed themselves for several decades. While the small minority of intellectuals and artists from the pre-Franco period revolted against the new order, the overwhelming majority of ordinary people simply cut themselves off from immediate reality.

Football was the primary escape valve to which millions of Spaniards turned to blot out the poverty and repression of the Franco years. Football offered a solace for the political bleakness of the dictatorship, and an outlet for frustrations produced by the pinched grayness of daily life. Along with cinema, radio and, from the 1960s onward, television, football offered the route to oblivion. Franco himself was addicted both to cinema and later to televised football, and never missed Spain's "match of the day." Football was at the heart of an emerging consumer culture devoid of political or intellectual content, and therefore innocuous. So popular did this consumer subculture become that, manipulated or not, an image emerged of a carefree happy-go-lucky Spain basking in the social peace achieved under Franco. Football also created a surrogate solidarity and emotional release otherwise crushed from this stiffly regimented society. Franco was happy to see popular passion and enthusiasm whipped up for non-political spectator sports that offered a harmless channel, a safety valve for more disruptive social energies. It was no accident that under Franco big football matches were always scheduled for May 1, the traditional labor day, as an additional deterrent to those tempted to march in support of trade union freedoms.

Those days are gone, but the passion for the game is if anything more fervent than ever, after a dip in popularity immediately following the dictator's death. So closely was football in Madrid associated with Franco that even today, more than 25 years after his death, there are still men in their forties and fifties who do not care for football, never attend a match, do not follow *La Liga* and discourage their children from showing any interest. This anti-football feeling among a generation of progressives, or *progres* as they are known, is only slowly dissipating as football in Spain has, in common with that in Britain and elsewhere, soared to unprecedented levels of popularity among men (and women) of all classes.

If you go into any bar or café on a Monday morning, you will probably be able to guess which team your barman supports, simply by watching his face for a while, or the enthusiasm or otherwise of his actions. Even if you have no Spanish at all, you may safely assume that the animated conversation taking place among the elderly, or young, men standing at the counter with a glass of brandy or beer, concerns the performance of their team, and the prospects for this or that player or coach. Football is of such all-consuming interest in Madrid that it is impossible to penetrate this dense and all-enveloping layer of the city's culture without having a passing knowledge of who is up, who is down and who are today's heroes and villains at any moment in the football season. Fortunately, it is not difficult to acquire such knowledge. The names are on everybody's lips: the taxi driver's radio will probably be tuned to a sports station—which delivers round-the-clock football and exhaustively analyses every detail until you would think that there was nothing more to say about this player's knee injury or the imminent replacement of that coach, and by whom he is expected to be replaced.

Football is a perfect vehicle for *Madrileños* who love to hold forth about a matter on which they may know very little. For a start, no one can ever be wrong. You may disagree with a fellow pundit's opinion, but since no one knows what the next match will bring, none of it is of lasting significance. Secondly, with national or international matches being played several evenings a week, the situation changes daily, providing endless permutations for comment and prediction. You could, indeed, spend your entire social and working life keeping up with football, without having to think very much, know very much or do very much.

Real Madrid

Only a small handful of giants really count in Spain's football hierarchy: either Real Madrid or their arch-enemies Barcelona usually top the league. Extra excitement is generated by the emergence of a rogue outsider, perhaps Valencia, or a strong Galician team. But supporters of Real Madrid consider theirs to be not only the best team in Spain, but in the world. This conviction has been strengthened in recent years by the team's winning of the European Cup for the seventh and eighth time in 1998 and 2000.

The spectacle of Real Madrid fans advancing across town after a big win is not easily forgotten. I remember once eating dinner in a good restaurant in the Salamanca district. The place was eerily quiet and empty, and waiters became more and more lugubrious as diners failed to materialize. We all knew this was because Madrid were playing local rivals Atlético in the deciding match of the league, and most of the city was at home glued to their television sets. By the time the waiter murmured with satisfaction: "three-one victory to Real Madrid," we already knew. A human tide was roaring through the club's prosperous heartland. Armies of fans, men carrying their young children on their shoulders, trailing purple and white banners, some embellished with the scarlet and gold of Spain's national flag, chanted and surged through pavements where little old ladies usually walk their poodles, past wrought-iron portals and window displays of designer textiles and soft leather handbags. Scooters and cars created instant city-wide traffic gridlock, filling the night with a deafening clamor of hooting. Young girls with velvet headbands leaned excitedly from BMWs, their glossy blazer-clad boyfriends flushed with joy. The sound of trumpets and kazoos floated through my bedroom window all night long. The dawn lull was shattered by a fanfare of car horns as revelers ejected from all-night bars protested at finding themselves double-parked. After victory in the European Cup in May 2000, celebrations went on for three days, with light shows, triumphal parades and all-night partying that prompted even hard-line *Madridistas* to wonder if they hadn't gone a little over the top.

Real Madrid's towering reputation was built on its still unbeaten record of winning the European Cup five years running between 1956 and 1960. Franco shrewdly took advantage of this success to promote the team as international ambassadors for Spain, injecting a much-needed boost of color, excitement and national pride into the life of his isolated and dispirited subjects. Victories by Spanish teams in international competitions were celebrated as national triumphs over historic foes. Spain's footballing victory over England in 1950 was hailed as a defeat for "perfidious Albion"; that against the Soviet Union—in the Santiago Bernabéu itself—celebrated as "bringing communism to its knees". The regime inflated the propaganda value of these achievements with such fervor as to create a virtual foreign policy. The myth was built up of a unique "Spanish style" of football that was "virile," impetuous in attack, the embodiment of those Hispanic values exalted by Franco's propaganda. But the international triumphs of 1956 to 1964 owed much to the massive importation of foreign players. Madrid's big clubs spent huge sums on transfer fees to acquire players from abroad. Those who believe that Franco cynically manipulated for his own ends a nation's desire for football glory retain a lingering distaste for the game and the all-embracing passion it can arouse.

The Santiago Bernabéu stadium is named after the club's most famous president, the man who took this once ordinary team to European stardom in the 1950s. Don Santiago Bernabéu hauled Real Madrid—or "El Madrid" as it is known simply, in a felicitous elision between the club and the Spanish capital—from bleak post-Civil War austerity to the peak of football's aristocracy. Madrid's white shirts with their purple trim became feared and respected throughout the world, while at home the color inspired the less-than-respectful nickname of "the meringues." Those white shirts also came to represent Franco's repressive regime. For Basques and especially Catalans, Franco's favorite team of international stars represented the omnipotent Castillian overlords. For Spain's historic regions, whose ancient rights were crushed by Franco, games against Real Madrid held a significance that went far beyond the pitch. Those games were no game: they were pitched battles in a visceral, political war that still goes on today, despite the fact that Catalonia and the Basque country have achieved a substantial degree of self-government. When Madrid meets Barcelona in the Bernabéu, taxi-drivers, zooming through the capital's deserted streets on such a night, remark menacingly "the Catalans are in town," as if warning of alien hordes assaulting the city gates. Police install a protective security cordon half a mile deep around the stadium on these occasions. It is easy to get a table at good restaurants, and the best seats at the theater or the cinema, but make sure you take the last subway train home unless you want your car or taxi to be caught in the interminable traffic jams at the end of the match.

Madrid Football Club was formed by students at the turn of the century. Originally the club had no fixed home, but moved from ground to ground. At one point the team members played next to a bullring and changed in the toilets of the bar next door. Early success prompted King Alfonso XIII to give Madrid his royal blessing in 1920—hence the *Real* (Royal)—and the club turned professional with the inauguration of the Spanish league in 1929. The player most identified with Real's miraculous rise is Alfredo di Stéfano, an

Argentine who is said to have developed his skills by dribbling the ball at speed down the straight grid-pattern streets of his native Buenos Aires. Di Stéfano was also wooed by Barcelona, who insist that they were cheated of the star player through political manipulation in Madrid.

When *Madrileños* tell you which team they support, they say they "are militant" in this or that team, as if it were a labor union or a political party. This verb, *militar*, suggests a much more passionate loyalty to a team than the feeble word "support." And one of the many colloquial Spanish words for "fans"—*hinchas*—has the connotation of uncontrollable addiction. Madrid is unusual in that the passion for football is a truly cross-class phenomenon. Real Madrid, in particular, is regarded—by non-supporters, naturally—as the snobs' club, the team favored by the prosperous yuppies, the *pijos* who live in smart area around the stadium or generally in the northern part of the capital. Real Madrid has, of course, legions of working-class supporters, but the club is also considered smart among the young professional set who would never dream of supporting Atlético.

Atlético

Madrid's other main club is less socially prestigious. No one with pretensions to social status would admit to supporting the club that is based in the rougher, southern part of town down the hill in the *barrios bajos*. Even Atlético's nickname—the *colchoneros* or mattress boys— indicates the club's humble origins. The label refers to the red-and-white striped shirts that legend says were originally made from surplus mattress ticking purloined from local factories. Or, since a similar scarlet-and-white strip is worn by Athletic de Bilbao (originally inspired by expatriate steelworkers from Sunderland) of which Atlético was originally the Madrid offshoot, perhaps the name refers only to the supposed occupation of its early players or supporters. Atlético has, in any case, always seemed in the shadow of its richer rival in the capital. For one painful season, in 1960, Atlético even had to suffer the ignominy of sharing Real's glamorous new Bernabéu stadium, while struggling to raise funds among its supporters for an upgraded home of its own. The club moved into the splendid Vicente Calderón stadium in 1966, by an old gasworks on the bank of the Manzanares river to the southwest of the city. There it sits, engulfed in the sweet hoppy aroma that wafts from the nearby Mahou brewery, which makes possibly the finest beer in Spain. Recently renovated, the stadium dominates the riverside scene and overlooks the lower middle-class and working-class neighborhoods that sprawl across the city's southern suburbs.

"Duel of the gods"

Sometimes the mighty sports papers *As* and *Marca*, Spain's best selling dailies, bill a local derby, when the capital's big teams face each other, as a "duel of the gods." Such reports are usually accompanied with stern nose-to-nose profiles of figures revered by each team that are spread across the billboards of the capital. The standoff depicted is not that between the idols of each side in honor of their superhuman goal-scoring skills, but between two eighteenth-century marble statues just a few hundred yards apart in the center of Madrid, adopted since the dawn of Spanish football as mascots for each club. The statue of Cibeles, goddess of plenty, in her chariot drawn by lions, is Real Madrid's sacred monument. And Neptune, with his trident and his sea horses, further south along the handsome Paseo del Prado, belongs to Atlético. These two lovely monuments, sculpted in 1777 by the master Ventura Rodríguez from Toledo marble, have defined this stretch of the city since ladies with mantillas and caped gentlemen strolled the unpaved promenades. After a trophy-winning victory by one or other team, the appropriate deity is besieged by ecstatic fans in the climax of a triumphal parade south from the Bernabéu or north from the Calderón stadium. Supporters clamber over the delicate limbs and rococo cherubs, and splash about the elegant fountains. They trample and maul the austerely beautiful figures, and irreverently festoon them with scarves, caps and flags amid scenes of wild hysteria.

So uncontrolled have these revelries become that the authorities have sounded the alarm at the damage inflicted upon the city's precious national monuments. When Spain beat Switzerland in the 1994 World Cup, Cibeles' hand was ripped off in the excitement. Days later, it was found dumped in a dustbin and painstakingly reattached with resin and fiberglass. Then Neptune was assailed in May 1996 after Atlético's

unprecedented victory in both the league and the cup, when the club's euphoric owner Jesús Gil y Gil bathed in champagne before joining the victory parade on his horse, Imperioso, garlanded and adorned with rosettes for the occasion. Fortunately, fans' threat to paint black the goddess of their rival did not materialize. Neptune suffered in May 1998 when Real supporters attacked the idol of their local opponents and ripped off his hand after winning the European Cup.

These two statues seem in recent years to have run a greater risk from enthusiastic football fans than they ever did from invading French troops in the early 1800s, Franco's bombardments during the Civil War, and the corrosive pollution emitted by today's traffic chaos. So concerned were *Madrileños* to protect their local gods from damage during the Civil War that they flung themselves into a defense effort, packing them in sandbags to the tip of their crowned heads. "How can we let such vandalism in peacetime happen to our precious heritage, which was protected and survived years of war, only to fall victim to football fans?" the authorities grumbled recently. "Having survived all that, why should they now suffer at the hands of those celebrating a sporting victory? Imagine if Italian fans scrambled all over Michelangelo's *Pietà* every time their team won." It was decided to cordon off the sites and allow only the players to celebrate their victories by standing upon the shoulders of their gods. But this plan had its opponents, who thought it would set a bad example to fans to see their living football deities treating their marble gods with such brutal disrespect. Hence the decision to board up the statues altogether on the night of crucial matches. But they remain the focal point of victory celebrations. For Real Madrid's great celebration of its eighth European Cup only two team members were given permission to assault the goddess, but the whole team climbed on anyway, although fans were kept well away.

Power-brokers and Hooligans

Atlético's delirious night in May 1996 marked the climax of the rollicking career of one of the most luridly colorful figures in modern Spanish football. Jesús Gil, disliked by some as a loudmouthed brute of a man, burst upon the Madrid scene when he bought Atlético in 1987. Long suspected of shady dealings involving vast sums, his glory days seem now to have entered a decline, along with those of his club, relegated to the second division in 2000. His bullying style and roller-coaster fortunes epitomize the buccaneering finances, the ruthless power struggles and high farce typical of Madrid's football world. Gil was born in Burgo de Osma, near Soria, north of Madrid in 1933. At the age of seventeen he shared a boarding house with a priest and nineteen prostitutes, keeping the establishment's accounts in lieu of paying rent. He mended gearboxes, then bought and sold lorries and eventually property. In 1969 an apartment block he built in Segovia collapsed, killing 58 people and injuring 150. There were no plans, no architect and no surveyor, and the cement was barely set. He was jailed in 1971 for five years for criminal negligence, but after eighteen months Franco pardoned him. He borrowed a modest sum and started again, some say with an enduring chip on his shoulder. Marbella, glitzy playground for rich Arabs and Russians, with possibly the densest concentration of powder-blue fringed suede cowboy boots in Europe, caught his fancy in 1979 when he attended a local weight-loss clinic. He homed in with his property deals with such disregard for the regulations that in 1988 the socialist town council declared him persona non grata. His way around that obstruction was to stand for mayor. He created his Independent Liberal Group (GIL) party and won a landslide victory in 1991. Throughout the 1990s his Atlético players sported the name of Marbella across their shirts in what Gil said was just an affectionate tribute to his favorite Mediterranean city. But investigations into Marbella's catastrophic finances gave rise to suggestions that Gil had been tipping the contents of the town hall treasury into the coffers of his club, and thence to his and his family's pockets. Throughout years of tortuous court cases, during which Gil was in and out of jail, sacked then reinstated as Atlético supremo, he insisted that he was innocent of any wrongdoing.

Curiously, for a phenomenon whose mass appeal originally drew much from the desire to blot out the horrors and boredom of Fascism, the football terrace is one of the last remaining visible redoubts of the far right in Spain. Nazi-inspired football hooliganism emerged in the mid-1980s under the influence of English skinhead "bovver boys" and Argentine *barras bravas* (wild gangs). Spaniards use the word for skinheads, *cabezas rapadas* or simply the English word "skins," to describe those disaffected young men who use the audience of a vast football stadium as a platform from which to chant their slogans and wave their Nazi symbols. Racist behavior has often been directed at players, and black players have been greeted with ugly taunts, accompanied by gorilla-like gestures and the hurling of bananas on to the pitch. This kind of behavior, confined mainly to the notorious *Ultra Sur* group of Real Madrid season-ticket holders who congregate at the southern end of the Bernabéu, is viewed with deep concern by the authorities, aware that it puts Spain, which has never fully disavowed Franco's legacy, in a poor light in the eyes of the world. Stringent laws have been passed forbidding "entry into public events of symbols that incite violence, racism and xenophobia." But the clubs are reluctant to take action against radical extremists; when racial incidents occur, they usually claim that the perpetrators are not genuine fans but criminals with whom the police, not the club, should deal.

Concerns have increased that football *ultras* have a sophisticated international communication network, with specialist magazines and especially Internet contact. In addition, fanatical Fascist organizations deliberately target young football fans as a fertile recruiting ground. A shudder rippled through Spanish society far beyond the football world in December 1998 when a young Basque fan of Real Sociedad, Aitor Zabaleta, who had followed his team to Madrid from his hometown of San Sebastian, was killed in a racist attack just before the match. He had come with this girlfriend to support his team against Atlético at the Vicente Calderón. Zabaleta went into a bar near the stadium shortly before kickoff, where he was taunted by Atlético fans for wearing his blue-and-white Real Sociedad scarf. He left with his girlfriend, but was followed, assaulted and stabbed to death in the shadow of the stadium. It was Spain's first ever football killing and plunged the nation into shock and self-questioning. How had this happened? A further twist was added in that young Zabaleta was Basque, from a region which, like Catalonia, has long defied the national predominance of central Castillian Spain. Within the fervent football world, unresolved regional and national conflicts still run deep.

On the whole, football, like all mass gatherings in Spain, is renowned for its relaxed, good-humored atmosphere. At half time, the stadiums fill with the sound of rustling tin foil as tens of thousands of home-made baguette sandwiches of sliced cold sausage are unwrapped and tins of fizzy drinks are popped. No alcohol is for sale inside the gates, but occasionally a leather *bota* or wineskin is surreptitiously passed round. A former socialist interior minister, José Luis Corcuera, once had a brush with the authorities when stadium security men picked him up for bringing a *bota* into the Bernabéu, in defiance of the law that his own ministry had passed. His response was typical of a certain kind of *Madrileño*; first he said "perhaps you are unaware to whom you are speaking." This is the centuries-old formula handed down from the years of the royal court and used by Spanish officials to evade restrictions placed on humbler mortals and to intimidate underlings who challenge them. When that failed to work—the police knew exactly who he was—Mr. Corcuera tried another get-out. "I didn't realize," he pleaded, "that the ban on alcohol included wine." This is a sentiment that most Spaniards would go along with. Alcohol, in popular Spanish parlance, means strong spirits; beer and wine do not count.

Rayo Vallecano

Madrid has a third football team based far from the usual tourist beat, in the unfashionable working-class neighborhood of Vallecas. Rayo Vallecano compensates in cocky pride for what it lacks in status and wealth. You catch a flavor of this by the slogans on the T-shirts the club sells in a corner shop attached to its modest little stadium. "Not only am I perfect," these garments swank, "I'm with Rayo Vallecano." Plucky little Rayo—*rayito* the fans call it, as if referring to a much-loved baby brother scampering to keep up with the big boys—has a fervent following among devoted local supporters, drawn from the industrial suburbs that form a vast sprawling belt around the south of the city. Rayo yo-yos in and out of the first division. Occasionally, as in the first part of the 1999 season when it was top of the league for several weeks, it achieves moments of glory. But Rayo's adoring fans are philosophical about the modest status of their club, compared with their twin rivals each of whose budget is more than ten times theirs, and say their only ambition is to stay in the first division. This down-to-earth attitude is typical of the gritty workers' suburb of Vallecas whose name the club bears.

This neighborhood of a million people is Madrid's industrial "red belt," home to pro-communist, strongly unionized workers who were the scourge of Franco's dictatorship. While Franco in the 1950s was eagerly promoting European superstars Real Madrid as unofficial ambassadors of Spain and basking in the national and international adulation their string of victories brought him, he was at the same time ordering baton charges and water-cannon to crush illegal strikes in the factories of Vallecas. That bitter contrast in the political fortunes of Madrid's clubs, a reflection of the "two Spains" that persisted in the Franco years, still has echoes today on the terraces. Skinheads at the Bernabéu or the Calderón shout Nazi slogans and wave swastikas, but Rayo fans wave banners of the revolutionary hero Che Guevara. Their rebellious spirit is not so much a serious statement of political loyalty— although the area is still largely pro-communist—but rather a gesture of thumbing the nose at more pompous and serious-minded football fans. The gesture implies a broad defiance of the establishment, a streak of non-conformity, and an irreverent championing of the underdog.

People from Vallecas are renowned for their boundless self-esteem, swaggering cheek, and impudent irony. These typically *Madrileño* traits are summed up in the local expression *chulería,* roughly translated as flamboyance or posturing. But the 15,000 capacity stadium is notoriously difficult to fill, even when Rayo faces Real Madrid or Barcelona at home. Fans tend increasingly to watch on TV and pile into local bars for collective enjoyment of the match, squinting up at a screen that seems invariably to be lodged near the ceiling in a corner by the entrance. Rayo fans enjoy an additional advantage; their little local stadium is the only one in Spain of which surrounding apartment blocks offer an unrestricted view of the whole pitch. Locals cram into the nearby balconies to enjoy the fun. These are no depressing high-rise slums but solid red-brick constructions. Militant neighborhood organizations fought in the 1970s to have shoddy dwellings transformed into good housing. For important matches, pseudo-postmen and pizza delivery boys bang on the blocks' back doors to try to bluff their way on to a balcony grandstand. It is very much a family affair. Football matches in Spain are generally played in the afternoon at about 5PM, or later. But Rayo, unusually, often schedules its matches at midday on a Sunday, so that the very youngest members of the family come along, and it is all over in time for lunch.

But like its two local rivals, Rayo is run by a flashy impresario with a lurid reputation. The flamboyant businessman José María Ruíz Mateos bought the club in 1991 and three years later, for ill-defined financial reasons, handed over chairmanship to his wife Teresa Rivero, mother of thirteen, and Spain's only female football boss. A deeply religious housewife who knew nothing of football when she took over, Doña Teresa swiftly became a fervent fan and participates actively from the presidential balcony in the triumphs and disasters of her players. She set up a local welfare association in Vallecas, and recently the stadium honored her by adopting her name, even if a few eyebrows were raised when the decision was bounced through a meeting of a handful of supporters.

Ruíz Mateos was a small-time sherry producer from Andalusia who created a huge conglomerate, Rumasa, which the socialist government expropriated in 1983 for allegedly shady dealings. The magnate spent years in and out of prison, trying to clear his name. At one point he skipped the country and was traced to Vienna, London and the Caribbean in the company of his business partner's wife, before he crawled home to face the music. He once ambushed Miguel Boyer, the economics minister who had stripped him of his fortune, in an exclusive restaurant in the Salamanca district. Mr. Boyer was enjoying an intimate dinner with his Philippine lady companion, later his wife, Isabel Preysler, when Ruíz Mateos approached the politician, an austere, rather lugubrious man, and flung a cream cake in his face. The cake episode was recalled recently in a hilarious television advertisement for Ruíz Mateos's current business venture, Dhul dairy foods, in which the entire Rayo team, plus Doña Teresa, extolled their boss's products. Players' shirts bear the "bee" symbol of Ruíz Mateos's Rumasa conglomerate, confirming the impression that Rayo is just part of the family business.

But the grizzled factory workers and giggling teenage girls of Vallecas who wait outside the changing room claim the players as their own. "We love them because they're our local boys," they say, and greet their idols with a gruff salute, or beg an autograph and a kiss. But behind the idolatry and the delirious joy when Rayo can get ahead of its wealthier rivals, players and fans alike recognize that Rayo just does not have the resources to compete on equal terms. Rayo is the eternal also-ran, David competing with—and sometimes outwitting—Goliath. "It's wonderful when we are ahead of our much bigger rivals, it makes us burst with pride. But we're realistic. We accept our position in the social scale," was how one team member, the American international goalkeeper Kasey Keller, shrewdly summed up the Rayo philosophy.

The Industrial Belt

Rayo's—and Atlético's—fans are drawn overwhelmingly from Madrid's southern industrial suburbs such as Vallecas, Orcasitas and Carabanchel. These are new communities that mushroomed during the economic boom encouraged by Franco's policy of "developmentism" (*desarrollismo*) of the 1960s. Those who live there today, often in handsome red-brick apartment blocks surrounded with sports centers, kindergartens and leafy squares dotted with benches, remember that sheep still roamed this nondescript scrub-land when they first arrived. Migrants from poorer parts of Spain who colonized suburbs like Orcasitas and Vallecas built low single-story shacks on these open spaces to the city's southern outskirts. Piped water came only in the 1970s. One elderly resident remembers how before then the settlers used to excrete into a can. She recalled how a lorry used to come round selling water from a tank at one peseta a jug, pretty much as water-sellers had done in the age of Velázquez.

Migrants flocked to these unpromising frontier settlements from the parched feudal estates of Andalusia to land steady jobs in the Peugeot car plant, the Marconi electronics factory, the Casa aeronautical complex and the glassworks, or to grub beneath the surface of the city, digging the underground railway in conditions not far removed from those experienced by miners in the Third World. Indeed, some impoverished miners from León who came to try their luck in the capital confessed that the conditions in the construction of the Madrid metro were worse than those down the pit. It was illegal to settle on these plots; Franco had them earmarked to build apartments for army veterans. But if a dwelling could be erected with a roof before nightfall, the authorities, to whom you might slip some money to turn a blind eye, did not have the right to knock it down. Hence the frantic scramble to assemble a ramshackle little hovel before sundown. The new residents organized neighborhood associations in the teeth of Franco's repression that became vibrant grassroots political bodies. Later they marched upon the ministries of new democratic government and fought off attempts to evict them to make way for speculative luxury housing. They defied the baton charges of the emerging young democracy and wrenched from the government promises to be re-housed. All this occurred within a single generation, practically within a decade, the 1970s, and the young pioneers—some idealistic, some just desperate—of these proudly self-conscious working-class areas of the capital, are still only in their middle years. Meanwhile, the factories have closed one by one, hit by successive recessions and technological advance. In a community whose strength was based on a booming manufacturing economy, unemployment of up to fifty percent is now more than double the national average. Those with one breadwinner in a family that typically comprises five adults count themselves lucky. This is the heartland of the fans of Rayo and Atlético, whose clubs, albeit for different reasons now, still offer the prospect of romance and glory.

Big Business

The football business has boomed in the last decade and is now estimated to be worth more than $4.5 billion. There are two main interrelated reasons for this spectacular growth: firstly, wall-to-wall broadcasting of matches on pay-per-view television channels, including special channels for the biggest clubs, means that fans can watch televised football practically around the clock every day. Secondly, huge budgets enable clubs to buy star foreign players, who also help increase popular enthusiasm. The change began in 1997 with the so-called "Bosman ruling," enabling clubs to buy players on free transfers from elsewhere in the European Union after their contracts had expired. This unleashed a rush of high-profile transfers and, for a while, prompted complaints that Spanish clubs were being taken over by foreign players and that local talent was being stifled. In addition, many players from Africa and Latin America gained EU citizenship through their association with countries like France, Spain, Portugal and Holland. The Brazilian and Argentine influx, in particular, had a stunning impact on Spanish football, and Rivaldo, Ronaldo, Roberto Carlos and others became household names and joined the ranks of the stars.

Money to finance these often expensive purchases came from lucrative deals struck between the clubs and the pay-per-view digital television channels that emerged in the late 1990s. Their main aim was to tap into the public's seemingly insatiable demand for televised football by providing non-stop coverage, including international as well as Spanish competitions. In a nation that considers free access to televised big matches to be an inalienable human right, it was feared at first that Spaniards might balk at paying a subscription for the privilege. There have been moments when the government has stepped in to declare some important games to be "in the national interest"—with echoes of Franco's concern to damp down any frisson of social unrest—and ordered the TV companies to broadcast them gratis. But such fears proved unfounded as millions decided to fork out their subscriptions for digital television. With the proliferation of televised football, gates fell somewhat after years in which they had been gradually rising. And with the increasing commercialization of the game and the astronomical sums now in play, complaints were raised that the bond of loyalty between local fans and their clubs were being broken, and that football was losing its original spirit of solidarity. Fans in Spain have never traveled the country in support of their clubs to the extent that British fans do. Perhaps the distances are too large and the journeys too expensive. Lucrative deals with pay-per-view television channels are now the big clubs' principal source of income, along with sales of kit and memorabilia: gate receipts come way down the scale of importance. These deals ensure massive receipts for years to come, and help offset the enormous debts of clubs like Real Madrid. Atlético is a different matter: its catastrophic finances seem to be linked to shady operations conducted by its owner, Jesús Gil.

Televised football overwhelmingly continues to be Spaniards' favorite form of entertainment: of the fifteen television programs most viewed in 1999, nine were football matches. And off the field, tales of the crazy sayings and doings of big club chairmen—especially their seemingly insatiable appetite for chewing up and spitting out coaches at the rate of several per season—are of immeasurably more interest to most Spaniards than the activities of their politicians, businessmen or pop stars. Huge interest was aroused one year when the entire Atlético pitch had to be re-turfed just before the start of the season after it had been chomped up and ruined by a plague of caterpillars. Atlético had eventually to seek the assistance of—horrors—Barcelona, who put the club in touch with a French turf specialist to solve the problem. This episode was reported in daily detail by the national press, although with typical Spanish vagueness about natural history, the one detail that fascinated the foreign media was never made clear: precisely what kind of caterpillars were capable of causing such havoc?

One of Spain's most popular football television personalities is an Englishman, Michael Robinson, whose pioneering program *El Día después* (The Day After) is Spanish television's most successful sports spot. An archetypal "cheeky chappy," Robinson, whose engaging English accent and halting Spanish form part of his enormous popular appeal, devised the program as a way of exploring all the fun and excitement of football off the pitch. Such programs, celebrating the private lives of stars, the little local clubs and the passion for the game in remote parts of the country, are commonplace now, but when *The Day After* began in the late 1980s, this was a revolutionary new way of showing football on television. The formula proved to be a gold mine that brought in millions of new enthusiasts who had never been interested in football before. Many Spaniards, it seems, are still trying to escape.

CHAPTER THIRTEEN

The Moriarty Gallery: Freedom and Excess

After Franco died in 1975, Spaniards—especially the young—sought sex and politics. "We wanted," they put it, "to recover what we had never known." Demonstrators filled the streets demanding political rights, and pornography was available at corner kiosks and in special X-rated cinemas that popped up all over town. The phenomenon of the "snogging bar" emerged, where couples groped their way through semi-darkness to sofas where they could engage in all the activities forbidden in their parents' front room and inadvisable on a park bench. It is astonishing to read brash and lively Spanish novels of the late 1970s and early 1980s by, say, the skeptical former communist and crime writer Manuel Vázquez Montalbán, and to realize how sexually explicit his early works such as *Mares del Sur* (Southern Seas, 1979) were—brutally so by today's primmer standards—and how sexually promiscuous were their main protagonists. With sex no longer taboo, the temptation seemed irresistible to describe and portray it as graphically and as frequently as possible, and to experiment in literature as in real life with homosexuality and transvestitism. The sexual frenzy calms down in Montalbán's later novels, perhaps as his hero, the private detective Pepe Carvalho, ages and mellows along with his creator. But it was a far cry from the time up until Franco's death when the Civil Guard would rebuke you for kissing your partner in the street. One magazine, typical of the period when liberty exploded upon a repressed nation, neatly fused the twin yearnings for sex and politics: *Interviu* magazine presented in the same glossy package an impudent blend of naked nipples plus no-holds-barred exposés of new, sometimes morally dubious, politicians.

In those overheated years of partying and experimentation, more than a decade after a comparable youth revolt elsewhere in Europe, young *Madrileños* demonstrated for, among other things, the right to bar-crawl until the early hours. Their celebration of newly won freedom settled into a more focused post-Francoist culture toward the late 1970s and early 1980s under the twin impact of a pair of wildly divergent figures who were each to become internationally known: Antonio Tejero and Pedro Almodóvar. The Francoist military officer and the avant-garde filmmaker between them define the extremes of the culture of modern Madrid. Tejero marked the last extravagant gasp of the old guard, Almodóvar the provocative synthesis of the new.

Tejero's Last Stand

Lieutenant-Colonel Tejero stormed Madrid's parliament building with a squad of civil guardsmen on February 23, 1981, firing his pistol in the air and shouting "Everybody on the floor!" The date is engraved upon the collective memory of all Spaniards. All but three deputies in the chamber panicked and obeyed the barked orders of this mustachioed, uniformed figure with his shiny flat-backed hat. Those who remained on their feet, as the endlessly replayed footage shows, were the communist leader Santiago Carrillo, the first freely elected prime minister Adolfo Suárez and the former Francoist general turned defense minister, Manuel Gutierrez Mellado. The chamber was interrupted as deputies were swearing in the newly elected center-right government of Leopoldo Calvo Sotelo, a tediously drawn out process that was transmitted live on radio and recorded on the Congress in-house television system. Suddenly, the nation—and shortly the world—gasped in horror and disbelief at the outlandish, frightening spectacle unfolding before them in jerky black and white images. Spaniards ran home, pulled down their blinds and sat terrified, glued to their radios. Many suspected with a sinking heart that Spain for all its pretensions as a modern European democracy was no more than a

backward, semi-Fascist state whose democratic trappings were barely skin deep. Tanks rolled on to the street in Valencia, and for several hours no one knew if the experiment in democracy would be cut short and drowned in blood. Several socialist and communist deputies later confessed that in their terror they had chewed and swallowed their party cards as they crouched upon the congressional carpet.

But in Madrid, troops stayed in their barracks, and in the early hours, King Juan Carlos appeared on television in his military uniform, saying that the army had sworn allegiance to him and that the coup attempt had been foiled. But as John Hooper observes in his unrivaled chronicle of modern Spain, *The New Spaniards*: "Tejero's abortive coup, while it may have fulfilled people's worst fears, also dispelled them—like the cloudburst that comes at the end of a thundery day." The next day, a million Spaniards poured into the streets of Madrid in an emotional gesture of support for freedom and democracy. In elections the following year, Felipe González's socialists swept to power with an absolute majority in a sign that democracy was here to stay and the Franco era was gone for ever. Congress opens its doors to the public once a year on Constitution Day, December 7, and the most popular sight of all, pointed out to eager visitors, are the bullet holes in the plaster and woodwork of the chamber. When the chamber was redecorated and renovated recently, it was decided to leave the bullet holes visible, as a reminder of that historic moment.

Polar opposites, Tejero and Almodóvar share qualities of melodrama, kitsch and excess that define *Madrileño* style. And between them they embody some of the characteristics that echo down the centuries of this curious, casual, hothouse culture. It is difficult to imagine either of these men being the simultaneous product of any other city. But while Tejero projected the brutal, monochrome authoritarianism of the Franco age, Almodóvar expresses the vibrantly anarchic technicolor of the *movida*. Both exude the manic extravagance and slight dissonance with reality typical of the best and worst *Madrileños*.

The *Movida*

The Spanish word *movida* means something like "shift" or "scene," with social connotations of "moving and shaking," although most dictionaries now carry a special entry for the *movida madrileña*, which they describe as something like "the Madrid scene of the late 1970s": a definition that leaves us little the wiser about exactly what it was and how it began and ended. The Madrid *movida* emerged as the city awakened from its forty-year-old slumber, and newly liberated youngsters started to *salir de copas*—going from bar to bar throughout the weekend, drinking until dawn. There are some parallels between the *movida* of Madrid in the late 1970s and early 1980s and London's swinging sixties. The dictatorship postponed for more than a decade the youth revolt and the permissive society in Spain, so young Spaniards' defiance of the inhibitions of their parents' generation, and of their own dull and fettered childhood coincided with the advent of democracy and a certain optimistic institutional fluidity. Notwithstanding obvious political differences between sixties Britain and seventies Spain, each reflected a joyous, hedonistic rejection of political conservatism and social conformism, especially for middle-class youth and students. Both movements spurred a flowering of artistic creativity that was energetically fueled by drugs in a newly tolerant climate, and by alcohol. And both reveled in a new sexual freedom. The *movida madrileña* was overwhelmingly nocturnal. Its center of gravity was the city's nightspots, clubs, bars, and the improbable parts of the capital that it claimed as its own, at night. In this city bombarded by the sun, the people of the *movida* came out after dark.

The *movida* coincided with the advent of an unlikely patron: the gently spoken professor of Marxist philosophy Enrique Tierno Galván, elderly and patrician, who was elected socialist mayor of Madrid in 1979. Tierno Galván was offered the job as mayor of Madrid as a consolation prize after Felipe González's Socialist Workers' Party (PSOE) swallowed up Tierno Galván's smaller Popular Socialist Party and ruthlessly expunged from PSOE statutes all reference to the traditions of Marxism that Tierno had defended. To universal astonishment, this shy, pedantic gent in double-breasted Prince of Wales checked suits proved perfect as mayor, and he seized his opportunity with relish. He celebrated the ancient customs of office, reviving, for example, the official proclamation or *bando*, traditionally declaimed from the mayoral balcony and a roll of parchment. But in his own archaic Castillian style he infused the old forms with modern principles of openness, tolerance, and enthusiasm, gleefully inaugurating a new era of liberty. "You know what to do: get stoned and watch out!" (*Así es que ya sabeis: a colocarse y al loro!*) was his exhortation to the youth of Madrid when the socialists won control of the city in 1979—three years before Felipe González was elected prime minister of Spain. The *Madrileño* slang expression—totally incongruous from the lips of "the old professor" who had translated Wittgenstein into Spanish—was incredulously reported verbatim in every newspaper in Spain. It was perhaps the most unequivocal exhortation to have fun ever to issue from someone in authority, and especially in Spain whose rulers down the centuries have always shown their fear of the free citizen, and who have always valued the concept of order over those of liberty and equality. Tierno Galván's message was taken as a blessing for tolerance, an encouragement of what became one of the most hedonistic, creative, and feverish social moments in recent European history. Many speculated that the old man was unaware when he spoke the hip-sounding phrase that the slang expression amounted to an unequivocal invitation to take drugs. He had ample time to find out afterwards what it meant, however, and never retracted or hinted that he regretted the indiscretion. The fun roared on until a moment in 1991 when a prominent actor was dumbstruck to be told by a security guard to stop rolling a joint in a well-known nightspot. Others mark the downturn from Tierno's death from cancer in 1986, which brought perhaps the majority of people in Madrid on to the street to follow his coffin, in an unprecedented demonstration of grief and affection. That year Felipe González strongarmed a referendum on Spain staying in NATO—a decision many felt crushed what remained of Socialism's promise of radicalism. For many, this event marked the mourning of a closing era. Still others cite the downturn from the catastrophic defeat of mighty Real Madrid by Inter Milan, beaten 0–5 in its own sacred Santiago Bernabéu stadium late in 1985. That result punctured the illusion of the omnipotence and invincibility of Madrid—club and city.

Even so, the excitement was prolonged by a speculative economic boom that accelerated during the late 1980s and became known as the *pelotazo*—"the big kick"—what we might call the boom years. By then, the years of partying and excess were beginning to show a darker side. Deaths from heroin addiction and AIDS depleted the ranks of the beautiful young things, and cast a shadow over their iridescent hedonism. Participants began to look to other things, studying economics, becoming rich. There remain few visible legacies of those years in the city today. The all-important nightspots—the Via Lactea, the Rockola, Stella, Ras, the Bobia and others—are either gone, transformed out of all recognition, or are a dreary, seedy shadow of their former glory. Does this mean that the cascade of freedom and euphoria gushed and vanished as if it had never been? Even those who were part of it remain unsure. But even to describe the things they did and the feelings they experienced demonstrate how intense a moment it was and how remote from today's more sober and pragmatic spirit. The yearning for sex and politics has muted, perhaps because throughout the heady 1980s, Spaniards could sate themselves with both. "It was like being in a toy store. You could have as much as you wanted of whatever was going. It seemed to be a constantly escalating stairway to cheap accessible pleasure. But then you just became sated, bored," recalls one survivor. But, adds one of those who were there: "Sometimes at an art opening you'll see people you remember from those days. And you recognize a shared experience and greet each other with a glint in your eye." Much of the joyous spirit that the *movida* pioneered still remains unquenched.

The important thing was to go to the right events at the right venues and be seen with the right people. The *movida* referred specifically to that group. They were, or aspired to be, artists, creative people, an initially small intimate coterie of friends. The bible of the movement was the monthly magazine *La Luna*, run by Borja Casani from 1982 to 1986, while the stylish Moriarty art gallery in still-cool Calle Almirante showed the works of key artists like Ceesepe and El Hortelano and photographers like Ouka Lele and Alberto García Alix. And everyone showed up at a number of clubs, particularly the Rockola, where Almodóvar first came into the public eye with his corrosively provocative act as a heavily made-up transvestite cabaret singer, singing songs about wanting to be a mother, to have a child, to call it Lucifer, and to teach it to be a whore. A proliferating gay scene boomed, as did a general outrageousness of dress, exaggerated makeup for both sexes, and behavior that criss-crossed sexual stereotypes. Those in the know moved from venue to venue as the night progressed. Constantly bumping into the same crowd was part of the fun and strengthened the impression of being part of a gilded elite that was at the cutting edge of everything new and exciting. Then you would turn up at dawn at some café for breakfast before heading off to a clutch of bars in the Rastro toward midday. One of the best loved of the Rastro bars was La Bobia on Calle San Millán, which filled up on Sunday mornings with black-clad, white-faced drag queens or men in fishnet tights and heavy eye makeup smudged by the ravages of the night.

It was considered cool to meet there those extravagant creatures you had been dancing with on a crammed disco dance-floor just hours before. La Bobia was repeatedly closed down because of the unconcealed dealing and consumption of all kinds of drugs on the premises, until the owners, who also ran the Café San Millán (which still exists and whose terrace dominates that sociable corner by the La Latina metro station), finally gave up and shut it down for good. No sign of it remains, to the lasting regret of many. But on Sunday mornings, there is still a louche buzz to that square with groups or individuals hanging around, waiting and posing expectantly as if—despite the feeling of ragged exhaustion proper to a Sunday morning after a night on the tiles—something exciting and unexpected might still happen.

"Madrid has died"

Drugs and promiscuous sexual activity were part and parcel of the scene. The consumption of cannabis was effectively decriminalized and the roaring nightlife fueled by good quality and freely available cocaine. One enthusiast remembers a David Bowie concert in the early 1980s at the vast Vicente Calderón stadium, home to Atlético de Madrid football club. "It was a sea of mirrors," she recalls, as everyone bent to snort rows of cocaine. Parties were thrown by rich freethinkers eager to welcome the fashionable into their homes and to be part of the alternative art scene. These parties were often in the smart northern suburbs of Pozuelo and Majadahonda, which presented serious transportation problems. Participants remember concocting elaborate arrangements to get lifts, recall perilous dawn scooter rides with two or three on the pillion following a night spent consuming vast quantities of whisky and other stimulants. "It was a constant search for the next great sensation, for pleasure and fun. People reveled and gloried in living as well as they possibly could, and we felt it would never end," my friend recalls with a mixture of nostalgia and incredulity. "*Madrid me mata!* " (Madrid's killing me!) was a common expression, conveying the sense of pushing everything to its outer limits. It was ten years before the process burned itself out and the motto became instead "*Madrid ha muerto!*" (Madrid has died!)—marking the end of the affair.

The writer Luís Antonio Villena calls his *movida* novel *Madrid ha muerto*. Written in 1999, he gives it the evocative subtitle "Splendor and Chaos in a Happy City of the Eighties." On the cover is a garish multicolored line drawing by one of the *movida*'s most prominent artists, Ceesepe (weird and wacky names were also part of the scene). The picture shows a dizzyingly anarchic Madrid skyline of cupolas, balconies, porticos and satellite dishes. Lying unconscious upon a roof of traditional curved tiles—as typical to the Madrid horizon as the skyscrapers and *fin-de-siècle* bronze statues—is a young reveler blissed out of his brain. Although unconscious, only his upper body is lying on the roof: his legs float perilously in the air, suspended above the void.

The image perfectly reflects the edge of danger, the frisson of fear that lay behind the frenzied pleasure of those years. Initially, the fear was political; Tejero's reckless escapade showed that the military still nursed hopes of turning back the clock. The paint was barely dry on the fresh new democratic structures and the atmosphere was tense and fragile. Even after Tierno had become mayor, it was not until 1982 that he legalized the traditional carnival celebrations. Before then, youngsters in their fancy dress and outrageous makeup celebrated semi-clandestinely, constantly on the alert for the *grises*, the security services, who might come charging around the corner flailing their batons and tear gas canisters to beat revelers out of the way, lock them up for the night, cause problems at the university, report miscreants to their employer or their parents. Who knew if the new freedoms might not be snuffed out at any moment? But political fear faded as the landslide election victory of Felipe González's socialists in October 1982 effectively set the seal on the young democracy. It signaled to the world that Spain's armed forces were now extinguished as a political force.

There remained, however, another sense of danger that participants in the *movida* actively courted. As Villena puts it:

> What I most remember of the night—those dives and nightspots that most fascinated me—is seeing, without explicitly seeking it out, a diverse and libertine atmosphere, of excess and laughter, heaven and tragedy, a mixture of perversion and affection, which could only be called vice. It was the liquor of life. No bar is any good without a few drops, like angostura in your cocktail, of this vice. All the haunts that we sought out, all of them, had vice.

At first this dark underside of drugs and sex seemed a stimulant for artistic creation around a few stars, comparable to Andy Warhol's factory that had flourished in New York in the late 1960s and early 1970s. Almodóvar's coterie of artists and actors are even today dubbed his "factory," in conscious homage to Warhol. The splendid nocturnal boulevard of bars and open-air discos that stretched during the summer months from Cibeles to Colón along the Paseo de Recoletos is still celebrated as Madrid's "beach promenade," although with every year it becomes more and more subdued as the improvised bars are subjected to increasingly stringent regulations. "The night I remember best," recalls Villena, "although there could have been several, it was summer and we slowly paraded up and down, like tall ships of modernity and delirium, the vivid splendor of Recoletos, between Cibeles and Colón, just letting things ride. Perhaps we did this several times. A Paseo that resembled the Phoenician dockside of a port of pleasure."

Those hot summer nights stretched out as endlessly and luxuriantly as youth itself, burning themselves out in pleasure. "We flew, night after night, amidst music terraces, videos, private houses and the long dawn until daylight, with sex and exhaustion," writes Villena. But in a premonition that such pleasure could not be sustained for ever, he notes recurring feelings of depression that descended just before sleep, the sun already high, or on waking up as dusk was falling to herald another night "when we felt empty and extinguished, as if the tide would never rise again, boats with sails limp and filthy, in a strange becalmed stupor." This was the moment to wind up again, to rise anew, for a process once begun "could not be put into reverse." The midday sun was something from which to flee, behind dark glasses, running to hide, in bed, until it was night again.

Survivors remember spending several years in this frenetic chaos in the firm conviction that it would never end. But then the uglier consequences began to impinge. On Recoletos, for example, all-night open-air improvised bars and discos known as *chiringuitos* had no lavatories. It became the custom to urinate in the passage that led to the underground entrance to Recoletos train station, a spot which became a stinking refuge for drug users and bag snatchers desperate to fund their habit, as ready supplies of drugs dried up and quality plummeted. One of Villena's concluding images of that crazy decade is of a young woman who seeks to relieve herself in the station entrance. She takes with her a gay man to act as her companion and possible protector in case she is threatened, not by someone with a knife, but by a desperate drug-user brandishing a syringe infected with AIDS.

Almodóvar

Almodóvar was the son of a gas station attendant from Calzada de Calatrava, a village in the parched badlands of La Mancha immortalized by the fictional Don Quixote. Recalling his childhood, Almodóvar once remarked, "I felt as if I'd fallen from another planet." He subsequently attributed his lust for color to the prevailing dark monochrome of this childhood, where his mother wore black for years while mourning a succession of relatives. He fled to Madrid in 1969 and started making underground movies while working at a desk job in Telefónica. His first full-length film *Pepi Luci Bom y otras chicas del Montón* (Pepi Luci Bom and Other Run-of-the-Mill Girls), shot in the nightclubs of Madrid, appeared in 1980. The work broached themes that would recur in all his later work; characters of almost unbelievable complexity and sexual deviance—lesbian masochist rock stars with a secret desire to sing Spanish boleros—would have the most commonplace conversations: "I personally am from Murcia. And you?"

Works that followed, drenched in lollipop colors, packed with hectic, improbable events and personalities, reflect the high-speed euphoria that swept young Madrid in the early 1980s. Nothing could have been more remote from the lugubrious blood-stained tragedies that

Spanish films had hitherto portrayed. *Mujeres al borde de un ataque de nervios* (Women on the Verge of a Nervous Breakdown) was nominated for an Oscar, brought him international fame, and was the highest-grossing foreign film in the US in 1989.

In the mid-1980s, an unknown Almodóvar had published in *La Luna* a series of tales full of spark and provocation, whose heroine—half transvestite, half madwoman, bizarre, fun-loving and full of cocaine—was called Patty Diphusa. She defined herself as "an international star of porn and fotonovelas" (*fotonovelas* are cheap romance magazines in which the story is illustrated by strips of posed photographs of the supposed protagonists): "My fotonovelas and some of my super eight films have sold very well in Africa, Portugal, Tokyo, Soho and in the Rastro." Patty was the alter ego of both Almodóvar and his former cabaret partner Fabio, or Fanny McNamara. It was all served up with generous dollops of kitsch, in a conscious attempt to reappropriate for the new iconoclastic youth all the traditional elements of Spanish culture that had been taken over by the Fascists, subvert them and return them to the new youth vanguard. Almodóvar made an entire film, *Matador*, in which he both celebrated and subverted the cult of bullfighting, blood, and death that had been presented in a "decaffeinated" form under Franco to define Spain to the new foreign tourist. (Decaffeinated, by the way, is a typical *Madrileño* expression of contempt.) The kitsch of the 1950s and 1960s, when Spain first promoted itself as an international tourist destination are a perfect illustration of how conventional national images were, critics felt, distorted and trivialized, stripped of their real human content during the Franco years. The tourist postcards of the time are a wonderful example of the innocence and toe-curling cuteness of those images.

Almodóvar and "the *Luna* boys" engaged in a subversive parody of traditional icons of Spanish culture—women's romantic fiction, sentimental songs, religious rituals, bulls, traditional folklore—in a way that was essentially frivolous, superficial, and sarcastic. This apparent dismissal of anything remotely linked to reality or political seriousness offended the traditional, sober-minded political left as much as the right-wing sympathizers of the former dictatorship. In a recent interview,

Almodóvar described how he and his friends stopped feeling afraid of the police and at the same time rejected the recent past of the early 1970s: the "*progres*, the beards, the crooners, the protest songs." They wanted to be feel free of all that, and looked to the exaggerated and provocative style of London's new wave punks, in which kitsch and color played a big part. A curious and engaging legacy remains: *La Parodia Nacional* is a popular television program in which grotesquely caricatured flamenco dancers smirk and twirl through numbers that are Spain's nearest thing to musical satire. The public is invited to submit satirical lyrics that are put to popular tunes and performed by professionals.

Bright clashing colors became the symbol of the *movida*, a hallmark of Almodóvar's films. A friend recalls flaunting her outrageously skimpy clothes in bright orange and green, and teasing her hair into spikes with hot water and sugar. She felt cool and provocative. Although inspired by Britain's punk new wave, this was all part of an attempt to create a peculiarly *Madrileño* sense of identity; something that was neither imported Anglo-Saxon culture nor the fake Spanishness of the Franco period. Almodóvar's early films are an extravagant parody of many themes and obsessions of sugary 1960s and 1970s films, especially religion and the family. They give back to modern Spaniards the real situations, dialogues and precious images that critics say the Franco regime distorted and defiled. Almodóvar also pioneered a revolution in sexual relations, creating a world in which transvestite fathers and prostitute nuns express genuine feelings of family honor and integrity. It is a source of astonishment in Madrid that Almodóvar has won international fame and Hollywood prizes by his quintessentially Spanish defiance of every convention you would imagine Spaniards to hold dear.

Another prospering survivor of the *movida* is the Moriarty Gallery, on the first floor of a handsome, spacious old house in Calle Almirante, up the hill from Paseo de Recoletos. The gallery's austere spaces, pie-crust cornices, creaking floor and fluted iron pillars exude a muted *fin-de-siècle* bourgeois taste that is rare in Madrid. The white walls are sparsely decorated with disturbing, almost indecipherable, avant-garde artworks and installations. Behind a tiny flat door, the former editor of *La Luna*, Borja Casani, whose wife Lola Moriarty runs the gallery, has an office that overlooks this chic street lined with discreet cutting-edge clothes designers and emporia of ethnic artifacts. The spectacle is an elegant, thrilling teaser to funkier, gayer Chueca further up the hill.

More than ten years after it is all over, it is much easier to say how the *movida* began and why it ended, Casani says. It was sparked by the fact that the political awakening coincided with an economic boom. People had money in their pockets, and as the fear of political upheaval fell away, they realized they could spend it on *tonterías*—frivolities. This was the trigger for a return to Madrid's great tradition of nocturnal revelry, the Mediterranean and Arab legacy of living in the street and frittering away vast sums on fun. The "23F," as Tejero's ill-fated intervention is known here, marked the turning-point, the moment when this bubbling fizzing underground movement burst into public view in the form of parties, discos, art openings, book launches, social occasions. These are the events that reflect *Madrileños'* preferred way of doing things. *Madrileños* do not tend to set up committees or hold meetings; they let things develop impulsively through social relations. Culture became fashionable. Everyone wanted to be an artist, a photographer or a rock singer, even if they had no talent and lacked even the rudiments of training. Suddenly, those involved became aware of the international impact of what they were doing, Casani recalls, as serious journalists covering Spain's political transition started joining in the fun and reporting it in the world's press. They described a city where people went out all night and caused traffic jams at 5PM, and conveyed the lightheartedly joyous, human aspect of this peaceful political phenomenon. No one, however, wanted to define the movement, or take it over or act as spokesperson. The whole celebration blossomed spontaneously without conscious effort. And it died away in a similarly untraumatic way.

Could the *movida* have occurred anywhere but in Madrid? Probably not. The shape of the *movida* defined the nature of the Spanish capital, that anarchic city formed by migrants from elsewhere in the country who came in search of a living. They were not single-minded or committed enough to establish a solid bourgeois class or style. It was not for them a matter of life or death to make it in the big city. They were happy to take things day by day, exploiting whatever opportunity might turn up, without too much concern for the future. If times got rough, *Madrileños* always had their provincial *"pueblo"* to fall back on. The *pueblo* whence they mostly came could be relied on to provide a sanctuary, a last resort, even though it might drive them crazy. The theme was hilariously developed in Almodóvar's *La Flor de mi secreto* (The Flower of My Secret), in which the heroine, an award-winning romantic novelist, suffers a personal crisis when her marriage to an army officer serving in Bosnia falls apart. Her mother persuades her to return home to the *pueblo* where she is nursed back to mental health, and promptly returns to Madrid before small town life drives her mad.

The *movida's* failure to generate a solid industrial or commercial infrastructure for this extraordinary creative flowering meant that many of its artistic achievements were transitory, Casani believes. People drifted into international production or cinema or simply wandered off into other careers. Being an artist went out of fashion as swiftly as it had come in. The speculative boom of the late 1980s and 1990s made flashy young entrepreneurs like Javier de la Rosa and Mario Conde the new fashionable role models and darlings of a nation. That was before their fraudulent business dealings landed them in disgrace and jail.

What remains? The gay scene that exploded during the *movida* is a permanent visible fixture in Madrid today. Homosexuals—coming out in defiance of one of Franco's strictest taboos—were the great vanguard of the movement. And the gay scene has grown irresistibly, undeterred by a decade of conservative local administration in the city that has made every effort to emphasize family values and conventional tastes. The nightlife, the *marcha*, the fiesta roars on. This is a surprise not only to bemused visitors who are constantly astonished by the cascades of people coursing down the streets all night throughout the week, but to locals, too, who find it difficult to believe that the passion for nocturnal socializing has not burned out. And this activity continues despite the city fathers' efforts to clamp down on after-hours bars and make them close before *la madrugada*, before dawn. But in this deeply ingrained habit, *Madrileños* are only recovering a tradition that goes back decades, if not centuries. *Trasnochadores*, those who stay up all night, have long impressed foreign visitors. "Nobody," Hemingway observed, "goes to bed in Madrid until they have killed the night."

But while the pursuit of drink and drugs continues, and the custom of live music performed in bars flourishes, the fiesta these days lacks the artistically creative buzz that characterized the real *movida*, veterans say. Casani recalls an occasion that for him sums up the *movida*:

It was a fiesta for La Luna *at the Hotel Palace in 1984. We hired the whole hotel and there were musicians everywhere, two or three thousand people drugged up and drunk lying on these gorgeous hand-woven carpets beneath crystal chandeliers smoking joints. It seemed like a miracle, as though we'd stormed the Winter Palace, a sensation of tremendous power, not economic or political power but a feeling of sheer physical force, as if to say: look at what's possible. But we had few expectations. We were bad businessmen and we let it all fritter away. What remains? Not a lot. Almodóvar, who was just one among many, is a world star and still embodies how we felt and what we were trying to do.*

Take-out fast-food outlets, video stores, and multiple digital television channels have all become enormously popular in recent years. Coupled with the sobering effects of a recession in the mid-1990s, people are more inclined to stay at home in the evenings. Almodóvar, now in receipt of an Oscar for his film *Todo sobre mi madre* (All About my Mother), has himself endorsed the "Madrid has died" slogan, and said recently that the city was set to become as boring as Oslo. He shot his Oscar-winner in Barcelona, the first time he had deserted his favorite city. But with the advent of the millennium, run-down areas in the center of the capital have been spruced up, little neighborhood shops that had suffered under the competition of out-of-town hyper-markets are holding their own, sometimes recycling themselves for today's tastes. New clubs and restaurants open every week and you have to book or get there early to secure a place, even on a Monday. No one in Madrid takes seriously the idea of living within their means. They just do not understand the concept: it's not in the blood. An unemployed youngster or a student may have only 1,000 pesetas (say six dollars) in their pocket, but they'll club together with friends and buy a carton of cheap wine and a liter of Cola and head off into the night. Because they know, and millions agree with them, that Madrid remains the most exciting city in Europe.

Further Reading

Arroyo, María Dolores, *Cayetana de Alba: maja y aristocrata*. Madrid: Alderaban Ediciones, 1999.

Baticle, Jeannine, *Velázquez, el pintor hidalgo*. Barcelona: Ediciones B, 1999.

Barea, Arturo, *La Forja de un rebelde*. Madrid: Editorial Debate, 2000.

Bennett, Annie, *Blue Guide to Madrid*. London: A & C Black, 1997.

Besas, Peter, *Strange Vignettes of Old Madrid*. Madrid: Peter Besas, 1969.

Brenan, Gerald, *The Face of Spain*. London: Penguin, 1987.

Brown, Jonathan, *Velázquez*. Madrid: Alianza Editorial, 1992.

Buñuel, Luis, *My Last Breath*. London: Fontana, 1987.

Burns, Jimmy, *Spain: A Literary Companion*. London: John Murray, 1994.

Burns, Tom, *Hispanomanía*. Barcelona: Plaza & Janes, 2000.

Carr, Raymond and Fusi, Juan Pablo, *Spain: Dictatorship to Democracy*. London: Allen & Unwin, 1979.

Carrete, Juan, *La Puerta del Sol*. Madrid: Real Academia de Bellas Artes de San Fernando, 1998.

Cabezas, Juan Antonio, *Madrid*. Barcelona: Ediciones Destino, 1971.

Calvo Poyato, José, *El Desastre del 98*. Barcelona: Plaza & Janes, 1997.

Carandell, Luis, *Madrid*. Madrid: Alianza Cien, 1995.

Cervantes, Miguel de, *Don Quixote*. London: Penguin, 1950.

—, *Exemplary Stories*. London: Penguin, 1972.

Cela, Camilo José, *Café de Artistas*. Madrid: Alianza Cien, 1994.

—, *La Colmena*. Barcelona: Editorial Noguer, 1982.

—, *La Familia de Pascual Duarte*. Barcelona: Círculo de Lectores, 1976.

Comella, Beatriz, *La Inquisición Española*. Madrid: Rialp, 1998.

Del Rio López, Angel, *Viejos oficios de Madrid*. Madrid: Ediciones la Librería, 1993.

Diaz, Lorenzo, *La España alegre: ocio y diversión en el siglo xx*. Madrid: Espasa Calpe, 1999.

Elliott, J.H., *Imperial Spain 1469–1716*. London: Penguin, 1990.

—, *El Conde-Duque de Olivares*. Barcelona: Mondadori, 1990.

Estebán, José, et al, *El Libro del Café Gijón*. Madrid: Encarnación Fernández e Hijos, 1999.

Fernández Álvarez, Manuel, *Felipe II y su tiempo*. Madrid: Editorial Espasa Calpe, 1998.

Fraser, Ronald, *Blood of Spain: The Experience of Civil War 1936-1939*. London: Penguin, 1981.

Fusi, Juan Pablo, *Un Siglo de España: La cultura*. Madrid: Marcial Pons, 1999.

García García, Bernardo, *El Ocio en España en el siglo de oro*. Madrid: Akal Ediciones, 1999.

García, Reyes y Ecija, Ana Maria, *Leyendas de Madrid*. Madrid: Ediciones la Librería, 1995.

Gautier, Théophile, *Viaje a España*. Madrid: Ediciones Catedra, 1998.

Gaya Nuno, Juan A., *Velázquez*. Barcelona: Salvat Editores, 1984.

Gibson, Ian, *Federico García Lorca*. London: Faber and Faber, 1989.

—, *Fire in the Blood: The New Spain*. London: Faber and Faber, 1992.

—, *Lorca-Dalí. El amor que no pudo ser*. Madrid: Plaza & Janes, 1999.

—, *The Shameful Life of Salvador Dalí*. London: Faber and Faber, 1997.

Gilmour, David, *Cities of Spain*. London: John Murray, 1992.

Gómez Rufo, Antonio, *El Desfile de la victoria*. Barcelona: Ediciones B, 1999.

González Martel, Juan Manuel, *Casa Museo Lope de Vega, guía y catálogo*. Madrid, 1993.

Haro Tecglen, Eduardo, *Arde Madrid*. Madrid: Temas de Hoy, 2000.

Hemingway, Ernest, *Death in the Afternoon*. London: Arrow Books, 1994.

—, *For Whom the Bell Tolls*. London: Arrow Books, 1994.

—, *By-Line, Ernest Hemingway. Selected Articles and Dispatches of Four Decades*. Touchstone Books, 1998.

Holguin, Antonio, *Pedro Almodóvar*. Madrid: Ediciones Catedra, 1999.

Hooper, John, *The New Spaniards*. London: Penguin, 1995.

Humboldt, Wilhelm von, *Diario de viaje a España 1799-1800*. Madrid: Ediciones Catedra, 1998.

Ingram, Kevin, "Diego Velázquez's Secret History" in *Boletin del Prado*, November 1999

Jacobs, Michael, *Madrid Observed*. London: Pallas Athene, 1996.

—, *Between Hopes and Memories: A Spanish Journey.* London: Picador, 1994.

Jaraulde, Pablo, *Quevedo.* Madrid: Castalia, 1998.

Julia, Santos, et al, *Madrid. Historia de una capital.* Madrid: Alianza Editorial, 1997.

Justi, Carl, *Velázquez y su siglo.* Madrid: Istmo, 1999.

Kamen, Henry, *Philip of Spain.* New Haven, CT: Yale University Press, 1998.

—, *La Inquisición Española.* Barcelona: Crítica, 1999.

Lacarta, Manuel, *Felipe II, la intimidad del rey prudente.* Madrid: Alderaban Ediciones, 1997.

Lafuente, Isaias, *Tiempos de hambre: viaje a la España de posguerra.* Madrid: Temas de Hoy, 1999.

Larra, Mariano José de, *Artículos y costumbres.* Madrid: Olympia Ediciones, 1995.

Lorenzo, Pedro de, *Guia de forasteros.* Madrid: Doncel, 1973.

Luján, Nestor, *Madrid de los últimos Austrias.* Barcelona: Editorial Planeta, 1998.

Madrid por dentro y por fuera. Guia de forasteros incautos. Madrid: Asociación de Libreros de Lance, 1996.

Mesonero Romanos, Ramón de, *El antiguo Madrid.* Madrid: Trigo Ediciones, 1995.

—, *Escenas Matritenses.* Madrid: Ediciones Felmar, 1989.

Montoliu Camps, Pedro, *Fiestas y tradiciones madrileñas.* Madrid: Silex, 1990.

—, *Madrid en la Guerra Civil.* Madrid: Silex, 1999.

—, *Madrid Villa y Corte: historia de una ciudad.* Madrid: Silex, 1996.

Morris, Jan, *Spain.* London: Penguin, 1982.

Muñoz Molina, Antonio, *Los Misterios de Madrid.* Barcelona: Seix Barral, 1998.

Nash, Mary, *Rojas: Las Mujeres Republicanas en la Guerra Civil.* Madrid: Taurus, 1999.

Orwell, George, "Some Notes on Salvador Dalí," in *George Orwell.* London: Penguin, 1994.

Parker, Geoffrey, *Felipe II.* Madrid: Alianza Editorial, 1998.

Pérez Galdós, Benito, *Fortunata and Jacinta.* London: Penguin, 1988.

—, *Misericordia.* Cambridge: Dedalus, 1995.

—, *That Bringas Woman.* London: Everyman, 1996.

Preston, Paul, *Franco.* London: Fontana, 1995.

Quevedo, Francisco de, *The Swindler,* in *Two Spanish Picaresque Novels* (with Anon, *Lazarillo de Tormes*). London: Penguin, 1969.

Tiemblo Magno, Alfredo, *Guia de Madrid.* Madrid: Innova Ediciones, 1998.

Thomas, Hugh, *Madrid: A Travellers' Companion.* London: Constable, 1988.

—, *The Spanish Civil War.* London: Penguin, 1990.

Time Out Guide Madrid. London: Penguin, 1999.

Tome Bona, Javier M., *Historia de la Puerta del Sol,* Ediciones La Libreria: Madrid, 1993.

Tudela, Mariano, *Aquellas Tertulias de Madrid.* Madrid: Editorial El Avapiés, 1998.

Villena, Luis Antonio de, *Madrid ha Muerto.* Madrid: Editorial Planeta, 1999.

Yarza, Alejandro, *Un canibal en Madrid: Pedro Almodóvar.* Madrid: Ediciones Libertarias, 1999.

Zuñiga, Eduardo, *Flores de Plomo.* Madrid: Alfaguara, 1999.

Index of Literary
& Historical Names

Index of Places